Love Revealed

Love Revealed

MEDITATIONS ON CHAPTERS 13-17
OF THE GOSPEL OF JOHN

by

*Rev. George Bowen
of Bombay*

UNITED STATES ADDRESS
Harvey Christian Publishers, Inc.
3107 Hwy. 321, Hampton, TN 37658
Tel./Fax (423) 768-2297
E-mail: books@harveycp.com
Int.: www.harveycp.com

BRITISH ADDRESS
Harvey Christian Publishers UK
11 Chapel Lane, Kingsley Holt
Stoke-on-Trent, ST10 2BG
Tel./Fax (01538) 756391
E-mail: jjcook@mac.com

Original Edition 1886
British Edition 1977
This Edition 2012
ALL RIGHTS RESERVED

Cover design by Grace Cawman
Thompson Bible Institute, Inc

ISBN 978-1-932774-64-1

Printed by
Lightning Source Inc.
La Vergne, TN 37086

Foreword

Our first introduction to the writings of George Bowen occurred some twenty years ago when browsing through old books at Smithfield Market, Belfast. Another book-lover paused long enough to engage us in conversation, and together we animatedly conversed concerning authors and titles. This aged saint and author recommended George Bowen as a writer of great spiritual insight.

It was ten years later that we found George Bowen's book, *Love Revealed,* in a Skid Row mission library in Chicago. The much prized book which was borrowed was eagerly devoured, read and re-read. We were loathe to part with such a mine of gold and so, ultimately, decided to reprint this long out-of-print volume to thus extend to others the rare opportunity for possessing those deeply spiritual meditations on the last words of the Lord Jesus Christ to His disciples.

George Bowen, a self-effacing missionary, labored from 1848 until 1879 in India without furlough. For some years he represented the Presbyterian Board but later took out membership with the Methodists in Bombay. He chose to be self-supporting, cutting off his salary that he might remove occasion from the heathen to impute the motives of gain which lucrative salaries afforded missionaries. The usual mission compound accommodation was exchanged for a humble, rented abode near the market in Bombay. Instead of making tents as Paul did, Bowen made books. He was editor of the Bombay Guardian for years, and his editorials, appearing there, were later collected to form three of his books, *Love Revealed, The Amens of Christ* and *Daily Meditations.*

We elsewhere submit a portion of an introduction, by Daniel Steele, which was written for the book, *The Amens of Christ,* but is equally applicable to *Love Revealed.* May God abundantly bless all who read.

Edwin and Lillian Harvey
Stoke-on-Trent, England, 1977

Introduction

More than a score of years ago I secured and read with great spiritual profit, Bowen's *Daily Meditations*—three hundred and sixty-five passages of God's Word, beautifully opened and applied with unction of the Spirit to the heart of the reader. Some years afterwards I obtained another devotional and expository volume by the same author, *Love Revealed*, which suggested to me a title for my own first literary venture, *Love Enthroned.*

All the books of Rev. George Bowen are strongly marked with his individuality. They are all meditations on the Holy Scriptures, exhibiting the same high literary finish; the same glowing love to God and men; the same freshness and striking aptness of illustration; the same vividness of conception; the same breadth of view, with power to discover the subtle, interior connections of thought in Scriptural exegesis; the same ability to illuminate a text as if an electric light had been suddenly hung in its very center; the same scathing rebuke of a merely formal type of Christianity; the same revelation of the sunlit heights of assurance and cloudless communion with the Father and the Son, through the Holy Comforter; summits on which the author himself is manifestly dwelling.

In reviewing the many influences which have become factors in molding my own Christian character, I wish in this public manner to record my sense of indebtedness to this good man whose pen, guided by the Holy Spirit, has, for nearly a quarter of a century, under the sultry skies of India, been a skillful sculptor, conforming me to the image of the Son of God.

Daniel Steele
Reading, January 1886

LOVE REVEALED

The Gospel of St. John
Chapter 13

John 13:1. *"Now before the feast of the passover, when Jesus knew that his hour was come that he should depart out of this world unto the Father, having loved his own which were in the world, he loved them unto the end."*

The long-expected hour of departure had arrived. The alternative was before Christ, either to refresh and animate His soul by the contemplation of that world to which He was about to ascend, or to fix His regard upon the disciples from whom He was about to separate. There was a bright, ascending pathway before Him, with principalities, powers and dominions, rising one above another, ready to rejoice in His ascent—a pathway terminating at that throne of pre-eminent glory assigned to the Son of God before the world was.

On the other hand, there were these few indocile [stubborn], unbelieving disciples, who had pierced His keenest sensibilities a thousand times with their unworthy surmises, and in whom lived, still too much unvanquished, the spirit of human selfishness. Is it possible that His heart could do otherwise than bound with joy at the prospect of escaping from the dark and deadly atmosphere of this world to realms of glory and perfect bliss? Say that He had thus long patiently lingered on the earth under the influence of a profound sense of man's need and of a hallowed determination to open up a pathway of life to fallen humanity, would He not permit Himself, in the hour which should terminate this long and bitter self-sacrifice, to rejoice with joy unspeakable at the thought of exchanging the companionship of these

7

dull Galileans for that of the heavenly hierarchies? Shall we not see Him sitting rapt and expectant, scarcely heeding the observations of His companions, mindful only of the seraphic sounds soon to burst on His ear?

Nothing of all this. Having loved His own during the long years of their fellow-pilgrimage, He loved them unto the end. To them His thoughts were given. All His solicitude was for them. Every emotion of their hearts, every utterance of their lips, had for Him the profoundest importance. They were "His own." The angels are not His own in any such sense, and therefore His thoughts were now given, not to the angels but to His disciples. If we would but know it, the preference given by Christ to the impure children of earth, whom He yearned to purify, over the unfallen sons of God, was repeated hour by hour during the whole of His life; and the triumph of His love was in the perseverance with which He maintained unto the last this preference, notwithstanding the new and sad revelations of their unloveliness.

"He loved his own." This was their testimony. On reviewing what had passed between Him and them during those years of His ministry, they were enabled to see that all that He had said and done, without any exception whatever, was fitly expressive of a marvelous love. Many things in His conduct and in His language appeared to them at the time, perhaps, dubiously expressive of love; but when they had at length reached a position from whence they could take an impartial and accurate survey of the whole of their intercourse, they saw that in all things He had acted toward them as toward His own peculiar treasure, and that if they had been the apple of His eye He could not have been more concerned for their interests.

The experience of those early disciples in this corresponds with the experience of those who are walking with Him in these days. Sometimes He leaves them for many a long hour toiling in rowing, but what they know not then they know afterward. He takes extraordinary liberties with us. Believing in His love and having our own particular conception of what love is, we settle it in our minds that a certain contingency can never, by any possibility, be allowed to come to pass. Against everything else we prepare—not against that. We feel that it would be an unpardonable outrage to His most loving nature to suppose for a moment that He should suffer *that* contingency to come to pass.

8

And yet that is the very thing that He brings to pass. We had boasted of the love of Jesus among our neighbors, and told them that He would not suffer our brother Lazarus to die, but would assuredly come and restore him to health, and, lo! Lazarus dies and is buried, and it is much if our sense of the love of Jesus be not buried with Him. He takes what seem to us frightful liberties with our sensibilities and with our trust. But there comes sooner or later, if we only stubbornly trust on, an hour when all His ways are vindicated, and those apparent unkindnesses become sanctified and precious in our memories.

Surely, He may do what He will with His own. The price He has paid to make them His own is a sufficient guarantee that He will never make light of anything in which their welfare is at all concerned. We are precious to Him by virtue of the blood which He has shed for us, and for Him to be found at anytime wanting in solicitude for our happiness would be for Him to treat that blood of His as the sinners of this world treat it. The persuasion of Christ's love must be graven in our hearts so deeply that no semblance of indifference on His part will ever make the slightest impression upon us. This is the victory which overcomes the world.

We are "His own." He has set us apart for Himself. He has absolute dominion over us, and may do what He will with us. There is no one in the universe that can call Him to account for any height of blessing and of privilege He may see fit to bestow upon us. He may fill us with all the fullness of God. He may make of us a new sharp threshing-instrument, and thresh the mountains with us. He may make us sit down upon His own throne and put into our childish hand His own sublime scepter. We are His. Not a tongue in the universe can dare to wag, for we have been bought with a price. There is no extravagance of love equal or at all comparable to that of giving His life for us.

We are His own, and He is therefore identified with us. We may boldly see the communication of all that ennobles His own character. We are His own, and His eye will dart flames of fire at all that would pluck us out of His hand. He will not suffer the world to write its name upon our foreheads beside His own.

John 13:2. *And supper being ended* (the devil having now put it into the heart of Judas Iscariot, Simon's son, to betray him)."*

This was not the first thing that Satan had put into the heart of Judas. Satan does not begin by putting in such monstrous thoughts as these; the mind would incontinently [spontaneously] reject them. It is by degrees and by a circuitous path that an individual is led up to some great act of iniquity.

The adversary begins by saying, "We will never approach so diabolical an act as that," and leads him by a path that promises to conduct him in a very different direction; but there is an imperceptible curve to it, and gradually it doubles on itself, and the thing once so bitterly repudiated is at length greeted gladly. Intemperance is, perhaps, the great means by which he effects the perpetration of huge iniquities in these days, and he has seduced the whole world to aid him in educating a multitudinous band of murderers and suicides. Or it may be that covetousness is the great means, for intemperance and every other passion enters into alliance with covetousness.

It was the love of money that was the root of the gigantic evil which was now witnessed in the heart of Judas. Before that passion had developed itself, Jesus saw the seed of it in the heart of Judas; and hence His exclamation, years before the evening in question, "One of you is a devil." Doubtless this exclamation met with no corroborative response in the heart of Judas. He was perfectly assured that he was not a devil. He was conscious of human affections; his breast was not unacquainted with gentle and kind emotions; he was susceptible to love and friendship; he listened with pleasure to the teachings of the Son of God; the society of this best of beings had attractions for him; none could accuse him of immorality or allege anything in his conduct that made it improper for him to be one of the twelve chosen companions of the Lord. Yes, he was quite satisfied that he was not the devil of whom Christ spoke. Whoever might be alarmed by the intimation, there was no occasion for alarm on his part.

---

* It should rather be translated "supper being come," or "there being a supper."

Alas! it was this very self-deception that showed the Satanic influence already, though subtly and unobtrusively, working within him. There was the slightest possible chink through which Satan had liberty to breathe into his mind without suffering his repulsive lineaments to be seen, and insensibly the whole atmosphere of his soul became what Satan wished it to be.

Judas had been for some time guilty of appropriating money put into the bag. Having been appointed to the honorable office of banker for the poor, a mediator to convey the gifts of the few to the suffering many, he had been guilty of an unspeakably great crime, treason to the poor. He stood between the benevolent and the needy, not to communicate, but to intercept. Treason to the poor and treason to the good! Men may make light of this crime; the poor are but the dregs of humanity in their opinion, and a little charity withheld from them is of no importance. But God has been pleased to identify Himself with the poor and needy, saying, "He that giveth to the poor lendeth to the Lord; and the defrauded poor shall be avenged by the Lord."

And there was no more fit preparation for the crime of betraying the Son of God than that of treachery toward the poor. Ah, but if we should go thoroughly into this matter, should we not probably find that many of us are guilty in some modified and yet sufficiently-alarming sense of treachery to the poor? Are we not, some of us, sent to them with benefactions which never reach them, and are only unconscious of guilt because so long accustomed to look upon the goods as bestowed on us, whereas the light of God's Word would plainly reveal upon those goods the names of the poor and needy?

Jesus disclosed on fit occasions His omniscience, but He made no parade of this any more than of His other divine perfections. Had He daily and hourly flashed on all around Him the evidence of His perfect knowledge, and made every man habitually to feel that his secret thoughts and untold acts were all fully in the gaze of Jesus, His presence would have been insupportable. Companionship would have been impossible. He gave them the evidence, and then He left it for them to remember or forget, according as faith or unbelief bore sway in them.

Ordinarily, He received men upon the footing which they themselves selected. He came not to condemn the world, but to save the world. Judas had no such perception of the divinity of Christ as hindered him from embezzling the money entrusted to him for the poor. At times, perhaps, there came over him a suspicion that he was known, and would soon be held up to the scorn of his acquaintances. This, which should have brought him to Jesus, only precipitated matters.

"Into the heart." This made the movement entirely his own. Though all the devils in hell had wished it and sought it, they could have had no power at all to accomplish it by his instrumentality, if he had not himself chosen it, willed it and given himself freely and heartily to it. Anything that is in the heart is the heart's own, and could not at all be there if the heart had not consented. If Satan had influenced Judas to do the thing in some mysterious way, without the voluntary decision and preference of Judas himself, then it could not have been said that Satan had put it into his heart.

The words "in the heart" fasten the responsibility upon Judas. And so it is with all the sinful volitions of men at the present day. They choose to do evil; they are not made to do it. God has given stupendous power to the will of man—power to resist God; how much more power to resist Satan! Yes, the hosts of hell, all of them, are utterly baffled in the presence of a will that rightly uses the power bestowed upon it. "Resist the devil, and he will flee from you."

John 13:3. *"Jesus, knowing that the Father had given all things into his hands, and that he was come from God and went to God."*

Thus is introduced the account of the washing of the disciples' feet. That action was not performed in a moment of forgetfulness. Jesus had the fullest consciousness of His true dignity—a dignity so great that it baffled every other conception than His. The consciousness of His sublime and ineffable superiority to all created beings was not allowed to check the flow of His friendliness toward the humble Galileans among whom He sat, or to hinder Him from performing the most menial of offices in their behalf.

Man, clothed in a little brief and dubious authority, is hindered by an intense consciousness of dignity from descending but for a moment, even in manner, to the level of his fellows. The consciousness of dignity is with him a barrier to free and loving intercourse. But with Jesus, to remember His own divine exaltation was only to immerse Himself anew in that ocean of love which fills the bosom of the Godhead. He had thought of these disciples when He had of old sat upon His throne of thrones in Heaven, and there consequently appears no reason why He should not remember them now. He had already descended for them nine hundred and ninety-nine steps leading from that height of glory to the place of His present humiliation, and should He not take the thousandth step?

That men of the world should have a false idea of dignity, and be deterred by considerations of personal importance from coming near to their brethren, is not to be wondered at, but, should we meet with any instance of a Christian hindered by the consciousness of his rank from manifesting an affectionate interest in his brethren, what could we do but wonder and grieve? For such a one this blessed act of self-abnegation on the part of the Savior has been in vain. This will become evident when we reach the fifteenth verse: "For I have given you an example, that ye should do as I have done to you."

We never shall have any proper conception of what true dignity is until we understand that love is upon the throne of the universe. He

13

that sits upon the throne came into the world and washed the feet of those Galilean fishermen, that believers might be blissfully aware that love is wedded to Omnipotence. If we see the glory of the infinite God in the face of Him Whose hands are pouring water on the feet of those twelve disciples, it will be impossible for us to shrink from any because they move in a different circle.

God sometimes bestows gifts just that love may have something to renounce. The things that He puts into our hands are possibly put there that we may have the opportunity of showing what is in our heart. Oh that there were in us a fervor of love that would lead us to examine everything that belongs to us, to ascertain how it might be made a means of showing our affection to Christ! Oh that we could one and all bring ourselves to believe that the largest amount of benefit to be derived from anything is when it is made the means of saying for us, "Lord, thou knowest that I love thee!"

"Knowing that he was come from God and went to God." Fixing our attention upon the great truth set forth in these words, we shall, perhaps, find that the incident of which we have an account in the verses that follow illustrates that truth in an interesting matter. Jesus was erst in Heaven. By Him all things were made—by Him and for Him. He was the Lord of angels, and all Heaven was bathed in the brightness of His glory and the beauty of His love. He lays aside His royal garments, divests Himself of His native splendor and dignity, makes Himself of no reputation and takes upon Him the form of a servant.

This, however, is only for a season, and with a view to the better unfolding of His glory in the redemption of sinners. The term of His humiliation ended, He once more ascends on high, leading captivity captive, and sitting down at the right hand of the Majesty on high, gladdens once again, and shall henceforth for ever gladden, the hosts of Heaven.

Now behold the illustration of this which was intended to affect the minds of His earthly disciples and assist them to understand that He was come from God and was going to God. He occupies the place of pre-eminence at the table where His disciples and He have met to eat the paschal lamb. They call Him Master and Lord. However imperfect their views, they know that never man spoke as this Man. No man was ever clothed with such authority. What now? He rises from supper and makes Himself as a servant.

Whatsoever there was in His apparel that unfitted Him to represent the character of a servant of servants He lays aside. He takes a basin of water and girds Himself with a towel, and bows down to His disciples that He may wash their feet. Should now any one enter the room, his eye would fall upon the twelve; not a glance would be given to Him Who is washing their feet, for what is He but a menial?

But stay. There is an unoccupied place; and when that servant has accomplished His task, He puts on other apparel, sits down in the place of distinction, and is recognized as the Lord and Master, the Messiah, the Prince of the kings of the earth.

Was there not in all this a striking illustration of that other great truth, that He had come from God and would return to God? Later in the evening He said to His disciples, "I came forth from the Father and am come into the world: again, I leave the world and go to the Father." And they were enabled to understand Him, for they said, "Lo, now speakest thou plainly."

Christ's acts of humiliation are to be estimated by the dignity of the agent, and inasmuch as the dignity surpasses conception, the condescension of this act also surpasses conception. In eternity, as we advance in the knowledge of Christ's glory, so shall we advance in the estimate of His humility. It is evident that we do not yet understand the action that is here recorded. We have not attained, neither are already perfect, with regard to any one of the incidents of our Savior's life, for the reason that we have not attained unto a proper understanding of that height of glory from which He descended in order to perform the acts of His earthly ministry. It is good for us to remember, as we read each narrative of the Gospel, that into the hand of Jesus the Father had given all things, and that He came from God and went to God.

John 13:4-5. *"He riseth from supper and laid aside his garments; and took a towel and girded himself. After that he poureth water into a basin, and began to wash his disciples' feet, and to wipe them with the towel wherewith he was girded."*

Here are seven acts, in themselves, under ordinary circum-stances, utterly insignificant; and yet, as here presented to us, of the highest significance; the seven thunders or the seven vials perhaps not more so. Acts are common and mean because they are ordinarily expressive of the common and mean thoughts of men. Let us not accuse the acts that make up our daily life of meanness, but our ignoble souls that reveal themselves so unworthily through those acts. The same act may successively mount up through every intermediate stage from the depth of unworthiness to a transcendent height of excellence, according to the soul that is manifested by it.

One of the glorious ends of our Lord's incarnation was that He might propitiate us with the details of life, so that we should not disdain these as insignificant, but rather disdain ourselves for our inability to make these details interpreters of a noble nature. Sin drags down with it not only the soul of man, but all that encompasses man about and stands in any relation with him. It falsifies the whole environing creation and stretches its dingy pall over all the glories of the universe. It makes not merely the nature of man contemptible, but all the offices of life, so that it becomes impossible for sin-governed natures to connect the ideas of honor, virtue and sublimity with anything pertaining to the path in which man is bidden ordinarily to tread.

There is nothing more desolating to society than the habit of viewing the ordinary functions of life as ignoble and unimportant. It was needful that the Son of God should come into this world and pass through the various stages of human life, religiously and joyously performing the thousand minute offices that make up the staple of life, in order that we might be reconciled to the common, and learn to recognize, in the trivial, undreamt-of opportunities of heroism.

With his poor, wrecked soul, man staggers into the presence of Jesus, expecting to behold a series of acts in all respects unlike what

16

man performs, and to his amazement beholds Him pouring water into a basin and washing the feet of certain Galileans. He says, "Is this all? I will do this." Will you do this? You must first go up to the throne of God and sit there, and then come down holy, harmless and undefiled. You see no beauty in this act? The acknowledgment is your own severest condemnation. It shows you unregenerate, a denizen of the defiled and disorganized world in which sinners dwell.

Look well upon this transaction. Who knows but a ray from the Sun of Righteousness may reach your soul, and through the very contemplation of this humble act, your need of infinite grace be made known to you? The heavens declare the glory of God; yes, and so do these acts of the Lord Jesus, the latter more than the former. The seraphim in Heaven veil their faces in the presence of nothing more divine than what is here witnessed. Does this language seem extravagant? Of necessity it must seem so, until it be taught you that God is love, that the acts which best reveal love are the grandest and worthiest, and that these acts were found in that upper chamber where Jesus laid aside His garments and took a towel, basin and water, and washed the feet of His companions.

Oh let us then look with affection and gratitude upon the daily details of life, seeing the sanctifying imprint of the hand of Jesus upon them all! He could have ranged through the world on mighty deeds intent, but only by adopting the wretched ideas of moral grandeur that obtain among men. The sublimity of Jesus appears in His rejection of the opportunity of moving in a path that men deem sublime. The incomparable excellence of the divine character comes out more strikingly in this obscure chamber than it could possibly have done in scenes that would have called Plutarch to seize his pen.

We should never forget that the disciples whose feet Jesus washed were our representatives. They were representative men, and Jesus dealt with us in dealing with them. "Go," He says, "and those whom you baptize teach to observe what I have commanded you." The commands given, the words spoken, were not for them alone. They were vessels to bear His Name before others. Every believer may understand that Jesus has washed his feet. He may by faith witness the very act performed in his behalf. But let him well understand the act, that his stony heart of pride may be broken within him.

But Jesus has stooped lower than to wash our feet. The filth of the human heart is something unspeakably more offensive than any material defilement. Sinners cannot easily know this; but ask the inhabitants of Heaven what they think: they will tell you that nothing startles them so much as to see the Godhead approaching the sin-steeped soul of man. There is nothing in the universe that has so odious and repulsive an aspect for a holy God as unbelief, selfishness, pride, envy, malice and the like. And there is no more wonderful spectacle anywhere than that of the blessed Spirit of God in the sinful heart of man, coming into closest quarters with his pride and malice, bringing Christ nigh to his rebellious will, and hewing for the triune God a holy of holies out of a rock of unbelief.

Whenever there is heard within us the still small voice of the Spirit, dissuading from evil, impelling to that which is good, there is an act of unutterable condescension and self-humbling on the part of the ever-blessed God which is altogether impossible to explain or justify without reference to the cross of Christ.

John 13:6-8. *"Then cometh he to Simon Peter: and Peter saith unto him, Lord, dost thou wash my feet? Jesus answered and said unto him, What I do thou knowest not now; but thou shalt know hereafter. Peter saith unto him, Thou shalt never wash my feet."*

The senses are not always the best interpreters. They convey their testimony, but it is sometimes in cipher and needs an interpreter. "What I do thou knowest not now."

But can I not see what You are doing? You are washing my feet, neither more nor less. Could an angel from Heaven inform me better than my own senses do concerning this act?

Nevertheless, O Peter, you know not now what your Lord is doing. Your information is in cipher, and needs to be expounded to you. Yes, He washes your feet; but what the thought of His mind which is expressed by this action is you have yet to learn. In fact, what is now said to you, Simon Bar-Jona, applies not merely to this transaction, but to all that you have seen Jesus do and heard Him say since He first spoke to you by Jordan until this closing scene of His life. You know not now, save very imperfectly, but you shall know hereafter, when He shall have risen from the dead; still better, on the day of Pentecost; still better, when you shall go to Cornelius with the Gospel; still better and better as you shall advance farther in the path of obedience, suffering and triumph; in higher perfection at your exodus from earth; in highest, when the Lord Jesus shall come, with ten thousands of His saints, in the glory of the angels and of His Father. When John, in the Isle of Patmos, saw Jesus, he fell at His feet as one dead—not but that it was the same Jesus with Whom he had spent years of intimate and hallowed fellowship, but the glory of the Savior, as it is now made known to him, he little understood in the days when He went in and out with him.

A new light shed upon the word makes it a new word, a new light shed upon providences makes them new dispensations, and a new light suffusing the works of God gives us a new creation. How much is there in the Old Testament that could only be glimmeringly discerned until the true light came, thousands of years after! The Spirit of God is symbolized by seven lamps. He comes to a generation in the infancy of time as a lamp dispelling the darkness, but beware how you entertain the thought that this is the fullest revelation. In process of time He will come in as a lamp of far-exceeding luster, and in comparison with the light now diffused, the former will appear darkness.

After a long interval He bursts upon the world with a far-surpassing glory; and so lamp after lamp translates the splendor of Heaven to earth. Yet it is all one Spirit. He that spoke to Enoch spoke also to Moses, and He that spoke to Elijah spoke to Paul. He that is least in the kingdom of Heaven is greater than John the Baptist. Our Gospel is the everlasting Gospel. If you will believe, you shall see the glory of God therein. There are some to whom the throne of God is there and the seven lamps of the Spirit burn simultaneously. Meditate therein, and what of glory you know not now you shall know hereafter.

"Thou shalt never wash my feet." This appears to be the expression of humility. How could Peter suffer that One so infinitely his superior should perform a service so menial? To many, perhaps, it may seem not only natural, but every way fitting, that Peter should object to be thus waited upon by his Lord. This only shows, however, that to entertain a false conception of humility is something not peculiar to Peter. For the sake of such, we remark, that whatever hinders us from receiving a blessing that God is willing to bestow upon us is not humility but the mockery of it. True humility will never betray the interests of the soul. That is not a true Christian grace which opposes the development of other Christian graces. By this test try the spirits. Humility desires the utmost communication of God's favor, and anything that teaches you to decline the spiritual blessings that God is ready to bestow, know that it is of the earth, earthy.

So, on a previous occasion, Peter said, "Depart from me, O Lord, for I am a sinful man." Now, Satan would have desired above all things a compliance with this request. What shall we think, then, of the humility that dictated it? It is well to have conviction of sin—we cannot

20

have it too deeply; we can scarcely take too dark a view of our own character—but humility, as a Christian grace, must ever draw the heart to Christ.

There is nothing more worthless than the self-deceit which leads some to say, "I am content to be an inferior Christian, and to be undistinguished by spiritual attainments; if I were a more devoted servant of the Lord, I might be lifted up with pride." That is to say, you are afraid you would lose your humility if you obtained more faith. Well, lose *your* humility; it will be no great loss. If you really obtain a strong faith, you will have along with it a very different humility from that which you now have. Consider and confess. Your present humility is something most base, for it gives God the lie direct, saying it is not good for a man to love God with all his heart and soul; and further it says that He is not worthy that you should serve Him devotedly. It tears almost all the pages out of the Bible, for almost every page of Scripture contains promises, invitations, commands, which it nullifies.

A genuine humility will ever feel the need of the largest measures of grace, and will be perfected just in the degree in which that grace is bestowed. Spiritual pride shows, not that there has been too much, but too little, of the operation of the Spirit. The only way to overcome it is to press forward. The truly humble man will seek to be filled with all the fullness of God, knowing that when so filled there is not the slightest place for pride or for self.

Peter had doubtless taken part in the dispute of the disciples as to which of them should be greatest—the very dispute which prompted our Lord to do what He was now doing. Peter's conduct in the after part of the evening showed plainly that he was far from being perfect in humility. It must be very offensive to God when we fail to give those proofs of humility which the occasion properly demands, and then insist that some unrequired thing done by us has the impress of that heavenly grace.

Some are deterred from communicating freely with God concerning this and that temporal affair which occupies their minds by the idea that it is beneath the dignity of God to take note of such matters. This, too, is sin baptized with the name of humility. They say, with Peter, "Thou shalt never wash my feet," and imagine themselves very religious. The only acceptable religion is to let God reign in your heart. To partition off a part of your thought-world, and call it a holy of holies, and hang a thick curtain before it, and then surrender the outer court to Gentile traffickers—this is no religion.

You may make God a prisoner and visit Him at times in sacerdotal garments, and then plume yourself on the deep tone of reverence that marks your approaches to Him. The disciples imagined that they were giving proof of an admirable veneration for the person of Jesus when they refused to allow little children to be brought to Him. They would cut Him off from a portion of humanity that had for Him a high attraction. Your minor cares Christ will not disdain. Without Christ, you will soon find that they are not minor, but insupportable; bring them to Him and every one of them will be made to yield you tribute in coin that has the superscription of Heaven upon it.

John 13:8-10. *"If I wash thee not, thou hast no part with me. Simon Peter saith unto him, Lord, not my feet only, but also my hands and my head. Jesus saith to him, He that is washed needeth not save to wash his feet, but is clean every whit."*

What our Lord here said to Peter concerning his soul was in reply to something that Peter had said touching his feet. "Thou shalt never wash my feet." Why not? What have I been doing these successive years that we have been together? Have I not been purifying you unto Myself? Am I not still engaged in this? Are there not multitudinous sins in you that are yet to be blotted out? There is no defilement like that of sin, and unless I wash you from your sins you have no part with Me in glory. Why, then, does it seem to you an insufferable thing that I should wash your feet?

Peter, without pausing to revolve these weighty words in his mind, simply seizes the idea that what is now being done has some relation to the glory and blessedness in which he hopes to participate with Christ, and exclaims, "Lord, not my feet only, but also my hands and my head." How long, O Peter, how long will it be before we learn to receive with due consideration the words of our Lord? He spoke as never man spoke, and yet how prone we are to receive His words as we do those of any thoughtless companion, and imagine that we can thoroughly master them without an effort, in the twinkling of an eye! How soon we are discouraged when our own weighty words are treated thus! How wonderful that Christ should not have been discouraged! Many of His most precious utterances have been for eighteen centuries waiting for someone to penetrate them.

The misconception of Peter elicited from Jesus an explanation of His words. Any doubt as to the spiritual significance of what He had said is banished by the closing words, "Ye are clean, but not all," glancing at the unsanctified Judas. This will assist us to understand other things spoken by the Savior that same evening. For instance, when He told His disciples to provide themselves with swords, we can hardly suppose that He wished to be understood literally, any more than when He said, "If I wash thee not, thou hast no part with me." If Peter had given heed to what took place in connection with the washing of his feet, and earnestly grasped the instruction then proffered, he would not have brought upon himself the reproof, "Put up thy sword; they that take the sword shall perish with the sword." With regard to the expression, "This is my body," there was no possibility of a misapprehension on the part of the disciples, as they saw the body of their Lord before them. It was necessary that men should get down into a deep, dark pit before they could palm off upon their besotted minds such a fantasy as that the bread in the hand of Christ was itself His hand.

It is supposed that in the words, "He that is washed needeth not save to wash his feet," there is an allusion to the fact that they who had been to the bath needed only to wash their feet in returning to the house. Whether or not there was any reference to the temple service (Ex. 40: 12, 31) I know not. The spiritual truth conveyed in the words does not seem difficult of apprehension. Jesus had before said, "If I wash thee not." The inference from these words that Peter had not been in any sense purified would be erroneous. "Ye are clean through the word which I have spoken." The work in their hearts had been commenced, but it was by no means terminated. Daily and hourly they needed the grace of God in new communications. They were regenerate, but they needed the sincere milk of the Word, that they might grow thereby. "Ye are clean through the word. Sanctify them through thy truth. Thy word is truth."

The words, "If I wash thee not thou hast no part with me," require us to believe that the Lord Jesus is not more intent upon the salvation of a soul than He is upon its sanctification, and assure us that the cry, "Lord, save or I perish," has not more power to touch the sensibilities of Heaven than the prayer, "Make me perfect to do thy will." Let it be understood that faith in Christ is as truly sanctifying as it is saving. The same Jesus Who bore our sins in His own body here presents Himself in the capacity of the Purifier. If there be any union, any commerce,

24

between Christ and ourselves, it is in the way of sanctification. "Ye are washed, ye are sanctified," wrote Paul to the Corinthians, and it was Christ Who had washed them.

The Spirit of God comes to us to make the words of Christ influential in us. This is sanctification, to have the word of Christ dwelling influentially in the heart; then Christ reigns in the heart. If then, a man has no part with Christ, where shall he appear? Scripture leaves us not in the dark. Men say, "Let us hope for the best." But what does the Bible say? "The fearful and unbelieving, and the abominable and murderers and whoremongers and sorcerers and idolaters and all liars, shall have their part in the lake which burneth with fire and brimstone." There is nothing less than this unutterably fearful doom awaiting all who are not sanctified by Christ so as to have part with Him.

Fearful ones, beware! You tremble and draw back affrighted from some rugged path in which Christ bids you come with Him, and yet you fear not the lake of fire prepared for the fearful. Deny Him not; He will not deny you. He will not save you unless you follow Him. You know Him not if you are appalled by the dangers that seem to stand thick along the path to which He summons you. Has He not overcome the world? Does not all danger turn pale at His presence? What can harm you if you keep your eye on Him? Be His partner here, and you shall be His partner in the day of His undisputed pre-eminence. It is enough for you to know that it is Christ that is purifying you; One so much your Friend can be trusted to do this; there cannot be needless severity in the process. He sits as a refiner and purifier of silver. Your faith is more precious than gold that perishes.

John 13:10-11. *"Ye are clean, but not all."* **In explanation it is added,** *"For he knew who should betray him: therefore said he, Ye are not all clean."*

He knew also who should deny Him thrice and who should forsake Him, yet only to him in whose heart was treason was the negative intended to apply. To the heart-searching eye of the Savior there was a very important ground of distinction between Peter and Judas. If any man love not the Lord Jesus Christ, let him be *anathema maranatha.* There was love to Christ in the eleven—most immature, a mere germ, a love ill-prepared to stand the fiery trial to which it was about to be subjected, yet nevertheless a genuine beginning of love destined ere long to triumph over all opposition. But there was not this in Judas. He loved not Christ. Something or other in the character or in the work of Christ had attracted him; but as the character of Christ became more unveiled to him, he experienced more and more of repugnancy. (He preferred himself, with all his sins, all his vileness, to the Son of God.) The disinterestedness and spirit of sacrifice conspicuous in Christ awoke no fellow-response in him, but on the contrary jarred strongly on his feelings. The words, the acts, the looks, that drew the other disciples to their Master, only served to widen the gulf betwixt him and the Savior.

Christians sometimes imagine that nothing more is necessary to subdue the heart of a sinner than to show him the character of Christ, but until his heart has been changed it is impossible that he should love Christ. It is not possible that he should love light and darkness at the same time; being what he is, the exhibition of Christ can only excite his hatred.

We flatter ourselves that by the abundant preaching of the Gospel and diffusion of the Scriptures, and by the vigorous prosecution of all our evangelistic schemes, we are gradually and surely filling up the chasm that separates the world from Christ. Well, it is so if the Spirit of God go with the Word, convincing and converting. Where His influences are not experienced, there—let us well understand it—*there* is no subjugation of the world's hostility, on the contrary, augmentation.

26

We could not wish for the world a better opportunity of knowing Christ than Judas enjoyed. In fact, we may consider Judas as the type or representative of that large portion of the world to which we are now offering the Gospel: the nearer it is brought to Christ, the more it rejects Him. "If I had not done among them the works which none other man did, they had not had sin; but now they have both seen and hated both me and my Father."

But knowing the disciples as He did, how could the Savior bear such an honorable testimony to them? How could He say that they were holy? In the great audience-chamber of this world, how many, hearing Jesus thus speak, begin to exchange whispers and smiles and looks of astonishment! We know what they say to one another. They are bringing to each other's recollection a thousand odious particulars concerning the eleven, citing innumerable instances of their pride, folly, unbelief, selfishness, ambition, covetousness, timidity, rashness, inconstancy, insensibility, malice, vindictiveness.

Very well; pile up these sins; rear them up, a pyramid, a mighty tower; and when you have finished it, we will write on it the names of the eleven and the names of all who are similarly sinful. Your names, too, it appears, belong conspicuously there, though you have reared the monument. In fact, we must inscribe the names of all men. And now over against it behold a multitude of angels rearing another monument, snow white, and upon the face of it inscribing the names of the heirs of salvation. But where shall these names be sought? Upon the sin-monument, for all the children of men are there; elsewhere they cannot be sought. We have only the proud, foolish, unbelieving, selfish, ambitious and covetous to choose from.

What hinders now that these eleven should be chosen? The only question is, "Have they received anything that constitutes them different in essential respects from other men?" They have. They have received the elements of a new life; they are born again; there is the seed of another nature in them—a nature that will first struggle with and then overcome and utterly destroy the evil against which you declaim. They are following Christ in the highway of holiness. As they proceed we see them ever and anon casting sins over the parapet, and it is certain that they shall at length appear, spotless, unblemished, unblamable, in the presence of the Father of lights.

In uttering the words, "Ye are clean," the Savior had respect to the measure of advantage enjoyed by them. Their advantages had undoubtedly been great, but there were other higher advantages to be enjoyed in the outpouring of the Spirit; and had these higher advantages left them morally what they now were, our Lord would not have addressed them thus. If we that now live should have simply an antepentecostal faith and love and courage and humility, we could not flatter ourselves that Christ would say to us, "Ye are clean." As they traveled the highway of holiness the apostles threw from it many stones that once deformed it, and wonderfully facilitated matters for those that should come after.

We have seen the Lamb die; have seen Him rise again and ascend into the heavens; have seen the Spirit poured out; have seen the apostles and their churches; have seen the visions of Patmos; and for eighteen centuries of the history of the Church in the world have seen the finger of divine Providence writing, very slowly, sometimes but one letter in centuries, yet beyond a question writing no other than the inscription first seen by Belshazzar, "*Mene, mene, tekel, upharsin.*" Where? Upon the Church? Upon that which calls itself the Church. Nevertheless, there is a chosen generation, a holy people, though mostly hidden.

But the thing is this, our responsibilities rise as the ages revolve. Men suppose the contrary to be the case. It is so long since the apostles lived, they think, that it would be preposterous to look now for piety like theirs. It is hoped that God will, every century, every year, abate somewhat of His claims and accept the mere crumbs of piety from us. What a delusion! The claim of God is adamantine, and no flow of time will ever wear it away.

Is there not too much reason to believe that, if Christ should speak to us, instead of saying, "Ye are clean, but not all," He would say, "Ye are unclean, but not all"?

28

John 13:12-13. *"So after he had washed their feet, and had taken his garments, and was set down again, he said unto them, Know ye what I have done to you? Ye call me Master (Teacher) and Lord; and ye say well; for so I am."*

"So I am." What delightful words are these to those who deeply feel their ignorance, the inability of their fellowmen to restore them from their ignorance, the utter privation of all claim to celestial teaching; who know that there is a way to Heaven and who desire to walk therein, to be educated for Heaven, to learn the laws and usages of the kingdom of Heaven! They have not to be educated in order that they may come to Christ, but He is their Educator, from the lowest form [grade] upward. They do not need to get rid of their gross ignorance before they approach Him. Who but He can dispel the stupidity and the darkness of their minds? Could any other do it, that other would be the true teacher.

Christ's glory as a teacher is that He can take hold of such ruined souls as yours and mine and pour light into them, first a single ray scarce relieving the darkness, then increasing radiance and heat, distributed with infinite wisdom among the valleys and chasms of the soul, until the whole is bathed in the light of Heaven. We need not fear that He will upbraid us and frown us away because we are so ignorant; He gives to all liberally and upbraids not; He upbraids those who remain away: "Ye will not come unto me that ye might have life."

The most surprising spectacle is when one of the wise of this world is brought to Him. What an enormous edifice has to be pulled down that Christ, the true foundation-stone, may be placed in the bottom of the heart!

Alas for those who are rearing up on high, story above story, a towering monument, intending, when it is done, to put the living stone somewhere at the top, and so get the whole transported to Heaven! No, it must all come down, every stone of it; and it is to be feared that there will not be time for you to get it down and the new foundation laid before the great earthquake flies rumbling through the earth, for the cement that you are using hardens rapidly, and the stones cling

29

together as though they naturally belonged together; and you are bestowing so much ornament and there are so many admirers that you are every day more and more fascinated with your own work. Day by day you become more and more intensely your own ideal; and the demolition of a structure so laboriously reared, so expensively, seems to your conception like the crash of an expiring world.

Then the schools of the world, so far from fitting their pupils for the school of Christ, make it less and less possible that those pupils should ever be brought to Christ. And here we discover a very important cause of the misunderstanding between the scholars of Christ and other scholars. The former condemn or disparage a great deal that which the latter have in high estimation, and do it not because the acquisitions are worthless in themselves, but because they block the way for Christ. They are not built upon the only true foundation. There must be life at the base—a living, life-giving stone; then will the superincumbent mass [structure above] be also informed with life and beauty.

There are a thousand forms of human knowledge that are now slighted by the scholars of Christ, not because, as is supposed, their minds are too contracted to form a proper estimate of them, but because they are aware that "in the present distress" and crisis one thing is needful. Their souls must first live, and then all intellectual acquisitions will participate in the life. While the soul is not possessed by the favor of God which is life, all mental acquisitions are but the tracery on the cornice of a sepulcher.

How wonderful a Teacher we have! Sometimes we seek Him in the house, but He is not there; we go forth seeking Him, and find Him perhaps in the wilderness or on a mountain praying, or leading some poor blind man by the hand, or eating with publicans or sinners, or asleep in a storm, or conversing with a Samaritan woman, or surrounded by wrathful men, or bearing a cross. It is not merely His words that instruct: His place, His occupation, His companions, His environment, His garment, His silence, His submission—all teem with instruction. And they that learn of Him are made like unto Him.

30

John 13:14-15. *"If I then, your Lord and Master, have washed your feet, ye also ought to wash one another's feet. For I have given you an example, that ye should do as I have done to you."*

The argument is two-fold. Because of what Christ has done for me I should serve my brother, and I should serve him because of what Christ has done for him. In each of these considerations there is, to the believer, an inexhaustible fullness of power. It would be an infinite reproach to me to receive such amazing benefactions from the Son of the Blessed and to retain my own wretched, churlish, selfish nature. In the parables of Christ, truth comes to us as she came to David in the parable that Nathan spoke, and before we are aware we have pronounced our own condemnation. When we read the parable of the steward who owed ten thousand talents, who was saved with all his family from lifelong captivity by the pure generosity of the master, and then displayed the base niggardliness and selfishness of his nature, unvanquished, undiminished by the exhibition of so large mercy, our souls are fired with indignation, and we exclaim, "Away with such a fellow from the earth! It is not fit that he should live." Then Truth lets fall her veil, and quietly asks us,

"Are you not the man?"

"I that man! That odious man!"

Well, perhaps not. Only it may be well to examine yourself and see what effect the unparalleled exhibition of love and mercy in the Gospel has had upon you. You are sitting at a banquet of promises, each of them worth more than ten thousand talents; you, that should be lifting up your eyes in torment, are sitting at the table of the Lord of life: His angels minister unto you. Now, what is the effect of it all upon you? Has this stupendous mercy made you merciful? As the Lord has sought you out, do you seek out the poor and needy? Do you readily cancel the claims against your brother? Do you value more highly the opportunity of serving him than the ability to make him serve you? Are you hindered by no feeling of shame from visiting the residence of poor and uncultivated Christians? When you enter their houses, is it as one

31

enters the house of his brother? Are you content that those Christians should come to your house as one goes to the house of his brother?

Again, Christ has forgiven your brother ten thousand talents; can you not forgive him three hundred pence? There has been joy in the presence of the angels of Heaven because of his liberation from a dread captivity, and do you insist upon hanging some chains upon him? Hearken to the kind utterances of the Gospel breathed in his ear by the Lord of glory. Will you cause the rude dissonance of your angry voice to be heard by him? The Lord has descended from the highest heavens, sweeping past the host of cherubim and seraphim, to become lower than angel, and has traversed the realm of death, that He might snatch this poor sinner from the devouring flame; and will you find it a costly sacrifice to ignore two or three contemptible conventional barriers separating you from him?

What a magnificent phenomenon would be witnessed if, throughout the Church of Christ, this appeal of the Lord Jesus should meet its fitting response! "If I then, your Lord and Master, have washed your feet, ye also ought to wash one another's feet." This would be, in some sense, the coming of Christ with ten thousand of His saints. He would live again in an exceeding great army. The Father would see Christ in us, and His love for Christ would come rushing down into our hearts a mighty torrent. John 17:26.

"For I have given you an example, that ye should do as I have done to you."

Do we understand, my friends? Christ came into this world not merely to act, but to show us how to act; not merely to suffer, but to show us how to suffer; not merely to love, but to show us how to love. If He has washed our feet, it is not merely that we should ascertain the depth of His humility, the vastness of His love, but that we should know also what humility and love to exercise. Have we read the entire Gospel under the influence of this great truth, looking at it as the portraiture of that better life which we ourselves are called to live? By the mere fact that we have taken up the cross to follow Christ we are pledged to follow Christ wheresoever He goes.

Ah, my friends, I am afraid that when Christ goes into yonder prison to visit a prisoner, some of us sit at the door talking with the jailer until the Master comes again; and when He stops to talk with a beggar, we leisurely stroll on and wait for Him at the corner; and when there is a whisper that the Jews will take up stones to stone Him, we go not up to that feast, but fulfill some other long-neglected duty. Is there not sometimes a phantom of Christ, saying, "I am Christ; follow me," that leads you in a pleasantly pious path, while the true Christ is making His way, attended by a little and despised band, through snow and ice, among precipices, in deserts and in the face of many foes? The thought is horrible; but the adversary is subtle and the heart deceitful. We have in the Scriptures an exact chart of the path pursued by Christ; and if we all duly give heed to this, we shall not go astray. Let us prove our Christ by the path and our path by Christ.

John 13:16. *"Verily, verily, I say unto you, The servant is not greater than his lord; neither he that is sent greater than he that sent him."*

Whence the necessity of so much emphasis in the statement of a truth so obvious? Do we not all know that the servant is not greater than his lord?—that the Christian is subordinated to Christ? Why introduce an announcement like this with a "Verily, verily, I say unto you"?

There was need, and there is need of this "Verily, verily." There is too much reason to believe that the great majority of Christians do not take their Master at His word in what He says. Notwithstanding His solemn reiteration of this truth, there are very few to whom it is a truth. Wherever we turn our eyes in the church we are met by the surprising spectacle of servants who put on the greatness which their Lord laid down. They disdain to be what their Lord was, to do what He did.

There is written over the door of a house, "Disciple of Jesus, servant of Christ." There come two men in ordinary apparel, but each of the twain is more than man: one is none other than the Son of Mary; the other is an attendant angel.

"Behold," says the Savior, "this is the habitation of one of My servants."

"A goodly mansion," says the angel.

"Ah, yes," responds our Advocate, "but it is not for his own pleasure; doubtless he has occasion to exercise hospitality." Several other remarks suggest themselves to the heavenly visitor. In fact, he finds it difficult to believe that a servant of Jesus here abides.

"To speak sooth [truly]," he says, "my heart is filled with admiration of the life whose memorials are in the Gospel. Whenever I think of a servant of Christ upon the earth, I seem to see before me one who has been reconciled by the life of Christ to a life like that of Christ—who has been caught away by the power of a blessed example from the vanities of the world; one who protests by all the force of his own exalted life against the pursuit of mere earthly honors and the pampering of the flesh."

34

"True," says the Master, with a sigh; "but it is possible for a servant of Mine to have the same mind that was in Me, though he be not a wanderer through the land as I was."

Jesus knocks at the door of His disciple. The servants, however, refuse Him admittance, assuring Him that their master is no friend of vagabonds or of hypocrites.

"Of course," says Jesus to the angel, "it is not surprising that these men should not know Me. They do not profess to be My servants. It is a pity, however, that their master, My servant, should not be aware of these impediments that choke the current of his own kindness."

The disciple of Jesus makes his appearance. He is going forth with his family to an entertainment given that day by a distinguished personage.

"The wife and daughters of this disciple," says the angel, "remind me very little of Joanna and Mary and Salome. Can it be that they have read what Peter and Paul have written by inspiration of God concerning female adornment?"

Jesus and His companion find difficulty in attracting the notice of the disciple. He does not recognize the Lord. Jesus says to him, "In the next street (I will show you the place) is a poor old man, a disciple of Jesus, whose sight is dim with age and who greatly desires that some brother should come and read to him for a half hour."

"Ah!" replies the disciple; "I am not a Scripture-reader. There are men especially appointed for this work."

"There is a youth, the only son of a widow," says Jesus again, "who has just been thrown into prison for debt; the sum is not large, and if you will pay it, there will be support for the widow and her family; if not, they will all be reduced to beggary."

"Ah!" returns the disciple; "I have acquired my wealth by industry, carefulness and prudence, and I know not why I should employ it in offering bounties for improvidence. The father should have insured his life. But we must away; I fear we shall be late."

"Stay!" says the unknown Jesus: "I wish your opinion concerning a passage of Scripture."

"You will find commentaries in yonder bookstore." With this reply, the disciple drives off with his family.

"Shall I not erase the inscription?" says the angel.

"Leave it," answers Jesus; "the day of trial cometh when the fire shall try every man's work."

The disciples had disputed with each other as to their relative dignity. Each was desirous of being the greatest, and each thought he could present some rather weighty considerations in favor of his own claim to pre-eminence. One had been called before the others; another had belonged to a higher social position; another had sacrificed more property; another had first borne public testimony to the Messiahship of Christ; another was more aged than the rest; another had been a more successful preacher; another had cast out many devils.

But Jesus says to them, "I am among you as He that serves. I have put Myself down below you. He among you, therefore, that seeks to be greater than his fellow-disciples, makes himself greater than Me. Study continually to keep lower than Me that you may occupy the right position relatively to each other. If you think it scorn to wash the feet of your associates, you do but show that you think it scorn to be as your Master. You make yourself greater than He is."

Let not the *poor* disciple think that the danger indicated in the words of our Lord is a danger peculiar to those who have abundantly of this world's goods. There are a hundred little ways by which the spirit that is here condemned may reveal itself. He that is impatient, he that is choleric [angry], he that is censorious, he that is sensitive and suspicious, he that prays little, he that is dogmatic, he that is unwilling in all societies to be known as a Christian—these and many others make themselves greater than the Master.

John 13:17. *"If ye know these things, happy are ye if ye do them."*

Who will show us any good thing? Where shall we find happiness? What is the secret of a happy life? These are questions that all men put to each other without being able to obtain a satisfactory and conclusive answer. Yet every one has already the information that he professes to desire. He puts into his vest pocket a scrap of paper given him by a person who is of no account in his eyes, and embarks for remote continents in a vain, life-long search of what is plainly enough pointed out in that scrap of paper. Socrates and Plato and Alcibiades discoursed together of the likelihood or unlikelihood of the advent of one from the skies to teach man what he so much needed to know—what, by himself, he never would know. Little, however, did it dawn upon their apprehensions that such a visitor would, unheeded, declare the secret so long and vainly sought by all mankind.

Happiness, we learn from our Lord Jesus Christ—(but do we learn? Are we not mocking Him in the use of this language, sitting at His feet as though to learn, yet giving our eyes and ears to some show discovered through the window?)—happiness consists, not in knowing, but in doing.

In doing! Who would have thought it? We should have thought to find happiness in exemption from work. We look with compassion upon the poor people who are obliged to work, and deplore the infelicity [unfortunateness] of our own position in being obliged occasionally to exert ourselves. Ah! I see how it is. Happiness consists in such work as that of carrying bags of pearls, caskets of diamonds and the like to our own treasury.

No, this is not the work of which Jesus speaks. The acts which He commends are acts of self-denial for the good of others.

The good of others! You mistake me quite. I ask how I may be happy myself; my question does not relate to the happiness of my neighbor. As you can give me no information on the point which interests me, I decline your instructions.

Ah, if the poor man would only suffer Jesus to teach him! "If ye know these things, happy are ye if ye do them." You yourselves shall find your happiness in a life of self-humiliation and self-abnegation. Be content to be as your Master, and your Master will not be content without making you as He is. Wash the feet of the disciples, deny yourself for their advantage, and the Son of God will take good care that you have a peace which passeth all understanding and a joy unspeakable. There is a woe where there is knowledge unaccompanied by obedience. It is fearful to think of the vast number who, at the present day, hear the sayings of Jesus and keep them not.

You have a very profound acquaintance with Scripture truth. A false doctrine is immediately betrayed to you; no disguise can hide it. How well and piously canst thou discourse! People feel small in your presence in view of your religious knowledge. You could write a discourse on the love of God that would carry off a prize from men. If Heaven could be won by knowledge, you would surely win it. But would you wash the feet of a disciple? Well, I think you would; for there is so much versatility in you that it would be strange if you were not at some time found doing this. But are your own hands clean? They are not. Even your kindly offices are mischievous because the truth does not sway you. You know the truth and serve falsehood. How can you be happy? The truth of God that is in you can only make you miserable, for your life is not subordinated to it.

How many are deceiving themselves with regard to their true condition simply because of their religious knowledge! They cannot understand how one should know so much without being a child of God. The truth of God is really, however, imprisoned in their mind. They receive the truth as though it were a king, and conduct it over a drawbridge and into handsome apartments, but soon it appears that the guest is a prisoner of state. When it pleases the host, the royal prisoner is brought forth and ceremoniously waited upon, but at other times it remains in seclusion. It has not the range of their being. Into the courtyard of their desires it is seldom allowed to descend, and a sentinel sometimes repels it from the terraced walk of their purposes. When they go abroad, it is confined at home; and when they are about to examine the interior of their palace, instructions are given to remove the prisoner from the apartments to be visited.

"If ye know these things." We have known them long enough, wondering all the while that we found so little joy in the knowledge. David and others esteemed the Word of God more than thousands of gold and silver. Why have I no similar appreciation of the Scriptures? Why is my joy in them so dubious and imperfect? For this reason— that you sought to find pleasure in the mere contemplation of the Word, losing sight of the plain declaration of our Lord, "Happy are ye if ye do them." The knowledge that leads to action is blessed. "That ye be not barren nor unfruitful in the knowledge of our Lord Jesus Christ."

John 13:18. *"I speak not of you all; I know whom I have chosen; but that the Scripture may be fulfilled, He that eateth bread with me, hath lifted up his heel against me."*

Christ had before said, "Ye are clean, but not all," knowing who should betray Him. The grace of Christ is free and full; the most precious promises and tender invitations fall naturally from His lips, but it is quite possible for a man to hear them with all familiarity, year after year, without having any part or lot in them. Judas may be considered as the representative of the countless host of the ungodly. They were tried in him. Peradventure it will come into their minds to say, "We would not have rejected the Savior if we had had the opportunity of drawing very nigh to Him, of living for some days in His society, of receiving His rebukes, hearkening to His promises. We would in such a case have undoubtedly discerned the divine excellence and attractiveness of His character, and would have believed upon Him unto everlasting life." But this conceit is without any warrant.

During the years that Christ suffered Judas to be associated with Him no one ever blamed Him for so doing. Neither the apostles, nor believers generally, nor unbelievers, had an unfavorable opinion of him. If we wish to know how blind a man is, we bring him out of darkness into light. If, with the full blaze of day around him, he is unable to see, then beyond all doubt he is stone-blind. And it is in the presence of the Sun of Righteousness that we learn rightly to estimate the deep depravity of man. We do not help the blind by simply increasing the intensity of light around them, we merely ascertain their misery. A change must take place *in* men. They must cease to love darkness rather than light.

How deeply should we have this impressed upon our minds while engaged in evangelistic labors! It is not enough to offer men the Gospel. If there be in us a tendency to trust in the mere proclamation of the Gospel for the salvation of men, long, long years of stagnation will teach us that we are offering to the blind what is profitable only for the seeing. It is the Gospel, accompanied by the Spirit of God, that is the power of God and the wisdom of God unto salvation.

40

"I know whom I have chosen." Christ knows; we know not. And even if we knew that certain persons were not chosen to eternal life, it would still seem to be our duty, after the example of our Lord, to offer them the words of life and spare no pains in the endeavor to bring the truth to bear upon them. For the Lord has chosen this concerning all men, that they should have the Gospel offered to them.

Judas was elected to be the companion of Christ, to hear His gracious words, to behold His wondrous acts; and a similar election is extended to all by the command to preach the Gospel to every creature. With regard to the election unto eternal life, we have nothing to do with it, except as an argument for our confidence. If God had not determined to save some, it is certain that there would be hope for none. A man who acts without foresight is a fool. God is the last being in the universe to act in this way. Whatever He does, He does by an eternal foreordination.

Christ had not chosen Judas, and Judas had not chosen Christ. Judas walked with Christ for years, and then chose thirty pieces of silver rather than Christ. Ten thousand reasons were presented to him why he should not make such a fatal choice as this, but in vain. He deliberately chose the pieces of silver and all their consequences, and all that he has since experienced or will experience is simply his own choice.

"That the Scripture may be fulfilled." By means of prophecy, our forefathers are spectators of the present. The Scripture is to them a window through which they look in upon us. The Psalmist, who had been dead and buried a thousand years, had not died without looking in upon Christ and the twelve gathered around that Passover-table.

"He that eateth bread with me, hath lifted up his heel against me." One is reminded by this expression, "Lifted up the heel," of the sentiment of Voltaire concerning Christ, "*Écrasez l'infâme* [crush the infamous]." In the fierceness of his hatred, Voltaire went far beyond Judas. In modern infidelity we see rather the spirit of the Scribes and Pharisees which caused them to gnash upon Christ with their teeth. Judas was not of those who cried out, "Crucify him, crucify him." He was appalled, indeed, when it became evident that the Master was to be crucified;

41

but he furnished them with their strongest argument for so exclaiming. They had not eaten bread with Jesus of Nazareth, but he had. "He has lived in closest intimacy with Him, has enjoyed unrestricted opportunities of knowing all about Him. To others something of mystery may invest the character of Christ, but not to this man; yet this is the man who betrays Christ into our hands for thirty pieces of silver.

"Of course, after such testimony, it is impossible to doubt. Here is a man educated by Christ Himself, and he informs us that Christ is an impostor. There could be nothing stronger than this, except the confession of Christ Himself. When he that hath eaten bread with Him lifts up the heel against Him, it would be a strange thing if we should let Him go free."

These considerations do not cover the whole ground. Physical nearness is one thing, and spiritual intimacy a very different thing. There was always between Christ and Judas a great gulf fixed. Judas could not know Christ, though he were to spend a score of years in His society, for his eyes were not anointed with eye-salve that he might see Him; the natural man discerneth not the things of the Spirit of God. The world, however, knows nothing of such discriminations: a disciple is a disciple; and it is perfectly satisfied with the testimony of one that has been in any kind of nearness to Christ, if that testimony is against Him.

There are some who shudder at the ribaldry of infidelity, and fail to consider that they themselves have opened the door to it. In some way or other the fact leaks out that they love thirty pieces of silver more than the poverty of Christ, the reproach of Christ, the work of Christ. It is understood that they have been initiated into the mysteries of the Kingdom of Heaven, yet it is evident from the avidity with which they enter into worldly pleasure and seek worldly honors, and the facility with which they remain away from Christ's work and Christ's audience-chamber, that they have tried Christ and found Him wanting. What further argument for infidelity does the world need? Voltaire can be left on the shelf. The very men that profess to follow Christ declare with a loud whisper that Christ is nobody.

John 13:19. *"Now I tell you before it come, that when it is come to pass, ye may believe that I am* **he.***"*

In the original it is simply, *"Ye may believe that I am." "I am"* is a name given in the Old Testament to God, and there would be nothing strange if Christ assumed it on this occasion. A little after, He speaks without any ambiguity of the Father dwelling in Him and doing the works. Or perhaps Jesus meant, "I am what I claim to be"; this will not differ essentially from the other view.

But did not the disciples believe in Jesus as the Messiah? Was there still a doubt in their minds whether Jesus was really He that should come, and whether they should still look for another? The expression seems to intimate that they sat there, unbelievers, and that Jesus was obliged to seek comfort in the thought that after the fulfillment of some prophecies they would believe. But no; the companions of Jesus were believers; they harbored no doubts; they sat together with Him in that chamber, as in a heavenly place, with an unquestioning joy and confidence. In an atmosphere so serene and ambrosial [fragrant] it was not difficult to believe; the difficulty was to entertain a doubt. Ah! if faith could choose her own moments to be photographed, and to have her likeness entered in God's book against that great day, she would be glad. But it is not so. God does not come forth to estimate our faith in the hours when faith is easy, but in the hours when there are many and fierce foes of faith.

The believer often thinks he is strong in faith, and wonders that the Lord does not make haste to answer his prayers, but the Lord knows that a fiery trial or two would make all the difference in the world in that faith. Faith that will hold its own, no matter what the tests to which it may be subjected, is what the Lord demands of us. The Savior knew that in a few hours the faith of His disciples was to undergo some terrible shocks, and He knew that the most of it would be dissipated under the deadly influence of the unexpected events that were about to transpire; therefore He sought comfort, not in the contemplation of their present faith, but in the anticipation of that better faith which would clothe their souls after the fulfillment of the prophecies concerning Him.

This was the joy which was set before Him, only He had to look at it through much gloom—gloom that became so dense in Gethsemane that scarce were it possible to see the star of hope athwart it.

The question for us is not, "Have we a faith in Jesus that answers all ordinary purposes in the day when Providence is smiling upon us?" but, "Have we in this, our hour of prosperity, a genuine faith in Christ, one that would enable us to march invincibly through any trials that God might appoint?"

The adversary of souls, the world and our own heart, all combine to make us believe that we have an excellent faith in Christ, and cease not to make such suggestions as the following: "Why should you trouble yourself to look at the evidences? Why search the Scripture for further confirmation? Why keep the words of Christ in your heart? If all had such a faith as you have, it would be well. No, thank God that you are a sincere believer, and leave it to those whose faith is faulty to study the proofs of Christ's power and grace."

These suggestions are as dangerous as they are subtle. A true believer is one who makes preparation against the assaults to which his faith may possibly be exposed. When sitting at the table of his Lord, he is not unmindful of the Gethsemane that may follow. Nothing whatever will satisfy him but the consciousness of a faith that will not be dashed to earth, even though the Lord should make him a mark for His arrows and withdraw from him the multitudinous benefactions that now speak to him so gratefully of a kind and considerate High Priest.

John 13:20. *"Verily, verily, I say unto you, He that receiveth whomsoever I send, receiveth me; and he that receiveth me, receiveth him that sent me."*

Moses, on a certain occasion, was alarmed by an intimation from the Lord that an angel would conduct the children of Israel through the wilderness and into the land of Canaan. He received it as a token of the displeasure of the Lord, and deeply felt that nothing but the manifested presence of the Lord of hosts, the God of Abraham, Isaac and Jacob, would ever inspire him or his followers with the confidence necessary for such an enterprise.

The disciples of Jesus, hearing from Him on the eve of His crucifixion that He was about to be taken from them, were not a little dismayed, but Jesus sought to reassure them by making known, so far as their dull apprehensions would permit, the character of the dispensation on which they were entering. He would soon appear to them again, and joy in their risen Lord would take eternal possession of their hearts, and He would send the Spirit of God to them.

How expedient it was that He should go away they did not fully understand till the day of Pentecost, on which day they found that Christ was with them more gloriously than He had ever been before. To thousands in Jerusalem, Christ was revealed that day for the first time, though they had often seen and heard Him in the flesh. They saw the apostles clothed with His wisdom, His power, His Spirit, performing the same miracles, preaching the same doctrines, leading the same life. Christ, in the days of His personal humiliation, had been accustomed to spend a few weeks in Jerusalem every year; they heard Him once or twice in the temple, and then missed Him for a long time. But now, in His apostles and in other of His brethren, He was constantly present in the city, daily in the temple, daily in the synagogues, in every street almost.

The enemies of Christ had drawn a deep breath of satisfaction on seeing Him delivered to be crucified. They were fully persuaded that the stone which would close His sepulcher would bury out of their

45

sight for ever all traces of the religion He had sought to establish. His lips, once sealed in death, would never more be open to torment them with unwelcome truths. But now Christ is risen, and mighty works do show forth themselves, not in Him, an individual, but in the company of believers, each of them clothed with His Spirit and power. They have crucified One, but from His cross hundreds and thousands have started into life. Whichever way they now turn they find a Christ exposing their hypocrisy, destroying their influence, denouncing their oppression, declaring the wrath of God, declaring also His love, and inviting them, with a broken and a contrite heart, to believe on Him and be saved from their sins.

Let us suppose that Christ, seated at the right hand of God, should send into this world, not men, but angels, to make known the story of the cross. These angels would come with something of supernal radiance, and would at first create no little sensation in whatsoever place might be honored with their advent. But what would be the impressions of men concerning the ministry of these angels if, after a short season, they were seen conforming extensively to the fashions of this world; contracting the love of money, of rank, of power, of reputation; exhibiting pride, anger, envy, malice, and limiting the performance of the task assigned them to certain stated occasions? It would be difficult for men to believe that the gospel preached by these worldly angels was in all respects true; that men were perishing; that the wrath of God was impending; that one thing was needful.

But now how is it with regard to those whom Christ actually sends to declare His Gospel? They are first called out of the world into the presence of Christ. They are made separate from men—for how can they be sent unless they be first called out? They come forth to us as it were from the state-chamber of Christ. They are a peculiar class of men—unlike all others. They are not of the world even as Christ is not of the world. They are ambassadors of Christ sent forth into this world to call men to another world—Christ's world.

Now, just in the degree in which they lose themselves in the common herd of men, conforming to the world at the sacrifice of what is distinctive in them, they will be disowned by Christ. Their commissions will be revoked; the Lord will not acknowledge them before the sons of men.

When we bear about us the evidences that we are sent of Christ, then he who receives us, receives Christ. "As thou hast sent me into the world, even so have I sent them into the world," for "they are not of the world, even as I am not of the world." This is most explicit. The sent of Christ are like Christ; they make known Christ; their words are the words of Christ.

Zacchaeus received Christ into his house, and soon he became aware that the God of Abraham had visited him, and that salvation had taken up its permanent abode under his roof. So, in later times, a humble applicant has sometimes found admission to a house, and the master of that house, before the departure of his guest, has received from him the bread of life, the saving knowledge of Christ. Let us look upon every Christian as one with whom Christ is identified, an ambassador in whom Christ is in a certain sense present with us, to receive our daily oblation of love.

John 13:21-26. *"When Jesus had thus said, he was troubled in spirit, and testified, and said, Verily, verily, I say unto you, that one of you shall betray me. Then the disciples looked one on another, doubting of whom he spake. Now there was leaning on Jesus' bosom one of his disciples, whom Jesus loved. Simon Peter therefore beckoned to him, that he should ask who it should be of whom he spake. He then lying on Jesus' breast saith unto him, Lord, who is it? Jesus answered, He it is to whom I shall give a sop, when I have dipped it. And when he had dipped the sop, he gave it to Judas Iscariot, the son of Simon."*

When He had thus said—that is, had informed His disciples that they whom He should send were to be in a certain sense clothed with His own dignity—that they were to be His ambassadors to the nations and His representatives on the earth. Not all of them, however! One of this very band should prove an emissary of Satan, and should betray Him. He was troubled in spirit as He made this announcement. It was not a new thought to Him. From the very beginning He had been aware that there was in Judas what no amount of influence—no exhibition of love, of wisdom, of power, of holiness—would subdue. The trouble that was now manifested in speaking of his treachery had hitherto inhabited his heart.

Jesus was a man of sorrows. He bore about with Him many sorrows that were unknown to others, and this was one of them. There was ever before Him this repulsive exhibition of humanity, suggesting that the heart of man is invincible in its hatred of good: "In vain your loving words and acts are lavished; the more you do for the recovery of fallen man, the more odious he appears; he loathes your purposes of redemption; he asks only that you should leave him to himself, to his sins, to his fate."

After so many years of silence and suppression, this trouble of the Savior's heart breaks forth, and reveals itself to His disciples. "He

48

testified, and said"—that is, He spoke the words with a peculiar solemnity and emphasis. This announcement fell like a blow upon the entire apostolic body. The treacherous intention was confined to a single breast; nevertheless, the reproach and the disgrace in some degree radiated through all the twelve. "The disciples looked on one another, doubting of whom He spake."

"Now there was leaning on Jesus' bosom one of his disciples, whom Jesus loved." This is the disciple which testifies of these things. John had a right to speak of himself as the disciple whom Jesus loved. So have I, so have you. Jesus loveth all that value His love. Anything beyond the gracious words and acts, the promises and largeness, the sufferings and death, recorded in the Gospel, John could not receive. And that same Heaven-embracing Gospel has been sent to me. John was emboldened to draw very nigh to Jesus, to take great liberties with Him, to lay his head on His bosom. As far as his faith suffered him to go, so far he found a warrant and a response in the love of Christ.

"We have known and believed the love that God hath to us," he wrote afterward. Having abandoned the miserable tendency of the human heart to measure and to magnify its own affection, and having given himself to the one vocation of apprehending the love of Christ to him, he continued so to do to the end of his prolonged life. Nevertheless, we speak of him as the loving disciple, and justly, for it is only he who occupies himself much about the love of Christ toward us that can easily and cordially love.

"Simon Peter therefore beckoned to him, that he should ask who it should be of whom he spake." How is this, Simon Peter? There are many that call you chief of the apostles and look upon you as having the keys of the treasury of Christ's grace, and do you get another to approach Christ for you?

"He then lying on Jesus' breast saith unto him, Lord, who is it?" He saw that Christ was not disposed to declare in the hearing of all who it was that should betray Him, and so he asked Him in a whisper, and in a whisper received the following reply, "He it is to whom I shall give a sop when I have dipped it." Jesus then gave the sop to Judas Iscariot. This shows that they were still at supper, and that the translation of the second verse, "Supper being ended," is not correct, as was already observed, and that in all probability Judas was not present at the institution of the Lord's Supper, as that took place after the Passover supper, and we find that Judas went out immediately after receiving the sop.

The act of dipping a piece of bread in the dish and giving it to another was an act of friendliness. Up to the very last the Savior continued to show kindness to Judas. There is something sublime about His conduct toward him. If generosity and amity could have overcome the hardness of man's heart, Judas would have been disarmed.

John 13:27-28. *"And after the sop Satan entered into him. Then said Jesus unto him, That thou doest, do quickly. Now no man at the table knew for what intent he spake this unto him."*

The principle of evil in the breast of Judas had much to encounter in that upper chamber at that supper-table, for the character of Jesus was arrayed that evening in extraordinary loveliness. A spirit of love inundated His heart and expressed itself in all His words and actions. Conscious that He was filled with all the fullness of God, He was nevertheless all grace, all condescension. Painfully aware that an hour of unparalleled sorrow was coming upon Him, He concerned Himself about the lighter and less-worthy sorrow that His disciples should experience. About to be broken and bruised and poured out for man, He sought to arm His companions against the trouble that threatened to invade their hearts. All the attractiveness of His united Godhead and humanity rested upon Him and appealed to the profoundest sensibilities of those who were permitted to be the companions of those sacred hours.

"Is there in all the world," I hear you say, "a heart whose malevolence would be proof against the sacred blandishments of such a Being in such an hour?" Yes; not one, but many. The Word of God favors the opinion that every heart is *potentially* deceitful and wicked to this degree, that there are germs of iniquity in every heart that need only a suitable train and combination of circumstances to fructify into just such marvels of malevolence as this. The good man who, seeing a malefactor go by to execution, said, "There goes John Bradford, had it not been for the grace of God," may look at Judas and say the same.

Looking at Judas on this occasion, and meditating on the celestial influences that fall around him without extinguishing his wicked intent, we might not unprofitably consider the similar victories obtained by the wickedness of our own hearts over the hallowed influences of the Gospel, of the people of God, of His providence, of His Spirit.

51

When the door of the heart is left open, Satan will not be long in entering. The thief is not more vigilant to notice every instance of a door or window left open than Satan to notice the open door of the heart. Men are so circumspect with regard to their earthly property that the robber wanders through many a street without seeing a single unguarded entrance. Men are so entirely off their guard with respect to the presence and power of Satan that he stalks through their hearts as despotically as a king through the chambers of his palace.

There are so many to open the door. Pride is ever ready to do it—is angry, indeed, when anyone for a moment shuts it. Covetousness will do it; resentment will do it; vanity will do it; so will self-indulgence; so will worldly care; the fear of man, too. All these things profess to be the servants of him whose heart they inhabit, and vehemently declare that they are altogether subject to his sway, but they are the devoted servants of Satan, and will never be content till they have seen him come in state and sway his scepter visibly over the heart prepared for him.

There was One there Who saw the advent of Satan to the heart of Judas; and knowing now that the unhappy creature's probation was at an end, He said to him, "That thou doest, do quickly." As this great crime was to be, Jesus wished that it might be committed *quickly*, but no man at the table knew for what intent He spoke this to him.

Judas had doubtless felt very uncomfortable during this supper. The kindness, the cordiality, the tenderness of Jesus toward His disciples were like daggers in his heart. He longed for some opportunity of taking his departure. He was unwilling to draw attention, and perhaps suspicion, on himself, by abruptly leaving. Jesus knew what was in his heart, and bade him do quickly what he was determined to do. He availed himself at once of the opportunity given, and went forth from the presence of the Prince of Life, leaving behind him all the promises of the Gospel, and all the invitations that had ever fallen from the lips of Jesus in his hearing.

John 13:29. *"For some of them thought, because Judas had the bag, that Jesus had said unto him, Buy those things that we have need of against the feast; or, that he should give something to the poor."*

These surmises of the disciples are mentioned to show how far they were from suspecting that Judas was about to betray Christ. The hour was not yet come in which they could understand that word of Christ. There are many words of Scripture which only become clear when the providence of God has brought us to the same table-land on which the fulfillment is to be found. Before that, we exhaust ourselves in speculations as to the meaning of the words; some of these approximate to success, but the majority are very wide of the mark; all are defective in some particulars. The history of the vain surmises of men with regard to the meaning of the more obscure words of Scripture would constitute a library in itself—some would say a monument of folly.

Scripture, however, tells us that there is more wisdom in endeavoring to understand its contents than in not giving heed to them at all. There is doubtless unspeakable folly in offering to interpret the Scriptures without earnest deprecation and renunciation of man's defective and carnal judgment. We must not, indeed, utterly stigmatize every conjecture that does not prove correct. The true meaning of a prophecy is often found at the end of a chain of opinions, of progressive reasonableness, along which we are necessarily conducted before we reach the true interpretation.

The inferences of the disciples give us incidentally some interesting information with regard to several points.

The twelve apostles and our Lord had a common purse (*case* or *box,* Gr.) out of which to defray the expenses that were common to them and to relieve the poor. We read of certain women that ministered unto them of their substance. Contributions in money were thrown into the common fund. Their expenses must have been inconsiderable, as they traveled on foot, met with frequent acts of hospitality, were content with little and sought to give faith its full expression in their lives. The state of things in the Church after the day of Pentecost, when no man counted anything his own and they had all things in common, seems to have been modeled upon this earlier exhibition of Christian socialism.

These poor disciples cared for the poor and gave away perhaps the larger proportion of what was given to them. They did not, as many do now-a-days, make their poverty an excuse for not giving, but rather made it a reason for giving. They would have need on the morrow, and therefore it was better to act in a way that was calculated to secure them the blessing of God upon the morrow. Doubtless they often gave away all that they had, that it might be manifest to men that they had a treasure in Heaven which God would open for them on the morrow. It is a fearful mistake when Christians act as though they had nothing but this perishable gold and silver of earth, clutching it as though it were their all. "Be without covetousness, for he hath said, I will never leave thee" (Heb. 13:5).

Judas was the steward and the almoner of this community. By whom he was appointed to this office we cannot say. I incline to think that Jesus asked them to choose one of their number for the office, and they chose Judas. He may have had certain qualifications that seemed to recommend him for such employment. Some may, perhaps, deem it surprising that Judas was not called to give an account of his stewardship at any time, or that Jesus did not expose his dishonesty.

But we must bear in mind that the company of the twelve were in an important sense a representative body; they represented the Church, and it was fitting that they should be trained and tried very much as the Church would be in after times. Our Lord was not with them for the purpose of depriving them of their freedom or of their fallibility, He was not present in His capacity of Judge and Assessor, and it was fitting that they should learn, as Christians since have learned, by sure and slow experience, the power of the adversary to waste and destroy even in the very heart of the Church.

John 13:30-32. *"He then, having received the sop, went immediately out: and it was night. Therefore, when he was gone out, Jesus said, Now is the Son of man glorified, and God is glorified in him. If God be glorified in him, God shall also glorify him in himself, and shall straightway glorify him."*

The heart of Christ experienced a feeling of relief when Judas went forth. It is an unspeakable advantage to the Church when they who are not of her go forth from her. The perfect fellowship of Christ and His people is hindered by the presence of ungodly men. He leads His people into the desert that they who are not of them may make it manifest by refusing to go. If persecution did nothing more than add to the strength of the Church, by freeing it from its foreign elements, it would be a pure gain.

Two glorifications are spoken of in the words that follow. One is to be immediately, the other is to result from it. One is the glorification of the Son of man and of God in Him upon this earth; the other is the glorification of the Son of God in Heaven and from Heaven. The latter depends upon the former: "If God be glorified in him."

But how shall we speak of that as glory which so greatly resembles infamy? The glory of God seems to be utterly trodden under foot in the humiliations and death of Christ: "I am a worm and no man, a reproach of men and despised of the people." "He was reckoned with the transgressors."

The believer, taught by the Spirit of God, sees the Son of man invested with unspeakable glory even in His sufferings and deep humiliations. Peter and John rejoiced because they were *counted worthy* to suffer for Christ. The spirit of glory and of God rested upon them. Apart from the glory of Christ, earth has no glory comparable with that of the martyr who joyfully testifies to Jesus in the midst of cruel torments. This glory, however, is but a feeble scintillation [spark] of the glory of Christ.

Look at Jesus as He stands before Pilate to receive sentence of death. He is the elect One of the entire race of man. All populations, all generations, from Adam to the last of the human race, were sifted, and He alone remained holy, harmless, undefiled and separate from sinners, and meet to be offered for sinners. All that was most glorious and admirable in humanity was found to be deeply soiled and stained when placed beside Him. He was not only the elect One of humanity: He that stands before Pilate is the elect One of the universe. All the inhabitants of the heavens were weighed and found wanting; the Lamb of God was alone found worthy to make an atonement for the sin of the world. Christ might, therefore, fitly speak of Himself as about to be glorified, and God in Him, since He was about to occupy a position that none besides could occupy.

God was pre-eminently glorified in the suffering Jesus, inasmuch as God is love, and the fullest exhibition of love is the largest revelation of the Godhead. By the "glory" of God we mean the manifestation of His perfections; and if we are not able to see it at the cross of Christ, then we can never behold it. The god of this world hath blinded the minds of those who believe not, lest the light of the glorious Gospel of Christ, Who is the image of God, should shine unto them.

Faith, then, is just a capacity to see the glory of God exhibited beyond compare in the death of Christ. The Christian is one who, under the guidance of the spirit of truth, exerciseth himself to discern in the humiliations and disgraces of Jesus of Nazareth all that can enrapture and elevate the soul. We are growing in grace just as we grow in the ability to discover the glory of God in those chapters of the Gospel and of the other Scriptures which speak of Christ's baptism of sorrow.

How little knew the world of God! The highest and brightest manifestation of His glory was made without their surmising anything but the shameful death of a heretic. How little is God yet known even in the Church! How very faulty still are our conceptions of glory! We pass from earth, and cross tremblingly, shrinkingly, the threshold of

Heaven, expecting to behold an intolerable blaze of glory, and we behold in the midst of the throne a Lamb as It had been slain. Did we think that amid the glories of Heaven we would leave the glory of the Gospel behind us? How different! It has rushed up before us and taken its place in the midst of the throne, and looking at us reproachfully, seems to say, "Will you know Me now?"

This is a matter of absolute importance, of inexorable necessity. We must come to God in God's way. We must come to Him through the broken body of the Lamb. We must find Him there with all His perfections, and must there rejoice in Him with joy unspeakable and full of glory, or we shall never, never see His glory. If Christ were now to come in the glory of the Father and of the angels and of Himself, it would be simply a terrifying spectacle to us if we had not first beheld His glory on Calvary. If Christ should speak to us from Heaven with an intent to save us, He could only bid us look to Calvary. After Jesus had appeared to Paul near Damascus, Paul abode some days in darkness; then Ananias came and communicated, not merely eyesight, but the Holy Ghost. Nor would Paul ever glory in anything save in the cross of Jesus Christ.

"If God be glorified in him, God shall also glorify him in himself." God was glorified in Christ; in Him alone of all mankind was He worthily revealed. We have all come short of the glory of God—very far short; even the men of most honorable life, how far short! But in Christ, in every action, every suffering, every word, in every particular of His life and death, we see the unmixed and uncontaminated glory of God. Taught of the Spirit, we say, "This place is Heaven; this cross is the throne of God." Here we enter into allegiance to the King of saints. God has glorified Him in Himself by raising Him up far above all principality and power and might and dominion and every name that is named, and placing Him at His own right hand, clothed with all power in Heaven and earth. And if we are willing to receive the revelation of the glory of God made at the cross, we shall not be left uninformed of the celestial glory of Christ. Indeed, it is at the cross that we are made to climb up, past the principalities and hierarchies of Heaven, upon the footsteps of the ascending Jesus.

By the cross we are crucified unto the world. By our readiness to suffer for the Savior we show our knowledge of the suffering Savior. If we suffer with Him, we shall also be glorified in Him. If Christ be glorified in us, He shall also glorify us in Himself. "Beloved, now are we the sons of God, and it doth not yet appear what we shall be, but we know that when he shall appear we shall be like him, for we shall see him as he is."

God straightway glorified Christ in Himself—namely, on the day of Pentecost. "Whatsoever ye shall ask in my name I will do it, that the Father may be glorified in the Son," and the Son in the Father. Heaven cannot satisfy Christ. His affections are set on things below, even on the souls of men. "He shall see of the travail of his soul and be satisfied" when His people come to the knowledge of that loving, longing, waiting heart of His, and, by this knowledge, clothing themselves with strength at the throne of grace, prevail to call down the mighty influences of the Spirit.

Where there is a genuine revival of religion, there the scenes of Gethsemane and Calvary are presented anew in something of their appropriate sublimity, with this difference, that the Heaven that once refused to be cleft by the cry of the sufferer now bows responsive, and sheds its own immortalizing influences upon the perishing multitudes around.

John 13:33-35. *"Little children, yet a little while I am with you. Ye shall seek me: and as I said unto the Jews, Whither I go ye cannot come; so now I say unto you. A new commandment I give unto you, That ye love one another: as I have loved you, that ye also love one another. By this shall all men know that ye are my disciples, if ye have love one to another."*

Jesus addressed the disciples sometimes as brethren, sometimes as friends, sometimes as children, sometimes as little children, and the different expressions are significant of various aspects in the relations between Him and them. According to the varying need of the believer in the voyage of life is the responsive adaptedness of Christ, and possibly there is not a single relationship of life which is not suggestive, to say the least, of something that occasionally occurs in the commerce of the soul with its Lord.

By the expression "little children" He here intimates that He is aware of their weakness, their exposedness, their need of protection and guidance; and the very expression on His lips implies a promise that He will not forget them nor abandon them.

There was something more in His mind that did not find utterance till afterward, when He said to them (14:18), "I will not leave you comfortless" (orphans); "I will come unto you." At present He simply makes the announcement that He is about to depart from them. "Yet a little while I am with you;" that is, only a little while. I am shortly about to leave you. "Ye shall seek me: and as I said unto the Jews, Whither I go ye cannot come; so now I say unto you." I am going away, and I am going far—farther even than to the ends of the earth. To the ends of the earth you might follow Me, but I am going to the realms of death, that I may obtain the keys of death and Hades. You shall seek Me and shall not find Me, and great wonder will fall upon you, that I should make no distinction between you and the Jews, going where neither you nor they could follow Me. Then will a sense of unspeakable

59

desolation come upon you, for He that was more necessary to you than parents are to their little children will be withdrawn.

Oh, if the invitations now given would only sink into your heart, how bravely would you meet that hour, how submissively and how hopefully would you bow as the dark cloud should pass over! You would then know that your crucified Lord had gone to disarm your enemy of enemies, even him that has the power of death—gone where it is your unspeakable felicity that you cannot follow, gone to shut for you the gate of the kingdom of hell, that He may then return and, ascending on high, open for you the gate of the Kingdom of Heaven.

"A new commandment I give unto you, that ye love one another; as I have loved you, that ye also love one another." I go away, He says. They look at Him in consternation. The words are like a thunderbolt. Oh, be not alarmed, He says: I am about to give you something that will take away your feeling of desolation; something that shall wonderfully compensate you.

I give you—hear!—I give you a new commandment that you love one another. But why do you look at Me with such a blank and unsatisfied expression of countenance? Is this a little gift? Know, then, that I Myself am love incarnate; I have clothed Myself with flesh that I might reign in your hearts. Love one another as I have loved you, and you will no longer find Me absent. You will behold Me as you never did before, and rejoice in Me with joy unspeakable and full of glory. All my life, labors, and sufferings have had this for their end— that divine love should tabernacle permanently among men. The throne to which I continually look forward is the throne of your affections; and if I ascend up on high, to sit upon the throne of Heaven, it is that I, by the Spirit, may accomplish what is now begun in the gift of this new commandment, and reign in you.

I give you the commandment, and I will give you the heart to obey it. Love one another as I have loved you, that earth, startled to see Me ascending up on high, may turn to you and behold, with glad surprise, Christ in you. It were a little thing that I should come into this world for the few brief years that are now drawing to a close. No, I have come into it for the purpose of identifying Myself with the life of humanity, and descending from generation to generation, from age to age.

I have been manifest in the flesh; I must be manifest in the Church. Love is about to have the highest revelation it has ever heard; but when you gaze on the cross, especially when the Holy Spirit enables you to look with intelligent eyes upon it, understand that the love there revealed is your model. You are to find a new life there, and a new character. That which dies upon the cross is to live in you. "As I have loved you that ye also love one another." "Walk in love as Christ hath loved us and hath given himself for us." The spirit that you behold exhibited on the cross is the spirit of Heaven. Let this spirit possess you, and Heaven itself will be in you.

Oh, when I say, "Thy kingdom come," come, Lord Jesus, let me show that I know the meaning of the words by seeking to obey the new commandment. All commandments are comprehended in this command, for in loving the disciple of Christ I love Christ, in loving Christ I love God. If I love God, I will love what God loves; I will seek what God seeks; I will be, as far as may be, a channel for His love to flow through, gladdening and irradiating all.

"By this shall all men know that ye are my disciples, if ye have love one to another." There is a call for the Church, the true church of Christ, to come forth from among the counterfeits, and give evidence of her divine origin. The Greek church presents herself with innumerable tomes, declaring that she is lineally descended from the church of the apostles, is indeed that very church, dwelling in the very lands and cities where she was originally planted. The Roman church comes forward with her keys, declared to be those of the Kingdom of Heaven, but suspected to be those of the prison-house peculiarly her own— Purgatory. The Armenian church puts in her claim; the Lutheran, the Anglican, the Presbyterian, the Independent, the Baptist.

"Which of the various churches is the true church of Christ? How shall we identify her?" is the cry of the age. Well, it is given unto all

61

men to know which is the true church of Christ. Christ has communicated to us a token by which we may identify her: "By this shall all men know that ye are my disciples, if ye have love one to another."

Any church that professes to be *the* church of Christ cannot be that church. The true church refuses to be circumscribed or parted by any denominational wall. It knows that Christ is repudiated when His people are repudiated. Not even a Biblical creed can yield satisfactory evidence that a specified church is the true church. True Christians are those who love one another across denominational differences, and exhibit the spirit of Him Who gave Himself to death upon the cross that His murderers might live.

"By this shall *all* men know." This is that evidence that none shall be able to resist. When Christians love one another with the love of Calvary, then the people who dwell in the heart of Africa, Australia, China, Japan, Tartary, Siberia, Arabia, Russia, Austria, America and England will know who are the people of God, and will hasten to them, ten men laying hold upon the skirts of one, to learn the way of life. For He Who bore testimony unto His well-beloved Son from Heaven will bear testimony to those in whom Christ, the hope of glory, is thus formed again. "That they may be one in us; that the world may believe that thou hast sent me."

John 13:36-38. *"Simon Peter said unto him, Lord, whither goest thou? Jesus answered him, Whither I go, thou canst not follow me now; but thou shalt follow me afterwards. Peter said unto him, Lord, why cannot I follow thee now? I will lay down my life for thy sake. Jesus answered him, Wilt thou lay down thy life for my sake? Verily, verily, I say unto thee, The cock shall not crow, till thou hast denied me thrice."*

"Whither goest thou?" If we suppose this to have been a question prompted by mere curiosity, Peter did not obtain much satisfaction. Our Lord did not inform him as to the "whither," but simply renewed the statement that Peter and his companions were to be left behind; only for a season, however. Very likely the idea in Peter's mind was, "What place is that to which I cannot follow Thee? I will follow Thee everywhere."

Jesus answered him, "You cannot now; you have an erroneous estimate of your ability; at a future period you shall have what you now lack, and difficulties will not hinder you then from following Me."

"Ah," says Peter, "You think that I have not the courage to suffer for You and with You; You know not the strength of my attachment; others may forsake You in the trying hour; that hour will only afford the proof of my invincible fidelity; I am Peter, and I will follow You, and, if need be, I will lay down my life for Your sake."

Well, this was no extravagant profession of attachment. Every one that professes to be a Christian professes as much as this. "He that will come after me," says Christ, "let him take up his cross and follow me." Over and over again He informs us that to follow Him is to forsake all.

A man with a cross is a man on his way to execution. The place of execution may be near or far—so far perhaps that the man will die before he reaches it; nevertheless, he and death are acquainted. Peter, then, went no farther, when he said, "I will lay down my life for thy sake," than he had virtually gone every day since he had begun to follow Christ. We all of us say the same thing every day, and must say it. We must, however, do a good deal more than say it.

"Thou canst not follow me now." What an inestimable blessing it is—if we are willing to know it—that there is One Who has perfect knowledge of our present state, and Who can tell exactly what strength we lack! We are continually trusting to some supposed ability within, and rushing into the thick of the fight of life, there to be jeeringly mowed down by some rude cut of an adverse sword. What frightful losses we sustain from self-ignorance! Oh for one to search and try us, and give us the exact measure of our abilities! Well, there is One. Jesus, named the Counselor, the Wonderful, the Physician, the Friend of sinners, comes to us, and lays before us a faithful statement of our abilities. "You cannot," He begins; but the willful patient exclaims, "Why can I not?" and rushes forth upon his fatal enterprise.

Men are ordinarily obliged to learn by experience. By failures, by disappointments, by egregious [flagrant] mistakes, by calamities, by immedicable [incurable] woes, they ascertain their own frailty, foolishness and dependence. But wherefore should the Christian abide under the pressure of this yoke? Why should it be necessary for him to make his way through miseries and sins to a just conception of himself? It is not necessary. It is a monstrous anomaly that he should do it. In the very fact that he has taken Christ to be Leader and Commander, it is implied that he has recognized his own incompetency to judge himself, his need of hourly enlightenment. He comes to Christ for instruction, not merely, like Nicodemus, with regard to the wonders of Heaven, but also with regard to his personal capacities and deficiencies.

He that refuses to receive Christ's testimony to his present weakness and the unsuspected treachery of his heart, and prefers rather to listen to his heart, which rises up blusteringly and says, "Do not believe a word of all this; I am strong, I am valiant, I am true: rely on me"—such a one must not think it wonderful if Christ should let him drop down into the very bottom of the abyss toward which he hastens.

The faith that does not hearken to Christ, that hearkens rather to one's own heart, is a mere phantom faith; it is the demon of unbelief under the angelic mask of faith.

The heart is deceitful above all things. Anything else deceives us one or twice, it may be; after that we will have nothing more to do with it; it may go down on its knees, we will not listen to it. But the heart, though it has been detected a thousand times in the most flagrant and detestable acts of deception, though it has ensnared us in all manner of calamities and disgraces, is, nevertheless, audacious as a robber and haughty as a king, whilst it unfolds before us some new scheme on which it requires us to enter.

To think, O Peter, that that wicked and oft-detected heart of yours should have the boldness in this solemn hour to give Christ the lie! To think of the Son of the Blessed receiving up to the very last such shafts of insolence from that heart of yours, from these hearts of ours!

If we could get the victory over our heart, and drag it to Jesus, and say to Him, "Yes, Lord, it is a vile, craven thing, capable of any treachery, any apostasy. Yes, Lord, I believe that I am capable of denying You times without number and under circumstances the most aggravated. But I have done with mine own heart. Believing on You, I have something infinitely better than this vile heart to rely upon: I have Your own heart of love divine and truth inviolable. To this I look. It is because I am capable of the basest treachery that I have made You my refuge. You are my strength, my steadfastness, my rock of ages. I am complete in You,—then Satan is baffled, and there shall be no denial of Christ."

Well, we do get this victory over our heart, and, perhaps—the Lord knows—the fall of Peter had something to do with this our victory. The exposure of the frauds of the human heart, made through such falls as his, has helped us to know our inward foe, and powerfully stimulated us to hide ourselves in Christ.

"You cannot follow me now." There is hope in the word "now." It seems to half open the door to a better, brighter future. Yes, the door opens, but you shall follow Me afterward. An unseen thread, made, however, of such stuff that no power of earth could break it, accompanied Peter as he fell into the bottomless abyss of unbelief. Down, down, he goes, the light of day is left far behind, the horrors of everlasting night seem gathering about him, yet still he plunges down, down. But at length he is arrested. The unseen thread checks him in his descent and draws him upward again. "I have prayed for thee that thy faith fail not." To any other eye but that of Jesus it had failed. He, however, sees not as man sees, for He sees with an eye of invincible love.

Chapter 14

John 14:1-2. *"Let not you heart be troubled: ye believe in God, believe also in me. In my Father's house are many mansions: if it were not so I would have told you. I go to prepare a place for you."*

There is here a slight ambiguity in the Greek. The same word which is translated "ye believe," and "believe," may be either in the imperative or in the indicative. On the whole, we incline to take it in both places in the imperative: "Let not your heart be troubled: believe in God, and believe in me."

They had gathered from the language of Jesus that some dread hour was approaching. The very agitation of mind which expresses itself in earnest protestations of one's own fearlessness is evidence, to a heart-searching eye, that there will be vacillation and flight in the trying hour. The trouble which is here deprecated is that which is inconsistent with faith. It implies a vanquishing of faith. It must be vanquished by faith.

It is not the wish of Christ that His people should be troubled. Have this point thoroughly settled in your mind. Christ often acts in a way that appears to a half-considerate spectator designed to trouble and confound his soul. One arrow after another, winged from the throne which he is taught to call a throne of grace, reaches him and drinks up his very life-blood. Must I remain thus a mark for the arrows of the Almighty and not be troubled? What am I that I should not be troubled by the strokes of divine Providence? If a mere earthly friend smite me, I am dismayed and confounded; and shall I regard it as a matter of little moment when the Lord of lords pours out His indignation on me?

Have faith, and those strokes shall not harm you. Lay aside faith, and they will be formidable indeed. What matters it if you be called to walk through a shower of thunderbolts if you be at the same time furnished with a shield tempered in the very armory where those bolts were forged—a shield on which they fall harmless? He that sends the terrors sends also the command, "Let not your heart be troubled." Take the shield of faith and walk scatheless. How shall it be known that you have such a shield if there be no missiles hurled against you? By this shall it be known that ye are the disciples of Jesus—by the serenity and freedom from anxiety with which you can meet the storms of life. There are troubles innumerable; but you, O believer, are entrusted with a secret by virtue of which those troubles become to you no troubles. What troubles are there for an untroubled mind? United to Christ by an invincible faith, tribulation, distress, persecution, famine, nakedness, peril, sword only afford new opportunities for faith to manifest itself and glorify its Lord.

"Believe in God, and believe in me." A strange combination, if Christ were what some think Him. The Scriptures, in a hundred emphatic passages, declare that faith in any besides God is a renunciation of God. He will not give His glory to another. That is the great sin of universal humanity, glorifying as God that which is not God. But God was in Christ reconciling the world unto Himself. To win men to trust in Him was one of the great ends of God's visit to earth in the Person of His Son.

However much the disciples might see of the glory of God in the face of Jesus Christ, it was all but impossible for them, from the nature of things, in thinking of God, to bring their thoughts down from Heaven and a throne of awe to that Being Whom they saw before them clothed in flesh and blood. The impress of deity was there, but how could they school their minds to recognize essential deity as dwelling in the temple of Christ's body? No, it was necessary, first, that the veil should be withdrawn, that Christ should ascend up; then it became possible for them to see these two blessed ideas, of God and Christ, interfused and mutually glorifying.

At present, their minds made a transition in taking up the two commands, "Believe in God, believe in Me. Believe in God, Whose power and majesty and wisdom you cannot doubt; believe in Me, Whose friendliness, kindness, condescension, long-suffering, gentleness, faithfulness you so well know." Progress in the spiritual life has a great deal to do with the approximation and unification of these two forms of faith. The believer obtains power just in the degree in which he is able to ascribe to the Father the perfections and the loveliness of Christ—to Christ the power, majesty and unlimited authority of God.

"In my Father's house are many mansions; if it were not so I would have told you. I go to prepare a place for you." Let not your heart be troubled, even should your life be threatened; for there is plenty of room in My Father's house besides which this earth affords. If you shrink back at the menace of men, and lose faith in God and in Me, then, alas! you are not in My Father's house. This is the frightful doom of unbelief.

But if you have an enduring faith, then men can only expel you from one chamber of My Father's house to another more desirable. Had there been no room in His Father's house above, He would have told us. Had it been necessary for us to spend some years or centuries in a place of fire called Purgatory, He would have told us. O blessed Savior! can it be that men calling themselves Yours have so calumniated You as to assert that the place prepared by You to receive your disciples after death is a place of torment? In Your Father's mansion You prepare a place for them whom by faith You prepare for it. The great preparation there effected is Your own presence. It is fitting that they should be with You, where You are, and behold Your glory.

The place where Jesus was thus communing with His disciples had been prepared beforehand by two of them dispatched for that very purpose. The language of Jesus, "I go to prepare a place for you," would come with a familiar sound to their ears. Perhaps they would picture to themselves some royal apartment having twelve thrones beside the chief throne. Soon, however, their ideas were to undergo a great change, and a very few days elapsed before the Kingdom of God and of Christ—the relations of this world to the next, the relations of Jews and Gentiles, the proper objects of Christian aspiration—were understood by them very differently from what they had been before.

On the day of Pentecost they found themselves in a place of dignity, power, and joy far transcending the unworthy conceptions of these things previously entertained; and viewed from this place, how glorious and attractive now seemed the Heaven of promise! In the fifth, seventh, twenty-first, and twenty-second chapters of Revelation we, too, catch glorious glimpses of that better Land. The more elevated the spot on which we stand, the more gloriously does it break upon our straining eyes. The more of Heaven we have here below, through the outpouring of the Spirit, the more rapturous become our anticipations of the glory that is to come.

John 14:3-5. *"And if I go and prepare a place for you, I will come again, and receive you unto myself; that where I am, there ye may be also. And whither I go ye know, and the way ye know. Thomas saith unto him, Lord, we know not whither thou goest; and how can we know the way?"*

The disciples had been some years learning to know Christ in the flesh; it was now needful that they should learn to know Him apart from the flesh. He tarried among them till they had begun to get glimpses of God manifest in humanity, and just then it was expedient for Him to go away. The invisible came to them in the visible, and when it had established a sure bond of connection between them and itself, then the visible disappeared.

Look upon the person of Christ as a vase filled with celestial gifts; the breaking of the vase is the diffusion of the gifts. "I go," says Jesus. The thought of it is to them unbearable. He adds, "I go to prepare a place for you." Well, there is comfort in this explanation. It is on our account He goes. But still He goes, and what are we without Him? Did we ever more need Him than now we do? We shall be of all men most miserable without Him, for He has stripped us of the semblances of strength and wisdom that we formerly had in common with other men, and taught us to find our life, our all, in Him. We have embraced His cause, and now, when men are beginning to understand that cause and are filled with an insatiate rancor against all connected with it, He takes His departure.

For Him to go away is for our sun to sink in perpetual night, leaving us to frightful darkness and desolation. It is kind of Him, doubtless, to go and prepare a place for us, but how can we reach that place without Him? Surely He overlooks our weakness, our ignorance, our helplessness: "how can we know the way?"

"Though I go," says Jesus, "I will come again and receive you unto Myself; that where I am, there ye may be also." If I go, it is in order that we may be the more perfectly united. It would be strange

71

indeed if I should go away for the purpose of preparing a place for you, and then should neglect anything necessary to bring you to that place.

We cannot but regard these words, "I am," frequently occurring in these chapters, as possessing a profound and special significance. While Jesus was on the earth He yet dwelt in a region far above the earth. He brought all that He could of Himself down to earth, but still there was a fellowship between Him and the Father, Him and the Holy Ghost, that others could not enter into or understand. He found it impossible to translate into the dialect of those who surrounded Him many of the most glorious thoughts of His mind. There was much of Heaven that He could not lay aside, any more than He could cease to be Himself. Into this Heaven His disciples could no more, at that time, enter than they could cease to be themselves. But His constant aspiration was to bring His disciples up to this blessed region of purity and light and strength and perfect love and victory and intelligence with God: "that where I AM there they may be also."

When Jesus rose from the dead and appeared to the disciples, then He began to receive them unto Himself. During the forty days succeeding, they found themselves gradually and mysteriously ascending unto a higher region, and by the day of Pentecost they had begun to breathe something of the very air which Jesus had been all along breathing.

Oh that we might be stimulated by these words "I am"! Our souls should dwell in the same region where the soul of Christ abode when He was on the earth. It is a light matter for the Spirit of God to lift us into that region. But have we the aspiration? Are we willing to cut ourselves loose from the vain clogs that chain us to the earth of common humanity? Do we consent to hear the voice which says to us, "Come up hither"?

Faith is like an ethereal gas that struggles to take itself and us away from the grosser airs of the lower atmosphere to a region free from storms and perturbations. It is not more true that Christ died to save us than that He died to procure for us the means of living a divine life upon the earth—a life of wonderful communion with God and with Christ, in which all Christian experiences should undergo a transfiguration, and Christian peace, joy and faith become a thousand times the things they are in an ordinary Christian life. This is that translation of the believer which is attended with blessings to the world at large, more copious, more precious than those which stood connected with the translations of Enoch and Elijah.

"The Son of man which is in Heaven," said Christ of Himself while yet on the earth. Well, this is where He would bring the believer. When our friends sleep in Jesus, with regard to us it is indeed a sleep. They may be blessed, but their hands no longer scoop from the urn of God, blessings for us.

Now that which earth intensely needs is that there should be ascension without sleeping—that the believer should by faith ascend to a region where he could hold perfect concourse with the skies without being lost to earth. The Romanist talks of his saint in Heaven; we need saints that shall be at the same time in Heaven for us and on earth for Christ. Then will be fulfilled the word, "Arise, shine; the glory of the Lord is risen upon thee."

"I pray not that thou shouldst take them out of the world." "I in them and thou in me, that they may be made perfect in one; that the world may know that thou hast sent me, and hast loved them as thou hast loved me." "Father, I will that they also whom thou hast given me be with me where I am." "I am glorified in them." Christians are to emulate one another in the great work of bringing down to earth the riches of Heaven. It is treason to humanity to propose working out your own salvation in a way that should secure your salvation and nothing else. The glory of that path of salvation which Christ has marked out for you is that it is a path umbraged [shaded] with trees of salvation; you are to go saving that you may be saved.

"And whither I go ye know, and the way ye know. Thomas saith unto him, Lord, we know not whither thou goest; and how can we know the way?" Ah, Thomas, this is not a creditable confession for you to make. Did you never hear the Master say, "I go unto him that sent me. What, and if ye shall see the Son of man ascend up where he was before"?

Here has this gracious Lord been spending years with you for the very purpose of teaching you these things, and now at the last you can find nothing better for His suffering spirit than the heartless announcement that all has been in vain. As yet your mind is all in the dark with regard to this most important point of the place whither and the way in which you are to follow Him. There is but one way in which to follow anyone: fix your eye upon him and tread in his footsteps. "He that followeth me shall not walk in darkness, but shall have the light of life." Thus I upbraid Thomas, and thus some one else may upbraid me, another Thomas; but happily our Lord gives to all liberally and upbraids not. After all, it is very unbecoming in us to get angry with Thomas, for we owe to his ignorance and dullness the precious declaration with which Jesus answered him.

John 14:6. *"Jesus saith unto him, I am the way, and the truth, and the life: no man cometh unto the Father, but by me."*

I am the way and the truth and the life; I am the way, the means and the end; I am the Alpha and the Omega of your salvation; he that is in Me is in the way, and he was not in the way before he looked to Me.

Just where the sinner is, in that very quagmire, begins the WAY. Christ meets him there and helps him there. Delusive and most dangerous is the idea—alas! too common—that the individual must make his way to some smooth rock, to some fair piece of ground, and there meet Christ. Not a single step heavenward can he take until he depends on Christ.

By the law he may become acquainted with his own sin and obtain a most poignant sense of his need of Christ, but it is an error that cannot be too stubbornly opposed that mere conviction of sin shows a man to be in the way of life. The devils are not unconvinced of sin. Judas had deep convictions of sin. A horror of great darkness gathers around many who find themselves about to fall into the hands of the living God. In all this there is nothing in the least degree saving. A man may open his eyes to the fact that some deadly disease has fallen upon him, but there is nothing recuperative in this perception.

Conviction of our need is necessary that we may turn to Christ, but the moment in which we so turn is the very earliest of which it could be said that we are in the path to Heaven. That conviction which leads a man to look to Christ, though so shadowy as to elude our diagnosis, is yet to be valued far above the most agonizing convictions which hold the soul in their own embrace and suffer it not to turn to Christ. Whosoever will, let him take of the water of life freely; it springs up at the very feet of every sinner. Men may spend some time in search before they embrace salvation in Christ; they may dignify delay by the name of search, but its true name is unbelief. Alas for the thief upon the cross, had he spent any time in such search! Look and be saved. *"This* is the way, walk ye in it."

"What is truth?" said Pilate. "I am the truth," says Jesus, but men will not hear Him; they hear nothing but the echo of their own question. There are men around whose feet the truth is springing thickly up, like grass, and who cannot take a step without treading on it, but who would laugh you to scorn at the suggestion that the truth is aught resembling that familiar and humble drapery of earth; yet these very men imagine themselves to be ardent truth-seekers, and never look to Heaven without a sigh at their inability to penetrate the void of space and make their way to the far-hidden world where Truth holds her sequestered court.

The truth is with the believer in Jesus, and it is with him abundantly. He knows what you, O Pilate, O Plato, know not; he knows his own weakness, ignorance, misery, sin and need. He knows that Jesus is the Savior—his Savior. The promises of God are glorious realities to him. At the cross of Christ he beholds the solution of the mysteries that perplex you. He washes in a fountain opened up for sin and for uncleanness. He overcomes the adversary. He is contented in the midst of sore privations, and is elated in the presence of appalling calamities. He meets death with a smile and goes on high with a shout of joy. Is not the truth with him?

Learn from him to abandon thy vain speculations, and to give heed to the despised words of Jesus. You sit as a high priest upon thy throne and bid the words of Jesus stand before you and be judged. It is impossible that you should discern their true character in this way. Let the words judge *you*. It is you that must stand before them. They will tell you all your sin, all things that ever you did. This only will they show you? Nay, before you have time to turn pale with alarm they will lead you into a mansion of great joy.

Christ is the truth; and they who reject Christ or neglect Him may sail over all possible seas, study in all schools, have commerce with all classes, yet the truth shall never be theirs. They reject Christ because He seems to be so different from themselves. His maxims are entirely different from theirs. There is an utter diversity between His beatitudes and theirs. His views of this world and of that to come are quite irreconcilable with theirs, and so they conclude that He cannot be the truth. Every man seems to go upon the presumption that he himself is the incarnation of truth, his mind the touchstone by which the possessions of all minds may be tested. But God speaks from Heaven, testifying that Christ is the truth, and by that one word casts the pretensions of all men to the ground.

Sin falsifies everything; itself, the universe, God and the individual are plunged by it into the center of a fictitious world. When the soul is united to Christ by faith, it is restored to the true center of the true world, and begins now to see aright both what God has made and what God is. In the fictitious world it had a fictitious life; it made many conquests, heaped up many possessions, clothed itself with dignity, power and wisdom; but all was fictitious, unreal, delusive.

In Christ the believer's horizon may appear at first to be very circumscribed; his attention is called to matters that were formerly deemed slight and contemptible. But as he continues faithfully to observe the new world in which he is placed, he becomes aware that that world is enlarging. No matter in what direction he sends his eager gaze, the curtains withdraw, the universe expands and he joyfully realizes that he is in the true center; in a word, that the truth is his—not a portion of truth, but *the* truth.

The truth is that which establishes a perfect correspondence between the universe and the percipient mind, between the knowable and the cognizant spirit. And the proof is found in the harmonious and unrestricted range of the mind. "The heavens declare the glory of God and the firmament showeth his handiwork"; to whom? to him alone who in Christ possesses the truth.

He that possesses a portion of truth may at first know a great deal more than he who has simply the truth, but his knowledge will avail him not; he is not in the true center; he is in the fictitious world, and sooner or later he must dash against existing things, and encounter the storm of God's misunderstood thoughts. But he that has the truth has eternity to grow in, and the entire universe is his home. He may range from the throne of God to the verge of the bottomless pit, and nothing shall by any means harm him or confound him. There is an understanding between him and God. There is in him that which all finite ministries are commanded to foster, namely, life.

No man comes unto the Father save by Christ. If you tell me that you have come unto the Father without Him, I tell you then that you must be arrested for having violated the sacred precincts of your Sovereign. It is a dangerous place for a rebel to be surprised in. Go back quickly, make haste to deny that you have ventured near God, and look imploringly to Him by Whom alone God hath solemnly declared shall any approach Him with impunity. Come to Him through Christ and you shall find Him a God of love; come otherwise, and He will be found of you a consuming fire.

John 14:7-9. *"If ye had known me, ye should have known my Father also; and from henceforth ye know him, and have seen him. Philip saith unto him, Lord, show us the Father, and it sufficeth us. Jesus saith unto him, Have I been so long time with you, and yet hast thou not known me, Philip? He that hath seen me hath seen my Father, and how sayest thou then, Show us the Father?"*

In what manner should a revelation be made? To many it would seem that the answer must be this: Whatever you have to declare, that declare in intelligible language. The answer is correct, but it involves a great deal more than is supposed. In order to know what language will be intelligible, we must know the mind of the individual to whom the communication is to be made; we must know what he knows, in order that we may know what he is prepared to understand. If we find that there is a great gulf of ignorance stretching from his knowledge to that which we wish to communicate, it will not do for us to ignore this immense blank and address him as though he had advanced in knowledge to the immediate neighborhood of the revelation to be made; for if we did so, our words would be entirely lost upon him. The gap must be filled up or bridged over. Preliminary information must be given. And whatever communications are made, their particular form and feature must be adapted to the measure of apprehension in the mind addressed.

It is easy to say that truth is one and should be boldly and simply outspoken. That which to a superior intelligence would be the simplest and most faithful expression of truth would actually convey a false impression to a mind more immature. If God, in giving a revelation to man, had used such methods and such language as would have conveyed the facts more clearly and impressively to the intelligence of Heaven, it is certain that the whole would have been unintelligible to man.

They that teach an infant to articulate do not address it in the language of adult men, but in some specially coined words believed to be more fitted to the condition of the organs. The child learns a language which it can afterward throw away; the great victory has been obtained: its organs of articulation have been developed and made meet for the exigencies of life.

Judaism was an all-important preliminary to that revelation of His grace which the Lord our God was bent on making from the very first. Jesus Christ was God manifest in the flesh, but it was necessary that the manifestation should be gradually made. It was fitting that He should have at the beginning divine attestations, that men might look on Him as One empowered to speak. It was fitting that those moral characteristics in which He was to be an example to men should have an abundant exhibition. It was fitting that His disciples should slowly and surely learn the unblemished purity of His character and His moral elevation above all the children of men.

As they became strengthened to bear it, increased vision of His nature was given them. As they grasped one truth, they reached a stepping-stone by which they could grasp another. At length they were informed that in Him was all the fullness of the Godhead bodily. "If ye had known me, ye should have known my Father also." They had actually been making acquaintance with the Father in making acquaintance with Christ. They were now to recognize that the kindness, friendliness, long-suffering and patience of Jesus were the kindness, friendliness, long-suffering and patience of God. He had been all this time with them for the very purpose of making known to them the disposition and the perfections of the Father. "From henceforth ye know him and have seen him." The words, the looks, the acts of Christ, were the words, looks, acts of the Father. This and all other statements of Christ, the Father has ratified by raising Him from the dead.

But no man has seen God at any time. No man has seen his fellow-man, for his fellow-man is an invisible spirit occupying temporarily a visible body. Light, hearing, etc. simply relate to the mediums of communication. God may give such a revelation of His glory as no creature could sustain. But let it not be supposed that a revelation of His glory and majesty such as would transfix the universe would be a greater revelation of God than that which meets us in Christ. The Christian knows that the contrary is true.

"Philip saith unto him, Lord, show us the Father and it sufficeth us." Show *me* not the Father out of Christ! Let me leave it to a thoughtless world to utter this request. They ask to see God, to see the dread Sovereign against Whom they have rebelled, to meet that accumulated wrath which they have been all their life-time heaping up. They that refuse to see the Godhead in Christ cut themselves off from all hope of seeing God otherwise than as the God of vengeances.

"Have I been so long time with you, and yet hast thou not known me, Philip? He that hath seen me hath seen the Father; and how sayest thou then, Show us the Father?" Not that Jesus had been telling him daily that He was the manifestation of God: far from it; but God was revealed in His acts and words. The implication is that these acts and utterances had been constantly testifying to the divinity of His nature. An intimation was given to Philip that he had lost the chief testimony that Christ had been uttering on earth.

Acting on the light now given, Philip, doubtless now or at a later period, re-examined the photograph of Christ's life—the Gospel in his memory—and joyfully recognized in a thousand minute deeds and expressions of the Savior a divine radiance. Things which he had seen with scarcely any emotion, and had straightway dismissed from memory as of no value, now suddenly assume the very highest value, and his whole soul kindles over the faded reminiscences with an ardor and joy unspeakable. And is it not just possible that the reader of this may receive an unction from on high, conveyed to him through the medium of some overlooked text, that shall suddenly clothe the whole of the Scripture testimony concerning Jesus with a glory and a power hitherto unknown?

John 14:10-12. *"Believest thou not that I am in the Father, and the Father in me? The words that I speak unto you I speak not of myself: but the Father that dwelleth in me, he doeth the works. Believe me that I am in the Father, and the Father in me: or else believe me for the very works' sake. Verily, verily, I say unto you, He that believeth on me, the works that I do shall he do also; and greater works than these shall he do; because I go unto my Father."*

Christ, with all His works and all His words, was in the Father, and the Father was in Christ, even in all His words and all His works. True faith in Christ embraces these glorious facts, and the believer lives under the power of them. It is impossible that faith should run away with us into the region of error if we identify Christ with Him that sitteth upon the throne of the universe. There is no danger of our carrying Christ too high. There is sometimes a timidity in the mind, lest one should go too far and find too much of the Godhead in Christ. But was there any timidity in Christ's expression on this subject? On the contrary, He luxuriated in the boldest language.

Were it right for any one to be scrupulous in this matter, it would have been supremely right for Christ to be so—and He would have been so. He was the last Person in the universe to use language that could possibly prove derogatory to God or savor of ambition in Himself. He sought not His own glory, but the glory of Him that sent Him, and He was never more intent upon the glory of Him that sent Him than when He spoke the words now under comment.

He thought it not robbery to use this language. He that robs takes from another, but Christ took nothing from the glory of the Father in saying that the Father was in Him, His words, His works. Neither does He rob us of anything when He asks us to make room in our minds for this mighty truth. Perhaps we are not willing to part with our erroneous conceptions of the Father because they have been long entertained. It is high time we were rid of them; they dispossess the mind of great treasures, unsearchable riches.

"Believest thou not that I am in the Father and the Father in me?" Oh, certainly I believe it. How could I be a Christian if I did not believe this? But ah! take heed; faith is something very different from subscribing to a formula. Many persons simply pronounce their own condemnation in repeating the words of a creed. Were you to hear a man say, as he sat quietly in a large building, "I believe there is to be a tremendous earthquake in a few minutes," you would say the man's profession is a lie, or else he courts destruction. There is too much repetition of creeds, and that is the reason there is so much infidelity in the world.

Instead of hastily saying, "I believe," test yourself, weigh what you call your faith in the balances of the sanctuary. Go carefully through the Gospel, take up the words of Christ one after another and see if you can hear in each the united utterance of the Father and of the Son.

Take, for instance, that word: "Seek first the kingdom of God and his righteousness; and all these things shall be added unto you." Do you hear in this the voice of the omnipotent God? Have you faith here? Your life must answer. Can you trust God to supply you with the temporal gifts you need, while you seek to secure for yourself or for others His blessing in Christ? Or do you make the supposed obligation of attending to your temporal concerns the excuse for neglecting those of your soul? Do you allow a small worldly difficulty to hinder you from attending the assemblies of God's praying people?

For a man to say, "I believe," is the same as for him to say, "I follow Paul." "The Father that dwelleth in me, he doeth the works." Consider these works, consider them carefully, one by one, and see if you can apprehend them one and all as done by the Father. You will find this a most profitable employment. You will become sensible of your want of faith, of the imperfect developments of your faith as to the power of the truth in vanquishing sin. Day by day your faith will be strengthened, and you will find that the apostles did not exaggerate when they spoke of the Kingdom of God as "righteousness, peace and joy in the Holy Ghost."

In like manner Christ has said, "My words, they are spirit and they are life." Let us look at all the words of Christ with reference to the discovery of spirit and life in them alone. Let us knock at every text till it gives forth to us its treasure of spirit and of life.

"Believe me that I am in the Father, and the Father in me: or else believe me for the very works' sake." Believe Me; believe My simple declaration; I am no visionary, no enthusiast; I have never been known to speak at random; no falsehood was ever heard issuing from My mouth; and it is in the nature of things, impossible that I should be deceived in regard to this matter. If you believe My other words concerning Myself, why not this word? If you find it difficult to believe this on My simple attestation, then believe it on the testimony of the works. Have not the power and other perfections of God been worthily exhibited in the miracles which I have wrought—wrought by virtue of the power and the perfections dwelling in Me? Surely you would not so disparage the majesty of Heaven as to give the glory of His works to a creature! I have spoken at this time, but My works have been speaking all along.

"Verily, verily, I say unto you, He that believeth on me, the works that I do shall he do also." The works that Christ performed bore testimony to the fact that He was God manifest in the flesh. Receiving this testimony, His people are enabled to perform similar miracles, or rather such miracles follow them that believe. The miracles performed by them bear the same testimony that those of Christ do. In fact, they are all of Christ.

Christ alone is possessed of miraculous powers. It was He that struck Elymas the sorcerer blind, though the word was spoken by Paul. Faith unites the believer to Christ, so that he receives of Christ's fullness even grace for grace. Had the power of Christ over diseases, devils and death not been exhibited through His disciples, there would not have been an impressive exhibition of the all-important fact that the believer is by his faith united to Christ even as the branch is to the vine. The influences and efficiencies of the vine all reveal themselves in the branch. As Christ is, so are we in this world. But the exhibition of His power may be, we conceive, limited or modified by the measure of our faith.

What we see of Christ in the Church is no true guide to the measure of His willingness to reveal Himself on this globe; it is simply a guide to the measure of His people's faith. This is certain, that He never intended by the translation of His body to Heaven to deprive earth of any of His energy or power or virtue. He ascended up on high that He might more widely diffuse His grace and His glory in the earth, that He might, in His disciples, visit every nation and flash forth upon the vision of all mankind the evidences of His power to bless unto the uttermost.

Oh for the faith that would bring us nearer to Christ, and bring Christ nearer to a world lying in wickedness! "All things are possible to him that believeth." "Help thou our unbelief."

John 14:12-13. *"And greater works than these shall he do; because I go unto my Father. And whatsoever ye shall ask in my name, that will I do, that the Father may be glorified in the Son."*

More and more it becomes evident that it is expedient for Christ to go to the Father, for we, His disciples, in a certain sense ascend with Him and enter into the very treasury of God's power. The way into the holiest is thus made manifest. Christ goes unto the Father that He may receive gifts for men. Seeing Him thus mount up and sit down at the right hand of the Majesty on high, our faith is emboldened to scale the heights of Heaven and ask the largest testimony from the Father to the worth of the Son. Christ is the Vine and His people are the branches, and it is only through the branches that the vine brings forth fruit. He uses language the most general; He says, not, "You shall do these greater works," but, "He that *believeth*" shall do them. What Christ can do faith can do. There is no fear that faith will misuse this power, for the same faith that looks to the power of Christ looks also to His wisdom, and is guided implicitly by Him.

Immediately after the promise, "Greater works than these shall the believer do," comes the information that it is Christ Himself that doeth the works: "Whatsoever ye shall ask in my name, that will I do." They who know that they can of their own selves do nothing, and yield themselves to Jesus for the accomplishment of His purposes, become a medium through which the fullest and most glorious exhibition of Christ's power can appropriately be made. "I have a baptism to be baptized with," said our Lord, on one occasion; "and how am I straitened until it be accomplished." During His life on earth He was very much restricted in the exercise of His power: "For the Holy Ghost was not yet given, because Christ was not yet glorified." But after the ascension, wherever there was a believer there was an omnipotent Christ. A thousand cities might simultaneously behold the displays of His power.

On the day of Pentecost a thousand of the fiercest enemies of Christ laid down their weapons and proclaimed Him Lord, to the glory of God the Father. He went forth conquering and to conquer the hearts of His own immediate disciples, so imperfectly subdued during His ministry, [but now] having been brought into complete subjection by the outpouring of the Spirit from the throne of their risen Lord.

The hoary mythologies of Egypt, Syria, Greece and Rome fled at the advent of His Gospel. Nations representing the larger part of the earth's population parted with their time-honored and art-honored superstitions, and acknowledged Christ as the Savior.

It was sufficiently manifest then that Christ had all power in Heaven and in earth. He had subjugated what was most formidable upon earth; He had done it in answer to the prayers of His people and through the instrumentality of His people; and in that day there might reasonably have been entertained a hope that the promise in Daniel would now be fulfilled, and the greatness of the kingdom under the whole heaven be given to the saints of the Most High. But the great works of Christ are indissolubly connected with faith; and when Christ was evidently declaring in providence His readiness to make all His enemies His footstool, then, alas! His people proved recreant. They attempted to join the strength of the world to that of Christ, to mix up something else with Scripture, to divide their faith between Heaven and earth, reality and falsehood, and the consequence was that the Church had to make a long and fearful and all but irrecoverable plunge into the abyss of the Dark Ages.

In these later days it is again becoming manifest that Christ giveth power unto His people. They are learning once again the lesson set forth in the words from which we are now deducing these thoughts. Yet it is more difficult now to learn it than it was in the freshened and unchastized hopefulness of the Pentecostal age. There is an almost insuperable disposition to receive our idea of the nature of this dispensation from the dispensation itself, overlooking the fact that man has fearfully vitiated what God purely gave.

The celestial theory of this dispensation, gainsay it who will, is set forth in these indestructible words of Christ: "He that believeth in me shall do greater works than these, because I go unto my Father, and whatsoever ye shall ask in my name, I will do it, that the Father may be glorified in the Son." From this it plainly appears that the dispensation of the Spirit is the dispensation of the mighty power of Christ, and that

87

there is no form or measure of opposition which Christ on His throne in Heaven is not competent, by the omnipotent Spirit acting through His Church, to overcome.

Behold what a Paul achieved! He that so overcame the depravity in the mind of Paul could do it in the minds of thousands, and in a day, as it were, multiply by thousands the achievements of Paul.

The only way in which faith can live is to grow, and it must be willing to grow in the direction in which Christ would incline it, else its expansion will be for naught. We must look upon the present processes of the Head of the Church, both among His people and among the unreconciled, as designed to develop the budding faith of His people. Oh, if they could once look without a veil into the clear glass of the Gospel! They are startled and delighted to find that, in answer to their united and specific prayers, thousands of individuals in remote parts of the land, or far off over the sea, are overtaken by the grace of God and converted, long afterward to be informed whose prayers obtained for them this grace.

"Concerning the work of my hands command ye me," says God in one place; and it is a truth that the infinite and blessed God does carry out the wishes of His people, when their wishes are right wishes, with a punctuality, a promptness and a fullness of accomplishment such as are not often found in servants. There are some who are doing their utmost in the attempt to enter into relations with invisible spirits—the spirits of dead men and women, in Heaven or on earth—by prayer or by mechanical means, hoping thus to obtain power for themselves in the unseen world, when there is the mighty God Himself, accessible through Christ and well disposed to do for us exceeding abundantly above all that we ask or think.

But the force of all that has been said comes home to us as individuals. Whatever obligation there is upon the Church to believe is upon me: and though all others should be recreant [cowardly] to it, yet woe is unto me if I be so. It is expedient for me that Christ is on the throne of Heaven, for He there has all power, not only in Heaven, but in earth; and if my faith be what it should be, there shall remain no reason why that power should not be exerted gloriously, first in my heart and then in the hearts of those within my reach.

John 14:14. *"If ye shall ask any thing in my name, I will do it."*

"The Father that dwelleth in me doeth the works," had Jesus said. This was said of the works wrought on earth. And now He says, concerning the future works to be wrought from Heaven, in answer to the prayers of His people, that He will do them. The Savior is still intent upon the conjoining and identifying, in the minds of His disciples, the boundless perfections of the Godhead with the grace of Him Whom they had known in the flesh. As the Son of man had power on earth to forgive sins, so would He have power in Heaven to answer prayer. You must conceive Me, He says, as actually invested with all power in Heaven and earth.

"In my name." What is it to ask in Christ's Name? It is to have a consciousness that in our own name it would be altogether vain to come with petitions before God. In connection with our own name there stands recorded a fearful catalogue of sins, every one of which appeals to the truth, justice and holiness of God to launch against us a sentence of everlasting destruction from the presence of His glory.

There are many who say in this day, "To whom shall we go but unto our Father in Heaven, Who is goodness itself and Who is ready to forgive?" Ah, do you think that God will show Himself a Father to you at the expense of the deepest interests of millions of His creatures? The welfare of the universe demands that God shall take such measures against sin as will tend to make it odious in the eyes of the universe and fill His subjects with horror at the thought of the most distant approach to it. For a man to present himself in his own name before God is to come before God with a declaration that the transgression of the commands of the Most High has nothing in it of special turpitude [depravity]. It is, in fact, asking God to repent that He gave such bad behests [commands], imposed such unnecessary requirements.

To ask aright in Christ's Name is to stake all our hopes of success at the throne of grace upon the work that Christ has wrought out in our stead, to rest with an undivided mind upon that, to feel that it is infinitely meritorious, and that the merit of it appears with infinitely more distinctness to the Father than it can to any creature. It is to believe that Christ has made a propitiation ample for all our sins, for all our depravity. It is to be strong in His strength, holy in His holiness; to put on His Sonship, His royalty, His influence at the court of Heaven; to take to ourselves the Name of Jesus, to go in the person of Jesus, to personate Jesus, so that the Father, as He reaches forth to us the thing we ask, shall say, "O My Son Jesus, the joy of My heart, can I deny Thee aught?" It is to stand in Christ before the throne and receive in Christ the expressions of the Father's love to Christ.

What a world of wealth breaks upon the believer's perception when he supplicates the Father in the Name of Christ for, in order to show the significance of the Name, he explores the treasuries of Christ's character and work. Every drop that fell from the brow of Christ in Gethsemane, in the praetorium and on Calvary, is found to be worth more at the mercy-seat than all the mines of Golconda. The Name of Christ is found to have an amplitude that stretches in every direction beyond the power of imagination to follow.

But, sad to say, some Christians seem to have come to the end of their Christ. Unlike the Thessalonians, whose faith grew exceedingly, the faith of these Christians does not grow. They come with cold, dead prayers, expecting nothing. Months, years go by without any perceptible kindling of expectation in their souls. Yes, they have expended the merit of Christ; they have exhausted the virtue of His Name; His little life with which He rose from the grave is extinguished. But what a foul reproach is this! What have you ever received from the throne of grace that you should think you had overdrawn your account and exhausted the virtue of Christ's Name? There is too much reason to believe that you never went to God with the true Christ, but rather with some phantom of your own.

We are to show our appreciation of Christ by what we shall ask in His Name. God gives us little to see if our Christ is little. Oh, let us feel the necessity of showing the unsurpassable greatness of our Christ by the greatness of our supplications! Let us ask to be filled with the Spirit of God; filled with all the fullness of God; filled with the fruits of righteousness; filled with joy unspeakable. Let us ask for perfect love and to be one in the Father and in Christ.

"If ye love me, keep my commandments." This injunction immediately follows the magnificent promise above noticed, and immediately introduces the promise of the Spirit of truth.

There is no fitter place for a commandment to stand than between two promises. The promise is a promise of help; help to do what? To do the will of God, to obey the command of Christ. The promises bring us to the commandments and the commandments to the promises. Thus lovingly harbored among the promises, who will approach the commandments with an unfriendly or murmuring spirit? "If ye shall ask anything in my name, I will do it"; and when I ask anything of you, surely you will not deny Me. I show you that My love has no limits, that I stand ready to evoke all within the range of possibility in proof of My love; in return I ask love of you. You, of course, are eager to know how you may express your love to Me. By keeping My commandments.

A new commandment I have given, that ye love one another, as I have loved you. I am about to disappear from your sight, but do not fear that you will be without a Christ to show love to; every disciple is My representative, and as many as there are around you, so many are there to represent Me at your gate and receive in My Name the expressions of your affection for Me. "If ye love Me, keep this commandment, and I will pray the Father, and He shall give you another Comforter, that He may abide with you for ever." Thus we see that a most important introduction to the outpouring of the Holy Spirit is the exercise of mutual love by Christians. We shall pray most fervently and believingly for the Holy Spirit when we shall pray disinterestedly with a pure desire for the edification of our brethren and the upbuilding of the general Church. And we must be careful to remember that genuine love for Christ's people is love for all Christ's people—a love for them because they are Christ's, not because they are associated with us in some particular communion; a love that rises superior to conventional laws and sectarian barriers.

John 14:15-17. *"If ye love me, keep my commandments. And I will pray the Father, and he shall give you another Comforter, that he may abide with you for ever. Even the Spirit of truth; whom the world cannot receive, because it seeth him not, neither knoweth him: but ye know him; for he dwelleth with you, and shall be in you."*

Men examine with liveliest interest the title-deeds that are to put them in possession of some valuable piece of property, and it would be strange if Christians did not search with a profound scrutiny and with kindling hopes those promises which exhibit to them the glorious gifts to be bestowed by a risen and triumphant Savior. Tell me what think ye of Christ, and I will tell you what you ought to think of the Spirit. Or tell me what think you of the Spirit, and I will tell you what ye think of Christ; for observe that Christ here promises another Comforter. "Let not your heart be troubled because I, your Comforter, your Monitor, your Advocate, am about to be withdrawn from you; another shall be given you."

Moses said, with reference to the offer of an angel to conduct the Israelites to Canaan, "If thy presence go not with us, carry us not up hence." And the Christian would esteem it but a mockery of his need if an angel or any number of angels were given to compensate him for the presence of Christ. It was because the Savior had such a perfect apprehension of the need of Christians that He promised them the Holy Spirit as another Comforter. Another? We are required to believe, on the testimony of this word, that in the guidance of the Holy Ghost we enjoy that which is fully equal to the guiding, comforting and strengthening influence of the Lord Jesus as enjoyed by the apostles. The word translated Comforter means Monitor, Counselor, Advocate. Counselor was one of the epithets assigned to the Messiah by prophecy. In Him are all the treasures of wisdom and knowledge.

But before going a step farther let me add the succeeding verse: "I will not leave you comfortless: I will come unto you."

The word here translated "comfortless" would literally be rendered "orphans." Taking this passage in connection with the preceding verses, it is evident that in the advent of the Comforter there is an advent of Christ to the soul, and the indwelling of the Spirit is the indwelling of the Savior. He could not come sufficiently near to His people while imprisoned in a body of clay upon the earth, and the body was broken like an alabaster box of ointment that He might come nearer to His own and communicate Himself to their very souls. Though we have known Christ after the flesh, yet now know we Him no more; His body disappears from our eyes in order that His blessed Spirit may be commingled with our spirit, and that we may be united to Him even as He is united to the Father.

We are never more impressively manifesting our love to the Savior than when we are praying for the outpouring of the Spirit. Christ is the truth and the Spirit is the Spirit of Truth, and it is not more true that no man comes to the Father, save by the Son, than that no man comes to the Son but by the Holy Spirit.

Christ is our Advocate with the Father, and the Holy Spirit is Christ's Advocate with us. As Christ pleads for us at the throne of grace, so the Spirit pleads for Christ in our hearts. The Spirit vindicates Him from our unworthy thoughts, shows Him to be chief among myriads and altogether lovely, declares His immeasurable love and our absolute need of His grace. If we ever, in any sense, become the advocates of Christ, confessing Him among men, it is only because the Holy Spirit hath wrought in us to this end.

"Ye know him." Christians, they that are indeed such, if they know anything, any one, know the Holy Spirit. When the Holy Spirit is given to any, you need not say to the Christian, "This is the Holy Spirit." Ignorant he may be of ten thousand things known among men, but he knows the Spirit of Truth, the Comforter, the Holy Ghost. He knows the work of the Holy Spirit in his own heart, and he knows the operations of the Spirit in other Christians.

When he obtains an insight into the meaning of the Scriptures, he says, "This is the doing of the Holy Spirit." When he is enabled to do that which is well pleasing to his heavenly Father, to resist temptation, make sacrifices, walk in love, renounce the world, give himself to prayer, he knows that he is taught of the Spirit. He knows how to distinguish between the suggestions of the Spirit of God and the suggestions of his own heart, and he advances in this ability just in the measure that he enjoys the Spirit's influences. Christians know each other because they know the Holy Spirit dwelling in each and all. Christians who come together for the first time enter at once deep into the sacred prerogatives of an intimate friendship because they know the Spirit by Whom both are led.

They that know the Spirit know that there is nothing in the world so much to be desired or valued as the teachings of this divine Being. They disregard the distinction conferred by wealth, fashion, rank, education even, in comparison with the distinction conferred by the presence of the indwelling Spirit of Truth. They who have been sealed in their foreheads as the sons of God know those who are similarly sealed. All the rest of mankind may fail to recognize these Heaven-born ones—they cannot fail. They that know the Spirit are ready to pluck out a right eye, cut off a right hand, rather than grieve the Spirit of God. They hunger and thirst after the sanctification which He alone can effect, and they earnestly desire that their fellow-men may be convinced of their personal sin and of the all-sufficient righteousness of Christ. If they hear of meetings for prayer, for the outpouring of the Holy Spirit, they are immediately interested.

Knowing the Spirit, they know that there is nothing earth so needs as it does His influences. They that know the Spirit are free from an overweening attachment to any one particular branch of Christ's Church, for the Spirit of God dwells in all the saints. He is without partiality, and He teaches the people of Christ to be without partiality. They who find themselves unable to sympathize with Christians belonging to other than their denomination show that they know not the Spirit.

John 14:18. *"I will not leave you comfortless: I will come to you."*

Literally, "I will not leave you orphans: I will come to you." The disciples had forsaken all to follow Him, making Him their all in all. They had broken away from all the ordinary helps and confidences of society, relying solely upon His presence with them, and His wisdom, strength and grace, to secure to them whatever they might need. But His very presence with them in the flesh for so many days had made it all but impossible for them to take in the idea that He could be otherwise present with them, that the grace and might of an *unseen* Savior would serve them in the battle of life.

That Jesus was going to the Father, to the glory of Heaven, was in itself an elevating thought, but what would be their position on earth in the face of a frowning world? They would be like orphans. Orphans are children peculiarly dependent upon the help of parents and deprived of this help—left alone in their incapacity to face trials to which only mature men are equal. "No," says Jesus, "I will not leave you orphans; I know that My presence and My grace are absolutely essential to you, and I do not intend that you should be deprived of them, save for a very brief season; I will come to you, and though you may not understand how I can both go to the Father and come to you, nevertheless the thing shall be."

John 14:19-20. *"Yet a little while, and the world seeth me no more; but ye see me: because I live, ye shall live also. At that day ye shall know that I am in my Father, and ye in me, and I in you."*

The "little while" was a period of less than twenty-four hours. After His crucifixion the world saw Him no more. His disciples saw Him when He had risen from the dead; He showed Himself alive unto them during forty days. We are not, however, to limit the announcement, "Ye see me," to the time intervening between the resurrection and the ascension. They saw Him on the day of Pentecost as they had not seen Him before.

The use of the present gives the force of perpetuity to the words. "You see me" means much more than "You shall see me." The world sees Him not, because, as He had already said, it sees not and knows not the Spirit. "For I live and you shall live," the last clause might fitly be rendered. "God hath shined in our hearts to give the light of the knowledge of the glory of God in the face of Jesus Christ." This is the great distinction between the people of God and others, that the former see Jesus by faith; He is manifest unto them.

These various expressions set forth a great truth which, it is much to be feared, the experience of many Christians does not permit them properly to grasp. The reference throughout is to a most powerful operation of the Spirit of God, annihilating to our spirits all that would hinder us from apprehending the presence and power and grace of the Lord Jesus. This familiar phrase, "Ye shall live," has a profound significance, a scope that knows no limit, for the life of the believer is here bound up with the life of Christ. The believer lives not as other men live, but as Christ lives. The Spirit of Truth is the Spirit of Life, connecting each believer with his risen Lord and with all other believers.

"The world seeth Me no more, but ye see Me, for I live and ye shall live; and if ye live indeed, then shall the world see Me through you, and ascertain in this way My righteousness, My power, My glory, as they could not ascertain them while I was corporeally present with them." The resurrection of Christ from the dead is a great and invincible fact, not merely with reference to believers, but with reference to the world. Believers started to life when He did, and their resurrection is a triumphant proof of His resurrection. On the day of Pentecost the Jews saw before them a hundred and twenty proofs of the resurrection of Christ. Each believer was seen to be clothed with a life such as had never before been beheld, and each believer was to the astonished multitude as a risen Christ.

Let no one imagine for a moment that the truth then illustrated was then exhausted. It is the vocation of every believer, in every generation, to afford in his own person the evidence that Christ has risen. Are you a Christian? You art one whom Christ has chosen to convey to men the proof that He is risen. This is your vocation. Will you roll back the stone upon the sepulcher and make the world believe that Christ is still there? This you are actually doing if you do not walk in the Spirit.

"At that day ye shall know that I am in my Father, and ye in me, and I in you." They shall begin to know this in the day of His resurrection, and shall make progress in the knowledge of it thence onward. That which they were slow to learn in the days of His flesh they will learn rapidly in the days of the Spirit. When Christ ascends on high, our conceptions of Him ascend also and unite themselves to our conceptions of the Father; so that we find the benignity, the love, the long-suffering, the grace, the tenderness, the gentleness, the sympathy, the cordiality, the friendliness, the brotherliness of the Son in the Father, and the majesty, dominion, omnipotence, omniscience, omnipresence, holiness of the Father in the Son.

But though our adorable Savior carries up into the Godhead the conceptions inspired in us by His earthly life and death, yet be it understood that the bond which binds us to Him is unrelaxed. It is indeed made infinitely stronger. He that speaks of Himself as in the Father says, "Ye in me, and I in you."

We not only rise with Him, but ascend with Him. Or if for a season we remain behind, it is that we may bring up a redeemed world with us. What inspires us with the hope of doing this is that the Redeemer dwells in us. It is evident that the believer is not far from the place

97

where Christ sits in glory. His words bid us take knowledge of Him ascending up to the Father, and straightway they bid us find Him in ourselves. "I in you"—words no less wonderful than those which light up another page of Scripture: "God was manifest in the flesh." Thousands beheld Him in the flesh who knew not His glory until they took knowledge of Him in the disciples that came forth from that upper room on the day of Pentecost.

How every word seems to burn in upon us the sense of our need of the outpouring of the Holy Spirit! In vain we profess to admire Christ, to desire His glory, to be hasting unto His kingdom, to compassionate the world, to hunger and thirst after righteousness, to love the Scriptures, to abhor falsehood and heathenism and Romanism and rationalism and infidelity, if we are unwilling to give ourselves, heart and soul, to the great work of supplicating God, in concert with our fellow-Christians, for the outpouring of the Holy Spirit.

If our fellow-Christians are bound up in slumbers of sin, if the opiates of this world are still holding them in dumb forgetfulness, we must seek to arouse them to the necessity of calling upon their God and ours without delay. If, in the garden of Gethsemane, James had been faithful to John and John to Peter, perhaps our Lord would not have returned from His place of agony three times to find them asleep.

"I in you." Jesus hath climbed the heavens, and hath made His way to a throne exalted above all principality and power and might and dominion. But there remains one great desire of His heart unsatisfied: He will not have seen the travail of His soul until in all His purity, beauty, power and glory He is seen in His saints.

The expression "I in you" has a present and important truth, but in its plenitude of meaning it is a thing of the future. Oh for that day when Jesus shall be fully seen in us!—the day of the manifestation of the sons of God. Come, Lord Jesus, come quickly. Come, thou Spirit of all grace, Whose office and joy is to form Christ in us, the hope of glory; come with Thy mightiest influences and effect that blessed metamorphosis.

John 14:21. *"He that hath my commandments, and keepeth them, he it is that loveth me: and he that loveth me shall be loved of my Father, and I will love him, and will manifest myself unto him."*

There are some who willingly speak of themselves as believers in Christ, but who would be displeased if you were to address to them the question, "Do you love Christ?" Love to Christ does not well express their idea of the feeling that a believer should have. There is something too warm, too personal, too enthusiastic about this definition of discipleship to suit them. They would view Christ at a certain distance, they would yield Him reverence, honor and trust, but to speak of loving Christ savors to them of extravagance. It is nevertheless certain that this is the very sentiment that Christ most persistently demands of His people. He freely speaks of it without the least hesitation. "Lovest thou me?" is His interrogation to every one who professes to be His disciple.

There are some who are very willing to make use of Christ, as they are of the servants of Christ in certain exigencies, but who prefer that there should be, for the most part, no great intimacy, no very decided warmth of affection. They would be united to Him by a cord so long that they may walk on one side of the way and He on another. They deceive themselves fatally as to the nature of a true union with Christ. Note the affection of the mother for her child, of the child for its parent. See how the glances of the bridegroom and bride seek each other! Search in the retrospect of your own heart-life for that which may best be expressed by the word "love" and you will be assisted to understand something of the strength of that feeling which binds the believer to Christ.

Do you consent to recognize the obligation thus to love Christ? Is it your heart's desire and aim thus to love Him? If not, you may immediately blot out your name from the book of candidates at the door of Christ. If you will not give up the idea that there may be faith without love, you must give up Christ. "Kiss the Son, lest he be angry and ye perish from the way."

Ah, what a great gain it would be to many to give up *their* Christ!—to know their utter penury of all that Heaven calls treasure, to take deliberate knowledge that there is no essential difference between them and the unconverted! How cruel of any to seek to confirm them in their delusion! How noble of us if we would help them to escape from the network of their imagination! How many there are whose hope is an unsatisfying one, and who yet cling to it with greatest tenacity. Ah, if they would only dare to die! "When the commandment came, sin revived and I died."

The apostle's hope died out, the consciousness of sin and hell-desert took possession of him again. It seemed to him that Satan had come back upon him and was reconquering him. But the fact was simply this—that Satan, disguised as an angel of light, had been hitherto leading him captive, bound by chains that were ornamented with passages of Scripture, and that now he had begun to see the diabolic lineaments of the guide whom he had deemed celestial. It was well that his hope and trust in such a mock savior should be destroyed, and it mattered little how much peace was dashed from him in the moral revolution. The ruins of his old confidence are simply the stones over which Christ, the true, the living, the all-mighty, the all-loving Christ, will haply be seen bounding on His way to the throne of his heart.

If any man love not the Lord Jesus Christ, an anathema will be his portion in the last day. It is the portion which he himself has chosen. All are under the curse, and all are pervaded by the curse (unforgiven sin is the curse), till the love of Christ comes into the heart to annihilate that curse.

He that truly loves Christ will be content to learn of Christ how he shall express his love. Some are willing to love Him, they think, but they must be allowed to express their love in the way their own heart may suggest. When He says "Go," they reply "Nay, but we will sit at His blessed feet." This sort of love is simply calumny. They prefer themselves to Christ in the very act by which they profess to show

100

their attachment. They prefer their will to His—that vile, corrupt, odious will; they prefer their wisdom to His—an abominable caricature of wisdom to the infinite wisdom of Christ. A parent may love a child and yet do what the child dislikes; a husband may show his love even in acts that oppose the will of his wife, for with him is authority, and with him, perhaps, superior wisdom; but what a monstrous position were this for a believer to take up with respect to Christ!

"He that hath my commandments"—hath them in memory, in meditation; hath them conspicuously in his mind where he can find them without delay and trouble—is filled with the knowledge of his Master's will in all wisdom and spiritual understanding. The lawyer, he that would know the laws of his state, with how much diligence does he apply himself to the study of those laws until he has mastered them, and is so much at home among them that none can throw him off his guard! The Christian must be a scribe instructed unto the kingdom of God.

See our Lord in the wilderness when tempted of Satan; what an admirable hold He had of the commands of God! He brought forth, in each instance, without giving the adversary the advantage of a moment's hesitancy, the very command that was needed. If Christ needed thus to have the commands of God about Him, surely the believer no less requires to have the commands of his Lord present to him. We must seek, by the grace of God, to make it a habit, an instinct, a second nature of our souls, to refer constantly to the will of Christ. The vigilant and faithful helmsman never acts as though he were the commander of the ship, but hearkens ever for the voice that shall bid him what to do.

The commandments of Jesus are not grievous—the very opposite; they are the means of giving expression to our love. Where there is love there is a necessity for expressions of that love, and the loving heart rejoices greatly in the opportunity of uttering itself. The commandments of Jesus are in fact responses to the question of the believer, "Lord, what wilt thou have me to do? In what way may I give utterance to my love?"

"He that loveth me shall be loved of my Father." Ah, Lord, there are some who deny that You are God manifest in the flesh, God over all, blessed for ever, by Whom all things were made, by Whom all are upheld. While they profess to love You, they declare You an impostor, guilty of one of the basest and most opprobrious [shameful] of all practices, the undue exaltation of one's self, and guilty of it in a greater degree than any other man ever was. To love *their* Christ were a sin indeed. How blessed the confidence of him who knows unwaveringly that he who loveth Jesus is loved of the Father! The Father loveth the Son, and therefore He loves him who loves the Son, rejects him who rejects the Son.

We love Him because He first loved us. Our love is elicited by His, and there are special revelations of His love granted to those who give proof of love to Him. As the believer makes progress in conformity with His will, he is enabled by faith to discover new measures of Christ's unmeasurable love.

John 14:21. *"I will love him, and will manifest myself to him."*

I will love him that loves Me, and will manifest Myself to him. We love Him because He first loved us; we are indebted to His love for the very first spiritual exercises of our souls, as well as for all that succeed in time and eternity. But there are special revelations of His love, and special manifestations of His glory, made to him who gives special evidence of love to Christ. One way in which this special evidence is given is in seeking very earnestly those special revelations. He that loves Christ counts all but loss for the excellency of the knowledge of Christ. His love "believeth all things"—believes that there are unsearchable riches in Christ, and that Christ is able and willing to impart of His blessed wealth to those that seek it.

We disparage Christ beyond expression when we rest satisfied with what we have seen and known of Him. It is sheer vanity for us to profess to admire Him if we do not, above all things, desire and seek, not in the distant future, but in the immediate present, those revelations of our Lord which made the disciples of ancient times to rejoice with joy unspeakable and full of glory. They saw Him not with the bodily eye, and let it not be thought surprising that the highest joys which our souls are capable of experiencing while they are in the body are awakened by spiritual contemplations.

Believers are spiritual. Even in Heaven it is not the beholding of a material glory that constitutes the crowning felicity of the redeemed; even in Heaven the redeemed look back to Calvary. A Lamb as it had been slain in the midst of the throne is what they gaze upon. The saints in Heaven excel us fully as much in their clear understanding of the sufferings and death of Christ as in other respects.

Christ hath promised to manifest Himself unto those that love Him. How will He do this? By His Spirit. The office of the Spirit is to take of Christ and show unto us: "Eye hath not seen, ear hath not heard, neither have entered into the heart of man, the things which God hath prepared for them that love him," said the ancient prophets; "Which things," saith Paul, "God hath revealed unto us by his Spirit." Does the word of the apostle seem to you to take away the glory of the prophetic aspiration? This only shows that you are shamefully ignorant of the power of the Spirit.

The Spirit of God is omnipotent; He is omnipotent with reference to these souls of others, with reference to the subjugation of sin and the communication of joy unspeakable. He is able to meet all the exigencies of our nature, to heal our corruption, our depravity, our carnality, to communicate His own hallowed and ecstatic perceptions of Christ, and to fulfill to us the visions that floated before the inspired eye of Isaiah. He is with us to make known Christ to us, and it will never do for us to think so meanly of His capacity as to doubt that He can make Him known to us so that He shall be to us the chiefest among ten thousands, the One altogether lovely.

If we wish, therefore, to sound the depths of this promise, "I will manifest myself to him," we must honor Christ and the Father and the Spirit by believing in the power of the Spirit. To have faith in Christ and not to have faith in the Spirit seems to be a great contradiction, yet we submit for the judgment of candid inquirers that this very contradiction is strikingly exhibited in the case of almost all who profess to be the followers of Christ. To know the Father we must know the Son; to know Christ we must know the Spirit. "He shall glorify me," said Christ. Do you believe this? Is this your conception of Christ's glory, that it is a glory that the Spirit of God can enable you to behold? When the omnipotent Spirit has been allowed, by our faith, to go to the full extent of His resources in the revelation of Christ, it will be time enough for us to turn away from Him to some more perfect way of bringing Christ near to us.

When Isaiah was in the temple, he saw the Lord (the Lord Christ, as we learn from John 12) high and lifted up, and the seraphim encompassing Him with shrouded faces overpowered with the sense of His unutterable holiness and glory; and the prophet fell to the earth, exclaiming, "Woe is me, for I am undone; for I am a man of unclean lips; for mine eyes have seen the King, the Lord of hosts."

You admit that this was a wonderful revelation of the glory of the Messiah. Well, it was after this that Isaiah penned that lofty conception of the Messianic times which Paul tells us is fulfilled in the operations of the Spirit in our hearts. And our Lord Himself tells us that he that is least in the kingdom of Heaven—the kingdom that He came to establish—is greater than any of the prophets that had been in the world before His advent. Greater? Why? Because he is a habitation of God through the Spirit, because that magnificent Gift of gifts which Christ died to obtain for us has been bestowed.

Now all these views of the glory of this present dispensation seem to vanish into night when we subject them to a comparison with the actual experiences of Christians in general. But we do them foul injustice in this way. We are rather to submit the experiences of Christians to the test of Scripture. When we do so, does it not appear that the Church has fallen back into an ante-Pentecostal state?—that it has slipped out of its own dispensation?

There was a measure, a feeble measure, of spiritual influence enjoyed by the disciples before the death and resurrection of Christ, else would they not have been able to call Jesus Lord; but it was nothing in comparison with what they received on the day of Pentecost. The day of Pentecost was a pattern day; all the days of this dispensation should have been like it, or should have exceeded it. But, alas! the Church has fallen down to the state in which it was before this blessing had been bestowed, and it is necessary for us to ask Christ to begin over again.

We, of course, in respect to knowledge—intellectual knowledge of spiritual things—are far in advance of the point where the disciples were before Pentecost. But it should be borne in mind that when truths have once been fully revealed and made a part of orthodoxy, the holding of them does not necessarily imply an operation of the Spirit of God. We deceive ourselves doubtless in this way, imagining that, because we have the whole Scriptures and are conversant with all its great truths, the Spirit of God is necessarily working in us. We need a baptism of the Spirit as much as the apostles did at the time of Christ's resurrection; we need that the unsearchable riches of Christ should be revealed to us more copiously than they were to Isaiah in the temple.

We profess to love Him. We profess, therefore—the inference is unavoidable—to desire to enjoy higher and more satisfying manifestations of Him than have been yet vouchsafed unto us. It follows, then, that we ought to feel very greatly the pressure of the obligation to seek the outpouring of the Holy Spirit.

Blessed be God, the Holy Spirit is being poured out in many churches, and many Christians are at this very hour enjoying such views of Christ as fill them with a preternatural joy and love and strength. But we have not yet entered into the fullness of this glorious dispensation. If we love Christ, we will press deeper into it, believing that Omnipotence will find ways of revealing itself in the spiritual world of which we have as yet no conception.

John 14:22-23. *"Judas saith unto him (not Iscariot), Lord, how is it that thou wilt manifest thyself unto us, and not unto the world? Jesus answered and said unto him, If a man love me he will keep my words: and my Father will love him, and we will come unto him, and make our abode with him."*

Jesus had spoken of a duty and of its reward. It was theirs to attend to the duty; God would attend to the reward. It was not necessary for them to embarrass themselves with the question as to how God would fulfill His promise, but solely with the question as to how they should fitly perform their part. Unbelief often uses this language: "Lord, how is it that You will do this?" Because it is not clearly seen how God will fulfill His promise, men refuse to go forward in the path of duty. They quite forget that the thing which they desire to see can only be seen from an advanced point in the path of duty. Outside of that path it is impossible to discern it.

If the rich young man to whom Christ promised treasure in Heaven, provided he would forsake all and follow Him, had only obeyed Christ, he would have soon, in the path of renunciation, obtained such visions of the treasure in Heaven, as would have made him think all terrestrial treasure to be dross in comparison. But before crossing the line which separated him from Christ he could not discern those compensating glories; it was necessary to believe Christ regarding them; this he would not do.

To many the palace of Christ upon this earth appears a very contemptible edifice. They walk around it, and see much to find fault with. They scorn the suggestion that there can be anything attractive or desirable, anything beautiful or costly, anything to gladden, to refresh, to elevate, in its apartments. But they are surely in a wrong position to judge. Let a man cross the threshold: he receives a wedding-garment; his eyes are anointed with eye-salve and it is not long before he is aware that anything more admirable, more regal, more suited to satisfy, is nowhere to be found on earth. There he is invited to sit at a banquet of life: the guests are kings, the Lord of the feast is the King of kings.

Jesus replies to the question of Judas by repeating what He had already said. Ah! how foolish do we show ourselves, coming to Christ with question after question, when the answer is already with us! There is very little encouragement for Christ to continue instructing us, when we throw away His words as fast as they are given and ask for new ones. Christ will not humor us in this. He takes up the very answers we have thrown away and gives them to us again. A thirsty man in the desert asks for some refreshing liquor, and a coconut is given him; instead of removing its husk and shell, he throws it away, saying that he asked for milk and had received a stone.

In the fifteenth verse we find Jesus saying, "If ye love me, keep my commandments," and this injunction introduces the promise of the Spirit. In verse 21 we have the same injunction, introductory to the promise of the manifestation of Christ. In verse 23 we read again: "If a man love me he will keep my words," and there is connected with it the promise of the manifestation of the Father, and of the permanent abode of both the Father and the Son with the believer. It would be difficult to conceive any addition to this promise. It contains within itself all conceivable wealth of blessing.

The question now comes home to us with irresistible force, How shall we obtain for our souls the verification of this magnificent promise? How shall the heart of the believer be changed into a holy of holies, where the fullness of the Godhead shall dwell? Let us fix our eyes steadily on the means that Christ has pointed out to us. Let us love Him and keep His commandments. Let our love to Him express itself in the utmost deference to His behests. Let us lovingly obey Him. Let us obediently love Him. Let us recognize Him in His Word, and render to His Word the honor due to Him. Let His Word rule in our hearts. We shall no sooner have begun heartily to do this than we shall find the Spirit of Truth, the Comforter, with us, and shall be wonderfully aided to discover Christ in His Word; and in Christ the Father will be revealed to us, and in all this nothing fictitious, nothing even symbolical.

It is not more true that God sitteth above the cherubim than that He, the triune God, is present with him that loves Christ and keeps His words. It is impossible, as we have said, to make this clear to one who does not love. The natural man does not discern the things of the Spirit of God; the semi-spiritual man even does not see how these things can be. But let us believe Christ that, by the Spirit and the Word in the heart of the believer, a glorious manifestation of God in Christ is made to him, such as elevates him in privilege immeasurably above the prophets of former days, and above the disciples who saw our Lord in the flesh.

How many are there in this world whose aspirations bear a reasonable proportion to these promises, who are endeavoring, at whatsoever cost, to obtain the largest possible measure of the grace of God, who are seeking to sound the utmost depths of the mine of wealth opened up to view in these words of Christ? Peradventure there be fifty. Peradventure there shall lack five of the fifty. Peradventure there shall be forty found. Peradventure there shall thirty be found. Peradventure twenty. Peradventure ten!

"We will make our abode with him." He that is surrounded by the seraphim with veiled faces, Who looketh and the earth melteth, before Whom the nations are less than nothing and vanity, *He* draws near to the believer and takes up His abode with him. It is evident that there is a length and breadth, a depth and height in this promise, as limitless as the character of God Himself. Ask the highest archangel what it means and he can only tell us in part. "I in them," said Jesus as He prepared to vanish physically from their eyes.

How little do we know of the unsearchable riches of Christ, notwithstanding the perfect arrangements made for the communication of them to us in this life! Is it right for us to be talking and thinking so much of a fixed Heaven when we refuse to take knowledge of the Heaven that waits to come down into our souls? Can it be said that we have the true Heaven in our eye of hope, when we neglect to give heed to these amazing promises? "We will come and make our abode with you," says Jesus.

"Not so," says the disciple; "tarry on high a while, and we will there rejoin You and the Father."

Nay, but today hear His voice. Grieve not the heart of Christ by repelling His advances. Keep lovingly His words, till, more and more glorious, the Day-star arise in your hearts, the Sun of righteousness fill your soul with effulgence.

John 14:24-26. *"He that loveth me not, keepeth not my sayings: and the word which ye hear is not mine, but the Father's which sent me. These things have I spoken unto you, being yet present with you. But the Comforter, which is the Holy Ghost, whom the Father will send in my name, he shall teach you all things, and bring all things to your remembrance, whatsoever I have said unto you."*

Christ represented the Father, and as men treated Christ they revealed their sentiments toward the Father. The Word of Christ represents Christ, and our sentiments toward Christ are revealed by our treatment of His Word. How many are laboring to settle the question, whether they love Christ or not? It would wonderfully help them in the solution of this if they would first seek to ascertain whether they love the Word of Christ or not. The Christian is one who keeps the words of Christ. He that does not keep the words of Christ, but suffers the adversary to take them away from him as often as they are given him, is not a Christian.

The words of Christ are the fuel of the soul. If we can imagine a fuel that is indestructible, that feeds a fire without losing any of its own virtue, our metaphor will then be a just one. Coal is not placed near an engine that it may remain there like so much dead matter, but that it may feed the fires of the engine and enable the machine to accomplish the work for which it was called into existence. There is no other fuel for the fires of the soul than the words of Christ, the Word of God. Our love to the Savior is a flame that was brought into existence by this fuel, and that absolutely refuses to be fed by any other.

When the Word is retained in the heart, then the renewed faculties of our being are found in lively exercise; prayer ascends unceasingly to God; right resolutions rule in the mind; self is denied; our property is bestowed in the relief of the suffering; we take a hearty interest in the work of God; we visit joyfully the assemblies of the saints; we engage in the praises of the Redeemer; we set our faces against the evil customs of society; our understanding is enlightened;—in a word, the Spirit of Life penetrates and possesses our whole being. But he that has the power of death does his utmost to hinder us from keeping the words of Christ. He has no unwillingness that we should keep them in the

110

head without self-application; then they cannot answer the purpose of fuel. It matters not to him where they are, so they are not found in the furnaces.

"These things have I spoken unto you, being yet present with you. But the Comforter, the Holy Ghost, whom the Father will send in my name, he shall teach you all things, and bring all things to your remembrance, whatsoever I have said unto you."

What Christ had now been saying to the disciples was calculated to elevate greatly their conceptions of the importance of the words of Christ, and it was natural that they should think, with dismay and utter confusion, of the immense number of words that Christ had spoken in their hearing, not one in a thousand of which they now remembered. He therefore repeats the promise concerning the Holy Ghost, the Comforter, the Counselor, Who should teach them all things by bringing to their remembrances the words of Christ. The Father would send Him in the Name of Christ, for Christ's sake and for the accomplishment of Christ's work. "He shall teach you."

Christ had been for years their Teacher, but what dull scholars had they been! The blessed instruction that fell daily from the lips of Him that spoke as never man spoke had for the most part fallen upon their ears in vain. Some of the servants of Christ that go about preaching in these days can say nothing that is not eagerly caught up by many pens and published far and wide. But even the intimate disciples of Christ, the choice of the chosen, neglected a great deal more than they retained of the words of Christ.

What then? Do they need another teacher—one more accomplished? There is none such. In all the universe there is none possessed of such an admirable fitness to instruct the children of men. There are not merely in Him the treasures of wisdom and knowledge, but He is moved by an incomparable love; He has patience, condescension, long-suffering and pity, so that our corruption and stupidity may not alienate Him from us. Not merely by words does He teach us, but by acts, by sufferings and by His whole life and death. His final lessons are from the cross. Yes, He is our Teacher; we are in His school, and in it we shall ever stay.

But His teaching on earth was merely introductory. He was there preparing the materials, the appliances, the conditions. He is at the right hand of the Majesty on high that He may effectually teach us. By His Spirit we are taught. We need the power of Christ brought to bear upon our very hearts by the Spirit of Christ within us.

When Christ was on the earth, He was yet at an immeasurable distance from His disciples. By the gift of the Holy Ghost this distance is annihilated. He comes nearer to His people now than when He washed their feet. He comes into their hearts and takes possession of their wills, their understandings, their energies.

These words present us with a wonderful spectacle—the Holy Ghost in the memory casting out the useless and harmful lumber that has so long choked it, and filling it with the very coin of Heaven, the words of Christ. It is not the legible word that suffices to refresh the memory; without the Spirit of Truth, our memories will remain un-acquainted with the words of Jesus. But before the Spirit thus makes the chambers of memory redolent [filled] with the fragrance of the things of Christ, He subdues the affections and guides the will. What we remember with pleasure we remember well. That which has the chief attraction for us will find our memory its powerful ally.

We remember to have read of a man who in his youth heard a certain word of Christ preached, lived in impenitence till he was more than fourscore years of age, and then was converted by that very word which he had heard in his youth, and which, after a long life of forgetfulness, he remembered when he was nearing the borders of the grave.

"He shall teach you all things." Who, of all the millions that have inherited these promises, has been taught by the Holy Ghost *all* that He is with us to teach? What magnificent revelations may we not expect from such a Teacher! What sublime views of Christ must those be that the Spirit Himself entertains! How far doubtless do they transcend our highest conceptions of Him Who is fairer than the sons of men! But the Spirit is with us that He may glorify Christ. There is not, there cannot possibly be, any indisposition on His part to give us the sublime discoveries which constitute His own felicity. We can only lay the charge against our unbelief and our contumacious [defiant] neglect of the Spirit's aid that we have such comparatively unworthy apprehensions of the excellency of Christ.

John 14:27. *"Peace I leave with you, my peace I give unto you: not as the world giveth, give I unto you. Let not your heart be troubled, neither let it be afraid."*

The disciples had been alarmed by the intimation that the Savior was about to depart out of the world. The repeated assurances concerning the marvelous compensations of the Spirit of God and the spiritual presence of Christ and of the Father, related to something of which they needed to have actual experience before they could understand it and fully rejoice in it. The words concerning the Holy Ghost, the Comforter, were words that none but the Holy Ghost could interpret to them.

The future looked dark to them, for they did not see there the bodily Christ Whom they knew, but a shadowy Christ Whom they knew not. It seemed impossible that there should be any peace for them in that earthly future. Their peace was in Christ; in Him they were strong; in Him they were wise; in Him they could encounter the malignity and violence of men; in Him they could meet and overcome the arguments and sophistries of Pharisees, Saducees, Scribes and Herodians. With Him they could go fearlessly anywhere, but without Him, exposed to the wrath of a Christ-hating world, under solemn obligation to bear a testimony that would cause men everywhere to take up stones and stone them, what remained for them but to take a lasting farewell of peace?

The Savior knew perfectly what was in their mind when He said, "'Peace I leave with you.' Strange as it may appear to you, I leave with you peace; I make it over to you; it belongs to you." The disciples of Christ are under obligations to have this peace. Christ gives; it is for them to receive. Let us not bring a cloud of suspicion over the words of Christ by living without peace. We shall not have it without an act of appropriation on our parts.

Let every one that names the Name of Christ understand that it is a sacred duty to have this peace. If he shut the door of his heart against the words of Christ, he will not have it. It will enter with the words of Christ. He that keepeth His words shall be kept in perfect peace.

This peace casts out fear and anxiety. It does not spring out of a consciousness of worldly wealth or honor. It abides where all these things that give men their momentary peace are taken away. The day of adversity is its day of triumph. False peace walks beside it while the sun of prosperity is shining, and claims that there is no essential difference between them, but the peace that Christ gives, lives serenely when the other has fled, unmasked.

"My peace I give unto you." Christ's own peace. Ah! here is a potent word of promise. The disciples had never seen anything like fear in the Lord Jesus. They had ever seen Him calm and tranquil in the presence of proud opposers. There was in Him the consciousness of invincible strength and inexhaustible wisdom and unimpeachable integrity. The natural result of such consciousness was peace that passeth understanding.

How could they ever possess His peace? Could they have His strength, His wisdom, His purity? Yes, they could have these. They should yet learn how intimate is the bond that unites them to Christ. This is the victory which overcometh the world, even our Christ made present with all His glorious power by faith, so that we may boldly say, "The Lord is my helper, whom shall I fear?" To fear is to have more faith in your antagonist than in Christ. When you have found one greater than Christ, then may you fear.

"Not as the world giveth, give I unto you." Very true, good Lord; You give Yourself. Thus You give peace. You give Yourself, the Just for the unjust, that God may be reconciled unto us and we unto God. The world can give us nothing by which we can present ourselves before the throne of a holy God in full assurance of faith. You give us that by which we can draw nigh to the treasures of Heaven and possess ourselves of worlds of wealth. The worldling adds coffer to coffer, with lifelong uneasiness, pursuing peace and finding it not. The Christian has peace amid privations. Contentment is just one aspect of his peace.

Observe, this is Christ's peace. It is not a mere imperturbability; it partakes not at all of the nature of indifference to others; it favors the fullest growth of sympathy; it weeps and is troubled at the grave of Lazarus; it sighs at the depravity of man; it spends whole nights in fervent prayer for the souls of men; it is not unaffected by the unkind treatment of men; it is affected by it, but not overcome by it.

But a formidable question presents itself: How can a child of Adam go down into the chambers of his own corrupt nature? How can he contemplate by the torchlight of memory, or the strong light of conscience, his odious transgressions of the law of a holy God, and still retain his Christ-given peace? Can he know himself and still keep hold of the hand of peace? Are thorough self-examination and peace compatible?

The Spirit of God sometimes tests the peace of Christians in this way: A man has been for years enjoying a good measure of what he regards as Christian peace. Suddenly he is made to see himself by the light of a most intense holiness, and his former conceptions of his sinfulness and of the evil of all sin are augmented a thousandfold. Straightway his peace is gone. His faith utterly fails. He finds himself sinking in deep waters. The mention of the righteousness of Christ fails to satisfy him. The Christ that he has been looking at all along was One that would save from a moderate amount of sin, such as he then knew of in himself; he has yet to become acquainted with a Christ able and willing to save from such a dire ruin as he is now conscious of. His past peace, his past faith, are now ascertained to have partaken very largely of the nature of delusion. Happy for him that he has discovered the inadequacy of his faith while it is yet the day of grace! Sad, unspeakably sad, is the fate of many whose faith is not thus tested in their lifetime.

We cannot have true peace without a thorough apprehension of our depravity and utter ruin. The peace that Christ gives His people is one that will bear any amount of revelation concerning the hatefulness of sin. It goes down with Jesus into the lazar-house [place of disease] of the soul, and sustains itself in the presence of so great corruption, by feasting on the infinite excellence of Christ. Expand a thousand or ten thousand times the conceptions which that soul formerly entertained of sin; faster than you can do this, its conceptions of the wondrous virtue of the blood of Christ and of the debt of love it owes to Him, expand. This is the peace which Christ gives. He digs deep in order to lay the foundation for it. He shows the sinner the utter blackness of his sin and the all-sufficiency of His righteousness. Let no man think it to his interest to remain ignorant of the evil of his heart. The peace thus purchased is treacherous. The great thing is to receive from the Holy Spirit at once, instruction concerning sin and concerning Christ.

John 14:28-30. *"Ye have heard how I said unto you, I go away, and come again unto you. If ye loved me, ye would rejoice, because I said, I go unto the Father: for my Father is greater than I. And now I have told you before it come to pass, that when it is come to pass, ye might believe. Hereafter I will not talk much with you: for the prince of this world cometh, and hath nothing in me."*

I have spoken to you of My departure. To reconcile you to this I have told you that My absence from you would be but temporary; I would come again and receive you unto Myself. As an additional and most potent ground of comfort, I have promised you that in connection with My departure the Holy Ghost would come unto you. It has further appeared, from what I have said, that there would be unspeakable advantage resulting to you from the fact of My being present for you in Heaven, interceding with the Father. If you have indeed heard what I have said unto you, you must now be aware that, so far from losing, you will gain unspeakably in wisdom, in power with God and with man, and in all perfection, by My departure.

Further, let Me now mention that I myself am to obtain great accessions of glory and felicity by My departure. My Father is greater than I; in ascending to Him I ascend to a far higher greatness than you have yet seen invested in Me. I am in some sense despoiled of My proper greatness by My life in the flesh. I have made Myself lower than the angels for the suffering of death. I have been encompassed about with the infirmities incidental to humanity. Even on the Mount of Transfiguration, you obtain but a shadowy glimpse of the greatness that awaits Me on high. I go unto the Father that I may be clothed with the glory of the Father. Dismiss the thoughts with which you have been accustomed to look upon a departure from this world. I go not unto darkness, but into light unapproachable, to glory inconceivable. If you love Me, rejoice.

Conceive a company of imprisoned men; a person of rank has voluntarily been their companion for a season. He is at length about to

117

quit the dungeon where they dwell; a cloud comes over their countenances at the announcement, but he assures them that, having come to reveal himself to them and satisfy their angered sovereign, he now goes to the presence of his august father that he may obtain gifts for them—the gifts of liberty, of wealth, of power, of honor; nor will he rest until he has brought them to the royal mansion in which he is himself about to appear. He has shared their bondage, and they shall share his royal state: his going should therefore be for them an occasion of exceeding great joy.

Believers in Christ are identified with Christ, so that they must regard themselves as enriched, honored, blessed, when riches, honor, blessings are bestowed upon Him. They now in this sense sit with Him in heavenly places. Tell them of the glorious extension of His kingdom, and you gladden them more than if you told them of great temporal honor or worldly wealth accruing to them.

It is evident that just in the degree in which our views of the greatness of Christ and of the glory which He has with the Father are exalted, shall our joys be of a more elevated character. What an incentive we have, then, to seek to understand the greatness of Christ! How fitting that we should count all but loss for the excellency of the knowledge of Christ Jesus!

"And now I have told you before it come to pass, that when it is come to pass, ye might believe." Our Lord intended that His people should have continually new arguments for faith. One of the reasons for which prophecy was given is that the fulfilling providence of God may be made to bear testimony to the Scriptures of truth. Thus the written prophecies answer the same purpose that was accomplished by the prophets themselves appearing amongst God's ancient people. Those men of God, speaking as they were moved by the Holy Ghost, and bringing with them credentials of their mission, brought Heaven near. They rendered visible the ladder that Jacob saw in his dream. The fulfillments of the prophecies relating to the vicissitudes of Christ's kingdom upon this earth do this. The God of the Bible is seen to be the God of centuries and millenniums.

"Hereafter I will not talk much with you; for the prince of this world cometh, and hath nothing in me."

Not only was Christ to depart out of the world, but even before He should do so, He was to be separated from His disciples. Brief as was the remainder of time to be spent by Him on earth before His death, yet during even the greater part of that, there were to be no communications between Him and His little flock. The Shepherd was to be smitten; the sheep were to be scattered.

"The prince of this world." This single expression, what a light it sheds upon the condition of this world! The prince of darkness, the father of lies, is the ruler of this world. This world is disposed according to his wish. Men yield obedience to him, and not to God. God says to man, "Love not the world"; Satan says, "Love the world"; and all obey Satan and disobey God. God says, "The love of money is the root of all evil"; Satan says, "Money is power, knowledge and blessing"; and all believe Satan and disbelieve God. God points to the narrow path, saying, "This is the way, walk ye in it"; the adversary points to the broad road, saying, "This is the way"; the multitude hearken to Satan.

The nations of the earth, even the nations of Christendom, how are they governed? Do the governors and legislators recognize themselves as the servants of God, take His Word for their counselor and wait upon Him in united prayer? The very question excites derision. The prince of this world rules in their councils. Even as he said to the Jewish authorities, "It is expedient for you that one man should die for the people, and the whole nation perish not," so he now with equal effect uses his doctrines of expediency to get the truth of God set at naught.

The prince of this world comes; I shall be delivered into the hands of his servants; they will wreak their malignity upon Me; and if there were anything in Me respondent to the nature and the principles of the sovereign of this evil world, any malice or wrath or impatience or pride or fear, then woe would be to Me. But he has nothing in Me, and the result of My approaching sufferings and humiliation will be, first the evidence of the fact that he has nothing in Me, and eventually, as springing therefrom, the destruction of his own sovereignty. Even on the cross, I will bruise his head.

Christ alone could say, "He hath nothing in me." Satan has a property in all until they are redeemed by the blood of Christ—in all, the least and the greatest. This may be to men a very offensive way of looking at sin, but it is the true way. The proud man bears in his very demeanor, the incontinent [unchaste] man in his glance, the angry man in his tone, the immoderate man in his thirst, the evidence of Satan's property in him. Look into your heart, O man! and see what Satan has there.

The believer is a vessel of mercy. He bears about in this world the mercy of God—the grace that brings salvation; but you are a vessel for the convenience of Satan. He puts into you selfishness, pride, profanity and a hundred other vile things, and sends you to and fro with these testimonials of his power. As men freight a vessel with goods for a particular market, so Satan has freighted you. You are full of his goods, and he is bringing you to his own haven. But Satan had nothing in Christ; God had everything in Him: He was freighted with infinite blessings for this world. When He died, three thousand men started to life in a single hour, and the mighty influence is still traveling abroad. This is My body which is broken for you. I, if I be lifted up, will draw all men unto Me.

John 14:31. *"But that the world may know that I love the Father; and as the Father gave me commandment, even so I do. Arise, let us go hence."*

Immediately preceding this verse are the words, "The prince of the world cometh and hath nothing in me." It is not difficult to trace the connection. I am to be delivered into the hands of the authorities, who, incited by the prince of this world, will do their utmost to shake My steadfastness, but in vain, for there is nothing in Me responsive to the corruption of their natures, and the fact that I shall pass through such a fiery trial unscathed shall furnish the world with evidence that I love the Father and am absolutely guided by a reference to His holy will in all that I do. The prince of this world was therefore signally unsuccessful.

Christ obtained His greatest victory in the hour when the rulers imagined that they were most triumphant. Even "the world" over which they ruled discovered in that hour (and more completely afterward) that Jesus was the Son of God, that He loved the Father, and that His life was the highest expression of the will of God. The multitude returned from the cross beating their breasts because of the death of One so great and good. The centurion exclaimed, "Certainly this was a righteous man"; or, as Mark has it, "Truly this man was the Son of God"—that is, "This Man was a true man, not an imposter; He was what He professed to be."

This centurion was wiser than many who live in these days, and who make great pretensions to wisdom. They admit that Christ was a righteous Man, but insist that much that He said was false. They deny that He was the Son of God, God manifest in the flesh, and that they who saw Him saw the Father. It would appear that they have a strange conception of what it is to be an honest man. They consider that a man may be righteous and yet assert the most blasphemous claims to a pre-eminence above creatures; blasphemous if unsupported.

It was on the day of Pentecost that men were struck with over-powering convictions as to the character of Him Who had been crucified at Calvary. Three thousand of "the world" then arose and bore testimony to the fact that Christ loved the Father and was in sentiment one with the Father, and that the highest exhibition of devotedness to God that the world had ever witnessed, was given on the cross of Christ. And from that time to the present, the world has constantly been compelled to give up new volunteers for the great army of Christ's witness-bearers.

What Christ rejoiced to do, believers should also make haste to do. They should aim to give full proof to the world that they love the Father and keep His commandments. They should seek by the grace of God, so to live as to give the most unimpeachable evidence of their disinterested devotedness to God.

The prince of this world said of Job, "Doth Job fear God for naught?" And he teaches his people to level the same sarcasm against the followers of Christ in these days. The fact that the reproach has such an origin is not a reason why Christians should neglect to furnish the best possible answer to it. Job obtained a complete victory over Satan. Amid the wreck and ruin of all sublunary [temporal] wealth, he proved that he truly loved God, and was bound to Him by something infinitely stronger and purer than the desire of temporal benefits.

And the truly consecrated disciple of Jesus will continually stand ready to renounce all that he has, in order that he may show the sincerity of his love to Jesus; nay, he will value everything that he has chiefly as it furnishes him with a means of expressing that love, and thus of showing to the world that Christ Himself is a Gift inclusive of all gifts, able to satisfy fully the heart of man.

Oh, is there anything whatever more demanded than this at the present hour? In all this world is there anything so much needed as the spectacle of men who are satisfied with Christ, and who are fully bent upon making it evident to the world that they are so? As Christ aimed to show the world that He loved the Father and walked in a divine path, so He would have evidences given to the world that His people do the same—evidences such as the world can appreciate. It will not do for us to slight this. It must be evident to those who search the Gospels, that Christ has dwelt very emphatically upon this point, and has given commandments that embody His conviction of the importance of it.

We may deem it sufficient that we draw nigh to Jesus and use the language of ardent affection, or that we find pleasure in the society of His people, or delight in His promises. There is also this required of us by Him Whose hands were nailed to the cross—namely, that we should seek to give the world the utmost possible proof of our love to Christ. What was it but this that gave such power to the life of Paul? Men had to do much violence to their consciences when they spoke of him as actuated by any other than the purest motives. He commended himself to every man's conscience in the sight of God.

"Arise, let us go hence." We may conclude from these words that what is contained in the three chapters following was spoken, not in the chamber where they had supped, but while they were on their way to the garden of Gethsemane. The words, "He went forth," in 18:1, refer, then, to His going forth from the city. It also appears from Matthew 26:31 that some of the words recorded in these chapters were spoken after they left the chamber.

As we have been permitted to dwell upon the words and facts of that upper chamber, so, if the providence of God permit, we will continue to prosecute our meditations on the gracious words that proceeded out of the Savior's mouth on His way to the garden of agony. In Christ are hid all the treasures of wisdom and knowledge—hid from the world, disclosed to His people; in these chapters we find these treasures—in a certain sense, only a specimen of these treasures—and the question is submitted to us whether we will come and receive wisdom like this, or prefer our own fictitious and treacherous wisdom.

Chapter 15

John 15:1-3. *"I am the true vine, and my Father is the husbandman. Every branch in me that beareth not fruit, he taketh away; and every branch that beareth fruit, he purgeth it, that it may bring forth more fruit. Now ye are clean through the word which I have spoken unto you."*

The relation between the Father and Christ, and the relation between Christ and His people, are here set forth under the parable of a husbandman, a vine and its branches. Inasmuch as the Father and the Son are one, the same office may be ascribed to both; the Son Himself appears as the husbandman in the third verse. "Now ye are clean through the word which I have spoken unto you."

In the fifth chapter of Isaiah, the Jewish people are compared to a vineyard which, after the greatest care had been lavished upon it, brought forth only wild grapes. Whether in the expression, "I am the *true* vine," there is an implied reference to that unfruitful vineyard against which the decree had now gone forward that it should be rooted up and destroyed, cannot be positively affirmed or denied. "My Father giveth you the *true* bread from Heaven." "That was the *true* light."

But let us find out what the vine signifies, and then we shall know what is the force of the accompanying epithet. The vine represents that by which believers are brought near to God, to be the objects of His care, and to bring forth fruit unto Him. By union to Him Who is represented under this symbol they are united to God. Christ is the true and the only Mediator by Whom this restoration of the lost soul to God is effected, through Whom it abides in union with God. It will not avail any to be united to a church. There are not wanting churches professing to be churches of Jesus Christ, yet shameless enough to declare that the sinner shall certainly find salvation in union to them, in obedience rendered to them. It is a question of infinite moment for every soul of the children of men: "Is Christ to me the *true* vine? Is He the fountain of life? Is He the Author and Finisher of my faith?"

There are some who are ostensibly in Christ, others who are really in Him. The relation between Christ and believers is set forth by a parable of a vine and fruit-bearing branches; that between Christ and merely nominal professors is set forth by the parable of that same vine and other branches, destined to be taken away because they yield no fruit.

The Lord Jesus accomplishes His purposes by His Word, His Spirit, His providence. His people are moral beings, influenced by moral considerations. This parable is one of the means by which He influences them. He shows them that their distinguishing characteristic is this—that they bring forth fruit; and He shows them this in order that they may bring forth fruit. He shows them that increasing fruit is expected of them, in order that they may diligently address themselves to this result. He shows them that His Word is a means of fitting them to bring forth more fruit, in order that they may give heed to His Word as a means of purification.

The great question of the day is, "Who are the true disciples of Christ?" Some say this cannot now be known. Christ says, "They that bring forth fruit are My disciples. By this shall all men know that ye are My disciples, if ye bring forth much fruit."

But the question recurs, "What is it to bring forth fruit to Christ?" The answer is obvious. He that is called in this connection the true Vine, is elsewhere called the Branch. He was a model Branch, bringing forth fruit to the glory of God. Believers are to bring forth such fruit as Christ brought forth. "He that saith he abideth in him, ought himself also so to walk even as he walked." They are to bring forth fruit by keeping His commandments. "If ye keep my commandments ye shall abide in my love." "Ye are my friends, if ye do whatsoever I command you."

Christ pleased not Himself. They that are true branches in the true Vine please not themselves, but study to please Him Who gave Himself for them, and for His sake to please and profit their fellowmen. He loved us and laid down His life for us, and we also should be willing

125

to lay down our lives for the brethren, and in the meantime to make those minor and multiplied sacrifices that are called for in the ordinary hours of life.

Christ was meek and lowly of heart, and they that are abiding branches in this Vine bring forth this fruit: they are meek, long-suffering, unworldly, contented, forgiving, contrite. Christ sought not the honor which cometh from man, but that which cometh from God only; and believers establish the fact of their union to Him by renouncing the honor of the world and aiming undividedly at the approbation of God. Christ was without guile; His people are distinguished by their truthfulness, their sincerity, their freedom from disguise. Christ was harmless; His people are like Him in this: they abhor the idea of wronging in any way their fellowmen; they prefer to suffer wrong.

But here we become aware of a confused din of intermingled voices, saying, substantially, "This record cannot be true." There are Christians, men who far outstrip other Christians in their pious conversation, their constant attendance upon the means of grace, their fervent and beautiful prayers, their affecting confessions of sin, their acquaintance with the Scriptures, who are yet notoriously men that cannot be depended upon to make good their word, who buy freely and pay slowly, who rashly contract and speedily violate their contracts, who have done and are doing much harm, who have caused many to rue the day that they ever knew them—in a word, whose standard of duty permits them to do things that worldly men even shrink back from. We admit it; and all we can say is that Christ repudiates these persons by His Word now, and hereafter by His providence. These are the greatest enemies of the cross of Christ because they so perfectly simulate, in may respects, the more advanced people of Christ.

There are some whose hearts seem to be tenderly affected by discoveries of the love of God, yet a little observation will suffice to show you that the goodness of God which thus affects them is nothing more nor less than a supposed liberty to sin. They weep over their sins, and in view of the pardoning mercy of God admire their own religious sensibility, and go away to do the very things of which they had professed to repent.

Some there are that limit their idea of bringing forth fruit to Christ to the performance of certain religious duties. Such satisfy their conscience by the fulfilling of these, neglect their obligations to their fellowmen, and yet claim to be regarded as eminent Christians. Christ will spew them out of His mouth. In the meantime the church suffers unutterably from the influence of such. One of these nullifies the influence of very many Christians with whom he walks, and hinders many from coming to the knowledge of the truth. The more he does for Christ, the more he injures Christ. He never opens his mouth in prayer without violating this command of Christ: "If thou bring thy gift to the altar, and there rememberest that thy brother hath aught against thee, leave there thy gift before the altar, and go thy way; first be reconciled to thy brother and then come and offer thy gift."

The principle here embodied is far reaching. If your fellowman has any just ground of complaint against you, if you have neglected to fulfill your obligation toward him, if you have made light of his interests, preferring your own, if you are not solicitous to do unto others as you would have others do to you, if you, through your own fault, have forfeited your good report among them that are without,—attend first to the rectification of these things. The church can wait for you; seek not to get a reputation in the church to compensate for the loss of that without.

For the third time we say it, and we say it with tears: The greatest enemies to the church are those who, under certain aspects, appear to be the most advanced Christians. The world sees them to be untrustworthy, fallacious, injurious, and concludes that there is no real power in Christianity, even in its best forms and highest developments. But in another point of view the matter is still darker. The presence of an Achan in the camp brought defeat upon the entire army of the Israelites.

"For afore the harvest, when the bud is perfect and the sour grape is ripening in the flower, he shall both cut off the sprigs with pruning-hooks, and take away and cut down the branches. They shall be left together unto the fowls of the mountains, and to the beasts of the earth" (Isaiah 18).

127

John 15:3-4. *"Now ye are clean through the word which I have spoken unto you. Abide in me, and I in you. As the branch cannot bear fruit of itself, except it abide in the vine: no more can ye, except ye abide in me."*

Now ye are clean or purged, referring to the process indicated in the previous verse by which the vine-dresser prepares the vine to yield increasing fruit. As though the Lord had said, "You are in Me and have brought forth fruit, and I have been preparing you that you should bring forth more fruit. I have given you the word by which your sanctification is to be effected; I am about to offer a prayer to the Father that you may be sanctified by the truth, and not many days hence the Spirit shall be poured upon you in order that that prayer may be fulfilled."

The words given to the disciples by Jesus are also given unto us, and unto us also is the promise of the Spirit. Let us, then, abandon the idea that we need persecution or disappointments or chastisements or special providences, or any new revelation or change of circumstances, in order that we may attain to a higher life. The Word is nigh us, even in our mouth and in our heart: unmixed with faith, it will not profit us. According to our faith it shall be to us the means of blessings unspeakable. Our Lord sought to lead the attention of His disciples to His Word as that which should remain with them when, shortly, He would take His departure, and as that in which they should afterward find His power, His wisdom, His grace—find Himself, find Him far more gloriously than they had yet found Him.

"Abide in me." The branch does not come to the Vine and take life and then go away with this life; it has life only by abiding in the Vine. There must be a never-ceasing communication—in fact, branch and Vine must be one, with one common life. Faith in Jesus Christ, when it is occasional rather than habitual, may be more correctly described as unbelief. Or if we speak of it as faith, it is because in a dispensation like this, where corrupt souls are struggling into life, we must deal tenderly with this dawning of life. When we shall have reached a higher walk of faith, our former trust in Christ will look to us like unbelief. He that says unto us, "Come unto me," says also, "Abide in me." And this abiding in Him is no mere passive state.

We abide in Him exactly as we come to Him; we feel our need; we feel that in Him alone is the supply of this need, and we look to Him for that supply. Our need is not so much of something that He can give, as of Himself. We find our strength, our wisdom, our righteousness in Him. We abide in Him when we come before God, so that the story of the Lamb of God that takes away the sin of the world—that story which is so enchanting to the ear of the Father—is repeated in all our prayers, and is yet new in every one of them.

We abide in Him for our happiness. He is our glorious dwelling-place—a palace of delights. He that says he abides in Him, and yet is not satisfied with that which Christ imparts to him, deceives himself. He is willing, perhaps, to abide in Christ for a future salvation, and is willing to adorn his present life with the hope of that salvation, but he is not content to abide in Christ for all his present happiness. He expects that Christ will make him happy through all eternity, but mistrusts that Christ can give him all that his soul requires during the brief term of this mortal life.

The command of Jesus is that we should abide in Him exclusively; not partly in Him and partly in a very different vine, the vine of this world—a most monstrous proposition, whoever may make it. "Whom have I in heaven but thee, and there is none upon the earth that I desire beside thee." Nothing in Heaven or in earth should possess loveliness or excellence in the eyes of the believer until he is able to see it in Christ. That which, not found in Christ, is excellent in his eyes, approaches him only to harm him. The more beautiful, the more harmful, for it weakens the measure of his abiding in Christ.

There are those to whom this demand seems exorbitant. They would be willing in some sense to abide in Christ—but to abide in Him exclusively, from this they shrink. One that delights in poetry covers the table with volumes of his favorites. He shows us in every volume the passages encompassed with marks of his enthusiastic admiration, and asks us if we would have him cease to find the noblest life of his soul in these, cease to surrender himself to these hallowed influences.

The lover of nature, the artist, the merchant, have similar protests to make on behalf of the respective objects to which they are so largely given. But our reply to one and all is, "Abide in Christ." Christ's reply to them is, "Abide in Me. In Me ye shall find a hundredfold over what you sacrifice for Me—poetry, music, painting, commercial excitement. Found in Me, it shall prove to you beneficent; found apart from Me, unbestowed by Me, it will pour into your heart a stream that must be known sooner or later as a stream of death."

Jesus Christ is not the enemy of art or nature—He is not the enemy of anything truly excellent or beautiful; all that is truly estimable and lovely owes its existence to Him. All things were made by Him and for Him. Whatever you lose and cannot find again in Christ is better lost. Who would not part with a phantom, especially a phantom sent to lure him to a realm where joy and hope are not?

"And I in him." The promise here follows swift upon the command. If we satisfy ourselves with Jesus, He will be the satisfaction of our souls. No language can express all that is comprehended in these three words, "I in him." Saints that have been for thousands of years before the Throne do not fully fathom it. There is but One Who knows Christ, and but One Who can estimate the wealth of that inheritance here made over to the believer. In Christ are all the treasures of wisdom and knowledge; the Spirit without measure; all the fullness of the Godhead; life inexhaustible; love unfathomable; glory, honor, dominion, blessing. Thus marvelously freighted, Christ offers to dwell in the believer; and as the believer does not occasionally visit Christ, but habitually abides in Him, so we are warranted to conclude that Christ proposes not to give the believer an occasional revelation of His grace, not to sadden him with intermingled periods of desertion, but as the vine abides with the branch, so will He abide with, in and for the believer.

John 15:5. *"I am the vine, ye are the branches: he that abideth in me and I in him, the same bringeth forth much fruit: for without me ye can do nothing."*

We learned from the second verse that the believer would bring forth fruit to Christ, and that he would bring forth fruit increasingly. Here we are told that he will bring forth much fruit. It is a false conception of the believer that he is one who brings forth little fruit. We are not to entertain the idea that it belongs only to the uncommon Christian, to the person of rare gifts, to bring forth much fruit. It is the essential characteristic of all, if we allow the Lord Himself to characterize His followers.

Christians are to bring forth much fruit, not because of peculiar incidental advantages enjoyed by them, not by the favor of circumstances, not in consequence of their social position or their wealth or their intellectual endowments, but because they are united to Christ. The virtue is in Him, and it freely flows to those who are united to Him. He is the source and origin of fruitfulness. All fruit is from Him, and it reveals itself in connection with His people just so far as they abide in Him.

The chief impediment to usefulness is the unsubdued feeling of independence on their part, the insidious idea that they have a strength and a wisdom of their own from which they can in some measure draw. Every Christian renounces this nominally, but the habit of self-reliance has so incorporated itself with his being during the life of nature, that he does not easily discover how much he is under the influence of it, at the very time that he is professing to look to Christ as the sole ground of confidence. How many there are who are looking to Christ simply to eke out their own inadequate strength and wisdom, as though it were the function of a vine to supply what was lacking in the inherent power of the branch to support itself! But the branch has no such power. Its glory is that it stands in a certain intimate relation to the vine, the source of its energy and fruitfulness.

It disclaims every other glory. It is no reproach to it that it has no fountains of sap and of blessing within itself. Its fountains are where they should be—in the vine. Its blessedness is that it is united to the vine. In order to bring forth much fruit to Christ, we must cease from our own fruit. If any man think himself wise, let him become a fool that he may be wise. Let him daily become a fool that he may daily become wise. Let him daily realize his own inability to guide himself in any matter, and look to Christ for guidance.

The fruit spoken of is fruit to Christ. A great deal that is called fruit in the Church is not fruit to Christ, and must therefore meet with reprobation in the day of Christ. Fruit to Christ is fruit like Christ's—the fruit of the Spirit. It is not limited to the mere exhibition of the life of believers, but it relates also to the extension of that life—the propagation of Christianity from one to another. But where we behold clusters of love, joy, peace, long-suffering, gentleness, goodness, meekness, temperance, faith, we may be assured that, sooner or later, there will appear results of this in the conversion of others.

Christians often err in estimating fruit. Success is often latent, coming slowly to light, and that which is more rapid and conspicuous may turn out at last to have been the opposite of success. He that is sincerely bent on bringing forth much fruit to Christ will rest with satisfaction in this conception alone, namely, that the favor of God is fruit. Am I doing that which has the approbation of the almighty Disposer of all? If I am, then I am bringing forth the best possible fruit. It will appear in His own good time, though it should be a thousand years hence.

One man insists on seeing his fruit, and God gives way to him and lets him have what he seeks; he sees his work prospering in his hands, but, unhappily, it does not endure; there is in the end the bitterness of disappointment. Another asks but one thing—that he may please to the uttermost Him Who has called him to be His servant. He is willing to wait in apparent sterility until God shall give the increase. He knows that God is the Author of all true fruit, and has the absolute control of all resources, and can accomplish by the wave of His hand the renovation of the world. Accordingly he puts his seed into the hand of God, sure that, in the best of times, he will see the best of harvests. Let us abide in Christ, bury ourselves in Him, be found in Him. "Except a corn of wheat fall into the ground and die, it abideth alone; but if it die, it bringeth forth much fruit."

"Without me (or apart from me) ye can do nothing"—nothing in the way of bringing forth fruit to Christ. What we do without a reference to Christ, without a conscious dependence upon Him, without a desire to please Him, we do without His approbation. It is not His will that we should do anything without Him, and, therefore, whatsoever we do without Him, we do against His will. In such a matter as finding the colt for Christ to sit upon, even, it was needful that the disciples should abide in Christ.

It becomes every Christian to recognize fully and distinctly that much fruit is expected of him. It is expected that he will give powers, energies, influence, wealth, time and talents in such a way to Christ as that he may bring forth much fruit. He is to place himself and all that he has in such a relation to Christ as that the fullness of power and of blessing that is in Christ, may flow freely forth through his instrumentality into the world. There is much fruit in Christ germinantly waiting for the channels through which it must obtain its embodied existence among men. Every one that professes to be a disciple of Christ really professes to be a branch for the production of this much fruit.

How much fruit? In the answer to this we are to look to the promises: "Whatsoever ye shall ask in my name, I will do it." "Ask and receive that your joy may be full." "I will send the Holy Ghost, the Comforter; he shall convince the world of sin, of righteousness, and of judgment." "Ye shall be baptized with the Holy Ghost and with fire." "He that spared not his own Son, will he not with him freely give us all things?" "Greater works than these shall ye do because I go to my Father." "This is the victory that overcometh the world, even our faith." "He shall come down like rain upon the mown grass." "A nation shall be born in a day."

John 15:6. *"If a man abide not in me, he is cast forth as a branch and is withered; and men gather them and cast them into the fire, and they are burned."*

Some there are who abide in Christ ostensibly, not really. They profess to be connected with Him, but there is no vital union between them and Him. Christ does not immediately disown any that profess to come to Him. It was long before He disowned Judas. These are the days of His long-suffering; the day of irrevocable judgment has not yet dawned. The branch which does not yield fruit, and which affords no indications that it is about to yield fruit, is still, perhaps, suffered for a season to remain, if peradventure it may receive the vivifying influence of the vine: when it has been fully tried it is removed.

There are many who are firmly persuaded that they are abiding in Christ who are yet not in Christ at all; nor is it likely that they will awake from their delusion until the hour when He shall say unto them, "Depart from me, I never knew you." The cause of their remaining so hopelessly bound in their delusion is that they are abiding in another Christ whom they choose to regard as the true Christ. They invent for themselves a Christ after their own hearts, by obliterating some of the features of the Gospel Christ and adding some from their own fancy. They ignore a number of His commandments. They reject a portion of His testimony concerning their sin, their dependence, their blindness, their danger, and concerning the character of the world, its pleasures, its riches, its honors. They leave out certain conditions of the promises.

The heart is deceitful above all things, and its triumph as a deceiver is most surprisingly seen when it binds an individual all his life long in the unfaltering conviction that the Christ of his fancy is the true Christ. How many are thus led captive! How incomparably difficult their deliverance! They believe in Christ—that is, their own Christ; they obey him; they honor him; they preach him; they are zealous for him; they make converts in his name; perhaps they raise up a church for him. And Satan opposes them in this their work only just so far as may be necessary in order to give them thus an additional evidence that they are in the way of truth.

Oh how great will be their astonishment when they shall at length be ushered into the august presence of the true Christ! Beholding Him as He is, they will look wildly on the right hand and on the left in search of the Christ whom they have been serving—the Christ of their fancy— but in vain. The Christ of the Gospel is there before them; the scales fall from their eyes; they awaken to a sense of their tremendous guilt in having trifled with the revelation of the Savior in the Gospel.

Think not, O believer, that you are in no danger of being found out of Christ. He that thinks he stands is welcome to think so, but only let him take heed lest he fall. Without much prayer, much watchfulness, much self-denial, you cannot abide in Christ. To abide in Christ it is necessary to attach the highest importance to communion with Christ; and you know there are a thousand currents sweeping through you every day all hostile to this. A single, trivial, scarce-noticed impulse of your heart is capable of leading you where you will find it difficult to realize the presence and the grace of the Savior. Seek constantly to have in mind how important in the eyes of the Savior is the perpetuation of this soul-communion with Him.

In the verse now brought before us, He gives us an appalling intimation of what it is to lose sight of Him, and be insensibly drifting into regions where He is not found. Not to abide in Christ is to abide in death and be fitted for everlasting destruction in hell. The Savior in His faithfulness brings all motives to bear upon the believer. Happy the believer who is held fast to Christ by the attraction of Christ!

Let us beware how we suffer coldness to spring up between us and our fellow-Christians. Inasmuch as you suffer it between yourself and one of the least of these My brethren, you suffer it between yourself and Me. Be reconciled to your brother or meet My frown.

Let us prefer Jerusalem before our chief joy, and give all heed to every proposition that invokes our aid in behalf of the church of Christ, the bride of the Lamb. If our brethren say to us, "Let us go speedily to pray before the Lord, and to seek the Lord of hosts," let us beware how we remain indifferent.

It may be that Jesus shall take a forward movement, and require the church to move at a quicker pace than that to which she has been accustomed. Let her be careful lest she be left behind. "And they were in the way going up to Jerusalem, and Jesus went before them: and they were amazed; and as they followed, they were afraid." There comes a time when the former measures of faith, hope, love and prayer are inadequate—wherein what formerly was life is now not life, what was before accepted is now rejected. The time for walking in the wilderness is past; the time for entering Canaan is come.

The voice of the Captain of the host of the Lord is heard, saying, "Be strong and of a good courage; be thou strong and very courageous; be strong in the Lord and in the power of His might; be strong, quit yourselves like men." There is danger at such an hour lest the Christian refuse to believe in the hour and its new duties, and insist that as he has abided in Christ, so he may abide in Christ. But Christ, in the new hour now given to His Church, will wait for no man. They who are with Him are called and chosen and faithful; the wise virgins, with their lamps trimmed, shall move swiftly on in the procession with the Bridegroom.

John 15:7-8. *"If ye abide in me, and my words abide in you, ye shall ask what ye will, and it shall be done unto you. Herein is my Father glorified, that ye bear much fruit; so shall ye be my disciples."*

Comparing this with the expression in verse 4, "Abide in me and I in you," we learn that Christ abides in us as His words abide in us. This is a most important thought—perhaps the most important of all truths for the believer. Our Lord had previously given a strong intimation of it. When Judas asked Him, "How is it that Thou wilt manifest Thyself to us?" He answered, "If a man love Me, he will keep My words." We are to seek Christ, not in the third heavens, but in His words—that is, in the Gospel. We shall find Him when that Gospel is taken into our own hearts and kept there. The Spirit of God takes of Christ and shows unto us by taking of His words and bringing them in their own appropriate beauty and authority before us.

Let the reader turn to 1 Cor. 2 and glance along from the ninth verse to the fourteenth, noticing the following expressions: "*The things* which God hath prepared for them that love him." "God hath revealed *these things* unto us by His Spirit." "The Spirit searcheth *the deep things* of God." "*The things* of God knoweth no man, but the Spirit." "*The things* that are freely given us of God." "Which *things* we speak." "*The things* of the Spirit of God." And compare with verse 2, "I determined not to know anything among you, save Jesus Christ and him crucified." The glory of God in the face of Jesus Christ is that of which the ancient prophets wrote when they prophesied of things prepared such as eye had not seen, ear had not heard, heart had not conceived. "The light of the knowledge of the glory of God in the face of Jesus Christ" (2 Cor. 4:6) is no other than "The light of the glorious gospel of Christ."

It follows that Christians are committing a most serious error when they neglect to seek in the Word of God for the answers to their prayers. If they believingly ask to see the glory of Christ, they may expect that the Spirit of God will cause them to see that glory in the ordinary words of the Gospel.

Ask any mature Christian concerning the blessings that have made his soul to overflow with joy unspeakable and full of glory, and he will tell you that they all came to him through the medium of the Word. "Say not, who will bring Christ down from above; the word is nigh thee, even in thy heart and in thy mouth." Say, who will bring the Holy Ghost down from above, so that Christ in all His beauty and majesty may be discovered by my soul, looking forth unto me from His precious Word.

Where, in this wide world, shall I find Elijah the prophet, to obtain for me by his effectual fervent prayer, the wonder-working fire from Heaven? Ah! call not for Elijah. Be to yourself your own Elijah. The word is nigh you, in your heart and in your mouth. It has as mighty a claim upon your faith as upon that of Elijah. "Ask, and it shall be given you." "If ye abide in me, and my words abide in you, ye shall ask what ye will and it shall be done unto you." You shall ask for the Holy Ghost, and He will show you the deep things of God in Christ, and Christ in the Word.

"If My words abide in you, ye shall ask what ye will." If His words abide in us, they will abide in our will, enveloping it and permeating it and making it Christ's will; and then what wonder if we obtain what we ask when we ask what we thus will! "This is the will of God, even your sanctification." "Sanctify them through thy truth." "Keep them from the evil of the world." "Hallowed be thy name. Thy kingdom come, thy will be done, as in heaven so in earth." "That their joy may be full." "Peace I leave with you." "Let not your heart be troubled." "That they all may be one." "That they may see my glory." These and such as these, are the words of Christ. Let them abide in us and become our own words, the expressions of our own will, our heartfelt desire, and we shall ask what we will without fear of a denial.

We see how it is that we are to bring forth fruit to Christ, how it is that other branches are to start from us, and thus the True Vine to extend itself to regions beyond, even to every nation, tribe and tongue. We are told, if Christ abide in us and we in Him, we shall bring forth much fruit, and we are told that if we abide in Christ and His words abide in us, we shall ask what we will and it shall be done unto us.

It is, then, at the mercy-seat that we are to obtain all our fruit, that Christ through us is to be loaded with fruit. How easy here to err! How many, in fact, overlook this all-important truth! How constant the impulse is to take the words of Christ and rush forth with them as though they would of themselves work out fruit! The first disciples hid them in their hearts and went to the throne of grace and continued with one accord in supplication until the day of Pentecost, nor did they afterward in the least intermit their prayerfulness. "Ye have not because ye ask not." "If ye shall ask anything in my name I will do it." Christ is as truly the Author of all the fruit-producing processes now as when He was bodily on the earth, and the believer loves to have it so. Not that Christ does anything without His people: through the branches the Vine bears fruit.

"Herein is my Father glorified, that ye bear much fruit." The Husbandman is glorified when the vines are loaded with excellent fruit. The hope that animated Him in all His labors is then realized. No one is justified in believing that there is an unwillingness on the part of God to witness the extension, elevation and glory of the Church. The end of all creation and all providence is that God may be glorified. Everything else must give way to this necessity. If we really and thoroughly desire that God may be glorified, there is no reason why we should not bring forth much fruit to His glory. If the much fruit is wanting, the glory of God is wanting, and we are responsible; it must be that His words are not abiding in us.

It may be a protracted process by which God will fit us for fruitfulness; though we see not the fruit, we may see the preparation for it. The fruit we are now speaking of is fruit in others, but until the day when God shall be glorified by such fruit through our instrumentality, let there be a constant prophecy of that future day of glory in our increasing patience, humility, prayerfulness, faith, submission, self-denial, love and gratitude.

Oh, let us lay hold of the gracious declaration that God is glorified in our exceeding fruitfulness, for in this there is the strongest possible affirmation of success accorded to our sincere prayers. What is here said does not affect merely the man of genius, the man of great natural energy and power of adaptation; it relates to Christians generally. Upon everyone is laid a solemn obligation to bring forth much fruit.

The command, "Glorify God in your bodies and in your spirits which are his," is no other than the command to bring forth fruit. To fulfill this command it is needful, first, for a man to know that the thing is possible; he must learn it from the promises. Second, to know that it is obligatory. Third, to cease from living unto himself, realizing that he is bought with a price. Fourth, to be willing to be anything in the hand of God, to let God treat him as something quite contemptible and worthless. Fifth, to be content to bring forth fruits in God's order— patience, meekness, submission—when these are particularly called for. Sixth, to beware how he dreams of glorifying himself with any fruit that God may give him, and gladly to leave his left hand ignorant of what his right hand does.

John 15:8-9. *"Herein is my Father glorified, that ye bear much fruit; so shall ye be my disciples. As the Father hath loved me, so have I loved you; continue ye in my love."*

The idea of the second verse is here reaffirmed. Christ had said, "Every branch in me that beareth not fruit, he taketh away." He here says, "If ye bear much fruit ye shall be My disciples." Not that by dint of bearing fruit, a man becomes a disciple of Christ, but he thus makes it manifest that he is a disciple. By his union to Christ he has life, and that life must reveal itself.

There is nothing in the Scripture to sanction the hope of him who does not bring forth fruit to Christ, but on the contrary there are countless asseverations [assertions] of the most positive kind that such a hope is vain. Faith without works is dead. Genuine faith reveals itself in obedience.

There are still a few in the world who insist that the question of their discipleship has no connection with the question of fruitfulness. They are sure that they believe on Christ, and they are consequently sure of everlasting life in Him; for what can pluck them out of His hand? What can separate them from His love? Shall sin or disobedience or spiritual slumber do it? What can take them away from the true Vine? Can fruitlessness do it? They scorn the idea, and look with contempt upon those twilight Christians who suppose that anything whatever a man does or leaves undone can affect the question of salvation. It is true that they are obliged to ignore a great deal of Scripture; but then they compensate for this by giving the utmost prominence to a passage here and there separated from its context.

They confound two things that are as far as Heaven and earth asunder—God's decrees and man's knowledge of God's decrees. "Make your calling and election sure." This is not an exhortation to you to live so that God may elect you unto eternal life and call you into the kingdom of His dear Son, but to live so as to make it evident that you are one of the elect.

"Oh, but," say they, "there can be no true peace if we are obliged to seek the grounds of it in ourselves." Granted: the only true peace is

141

that which springs out of your union to Christ; but the question is, "Does my peace spring out of my union to Christ, or is it the offspring of a mere imagination that I am united to Christ?" Christ says, "He that heareth my words and doeth them is like a man who built his house upon a rock; he who heareth them and doeth them not is like a man who built his house upon the sand."

The obligation to obey is like an enemy and like a tyrant to the heart of the natural man. He is a child of disobedience; his whole frame is cast in the mold of self-will; all his powers, his affections, his thoughts, his habits, are in a state of rebellion and have continually been so; the King is driven out and forgotten, and there is a certain kind of peace in the mind in consequence of the non-realization of the presence of a law-giver.

When, by a superior power, the mind is compelled to take knowledge of the long-forgotten law, then farewell to peace! The elements of a fierce conflict start into activity. The more the necessity of obedience is pressed home upon the mind, the more it abhors that necessity—as the resistance of a spring increases with the tension. A life spent in sin has utterly unfitted the mind to obey a holy God; and the obligation to obey is like the setting up of an inquisition in the mind, with its consummate enginery of torture. There is no peace until Christ, the Redeemer, is revealed to the conscience. The sinner believes, and obtains peace through the discovery of God, reconciled to him in Christ. The sense of obligation was agonizing to his soul; the sense of free forgiveness enraptures him, and he is ready to conclude that obedience and faith are diametrically opposite—to look upon the former as the eternal enemy of his nature, and upon the latter as the ever-living benefactor of his soul.

But the glorious office of faith is to reconcile him not only to God but also to obedience. God in pardoning him does not change; His character remains the same; His requirements are the same, for they were never arbitrary. Faith introduces the individual to the principle of obedience under altogether new circumstances—for obedience and grace are commingled—and the sense of obligation, so far from coming

142

to desolate a heart sensible of its weakness and folly, is accompanied by a revelation of the all-sufficient grace of Christ.

The sinner, pardoned through the merits of Christ, rejoices that the grace of obedience is now given to him, and that he has the opportunity of testifying his love to the Savior. He would count it in the last degree dishonorable if, in the presence of the cross of Christ and of such exceeding great and precious promises, he should retain his former animosity to the sense of obligation. The commandments of God are not grievous to him, for he knows where to find the strength which they demand; and there is a sentiment of gratitude within him which only waits for these indications of the way in which he shall honor Christ.

Disciples are those who learn of Christ. They learn from Him what they are, what He is; they learn from Him what to love and what to hate, what to desire, what opinions to entertain, what words to speak, what places to frequent, in what to rejoice, for what to weep, what life to lead, what prayers to offer, what labors to engage in, what death to die. To show that they have learned of Him is to bring forth fruit to Him. A disciple is necessarily a fruit-bearer. The Lord Jesus will not continue to teach one upon whom His teachings are thrown away.

"As the Father hath loved me, so have I loved you." These words should fill the soul of the believer with joy unspeakable. This declaration cannot, of course, tell us more than the cross of Christ tells us; but we are so unutterably sluggish in the apprehension of the deep things of God, that it is well we have this comment on the cross from the lips of the Savior Himself.

We understand without difficulty that the love of the Father for Christ was and is a boundless love. All the wealth of love residing in the Godhead, pours itself upon the head of the Beloved. We are taught to retain intact the conception of this love, even in the garden of Gethsemane, and when Christ was numbered among the transgressors.

We know that Christ is the image of the invisible God; that He was without spot or blemish, He alone of men; that there was everything in His character, His work, His humiliation, His sufferings, to carry to

143

its highest pitch the love of the Father. Do you recognize the love of the Father to the Son? Then let that be to you the measure of Christ's love to you. Is the former forever indubitable? Then let the latter be.

"All very true," says one, "but the simple fact is, that I experience cruel pains in my body, accompanied with gloom of mind. That state of suffering interferes with the exercise of right feelings toward God. I can scarcely think of anything but my suffering; even prayer is seldom a relief to me. It is certain that Christ has power to banish at once these pains, this darkness. He has but to speak, and I shall have something worthy of the name of life—faculties, and a heart to use them for His glory. Now why does not Christ speak that word? He has all grace—why does He not reveal it by granting me deliverance? How can I be expected to appreciate His love, when, in the day of my trouble, He suffers me to remain days, weeks, months, without alleviation? A little kindness shown in my restoration would affect me more than a multitude of mere assurances, or even of acts that do not meet this my urgent need."

Well, if you wish for an inferior expression of Christ's love, you shall have it: Christ will hear your prayer and banish your ailment. But if you wish that He should love you with the highest love, even as the Father loved Him, then you will beware how you dictate as to the expressions of that love.

He loves you with an infinite love. He is preparing you for eternal happiness, for inconceivable glory; and if you now thrust in your own paltry ideas of blessing, you will fearfully endanger your prospects of that sublime inheritance. You are to believe in His love. You are to believe that that which torments you embosoms some great advantage. You are to say with Jesus, "The cup which my Father hath given me, shall I not drink it?" You are to let patience have her perfect work, and glorify God in the fires by submission, unrepining acquiescence in His appointments and a persevering grasp of His promises. God is faithful, Who will not suffer you to be tempted above that ye are able; and this ability you are not to look for in yourself, but in Him Who is made unto you strength and wisdom and sanctification.

John 15:9. *"Continue ye in my love."*

We are not satisfied with being insincere—we must also impute to Jesus the insincerity that belongs to us. We profess to regard Him as a Being of irreproachable truthfulness, and yet the most positive statements from His lips fail to convince us of His willingness to keep our hearts perpetually irrigated with the living water of His love.

The Christian in some happy hour finds himself enraptured with a sense of Christ's love; it is like the advent of a bridegroom—his whole soul is permeated with a celestial life. He is startled as well as delighted. He has been seeking the blessing, but even when he sought it he had not adequate conception of it. A troop of angels have run down the ladder that Christ has made to reach from earth to Heaven, from Heaven to earth—run down to him and chanted in his ear the assurance that they have seen his name written in the Lamb's book of life. Before they return one of them takes up the Bible that has fallen from his hand in the glad surprise, and places it open in his hand again. He looks at it and sees the word of Jesus, "Have I been so long time with you, and yet hast thou not known me?"

As he turns over the pages, a beauty and a power never before noticed are seen investing the words of Christ. What unmistakable evidences of love! What long-suffering! What fidelity! What reassuring acts and tones! What a precious Gospel! How suited to satisfy the most ardent aspirations of the soul! How strange that I never saw these things before as now I see them! It is strange, for they were always there.

No change has passed upon Christ or upon the words of Christ. The change wrought has been simply in the dissipation of your unbelief. You see in what an odious enterprise your unbelief has been persistently engaged. You have been falsifying Christ. You have written upon a hundred of the most burning declarations of the Savior's love, "This means nothing." Upon others, "Poetry." Upon others, "Make a large allowance for Oriental imagery." Upon others, "For the prophets and apostles." Upon others, "Fulfilled and buried." You think what kind of a gospel you, with your insincerity, would give to men, and conclude that Christ's Gospel is such. A mirror with inequalities upon its surface presents a distorted and repulsive image of the loveliest face. Your unbelief made of the Gospel such an image.

The Savior has pardoned the frightful injustice thus done to Him, has dismissed from His thoughts the long-protracted calumny, and has inundated your soul with a blessing more ample than your frail nature can well sustain. He sustains you under it. And now the question arises in your mind, "How long will this last? A week? A fortnight? Three days? Five days?" You awake in the morning and wonderingly look into your heart to see if the blessing is still there. You are sure it cannot last. The question is, "How far will you be permitted to carry it?"

Oh the terrible unyieldingness of unbelief! Do you not see the word of Christ as plain as day, "Continue ye in my love"? So far from having any desire to withdraw the communications now made to you, He charges you to see to it that you continue to enjoy them. He puts you upon the distinct obligation to continue in the enjoyment of His love. There is something most dishonoring to Christ in the idea that He is willing to draw near to you in love in a certain month, on a certain day, and then during a long period absent Himself from you.

The Gospel makes no mention of any fitful love on the part of Christ. The only love it reveals is an unchanging love. The words that embosom it are surely unchanging. They have as much meaning on Tuesday as on Monday. If there be a difference in your perception of that love, impute it to your unbelief, and abhor yourself for that unbelief, the sin of sins.

If you expect to have the blessing disappear after some days, it will disappear. But know that it is frightened away by the resurrection of your unbelief. Unbelief lies very quiet in its grave for a few days; then gradually, stealthily, it lifts the ponderous stone—it is strong enough—and thrusts its hated face into the light of your consciousness;

146

soon it is on its old throne, or at least on one of the steps of it, masked, it may be, as prudence.

This, however, is not the history of every Christian heart. We turn to another, and a more shining record greets us. This poor man, this loved disciple, having learned by experience the subtlety and wickedness of his heart—learned that it was capable of taking one after another of the jewels handed down from Heaven and throwing them into the Dead Sea—resolved to be on his guard when the next blessing should come, and by prayer, fasting, faith, vigilance, self-denial—by the armor of righteousness on the right hand and on the left—to fulfill Christ's command and continue in His love. He believed that the Savior was not more willing to grant him His love than to grant him the continuance of it. He confidently fled to the Savior to enable him to continue in His love. He was sure that the same all-sufficiency which causes the mountain lake to abide in undiminished fullness, notwithstanding the evaporation and the percolation and the streams sent forth from its bosom, could fill his heart from the heart of Christ and keep it full.

There is an analogy between a blessing bestowed on an individual Christian and one bestowed on the church generally. If the individual suffer the idea to lurk in his mind that probably after some days his present fervency of love, joy, faith and zeal will subside—if he neglect to use the utmost circumspection, greatly to watch, earnestly to pray, eagerly to keep pressing forward—then assuredly he will lose it.

Just so with a revival in the church. A revival is simply the church's recovery of health. Anything less of fervor, faith and joy is a condition of unhealthiness; and the church should never be contented to live below the blessed elevation she has now, by the grace of the good Physician, attained. If now she allow the idea to creep in that this state of revival is a state above health, and that she is moving in a region where she cannot long continue—if she give place for a moment to such an idea—then there will be reason to apprehend a speedy termination to the blessing.

147

As the individual, made wise by his past losses and by the consciousness of unspeakable difficulties arising through the interception of the blessed light once granted, resolves that in whatsoever good hour it may please his sovereign Lord to bring him back to that state of heavenly assurance, he will cut away and cast away, on the right hand and on the left, everything that may in the least degree jeopardize the continuance of the blessing. He will count all things but loss that he may abide in Christ's love; so the church, admonished by those dreadful intervals of slumber, resolves that when the refreshing from the presence of the Lord shall once again be granted, she will watch with inconceivable vigilance for the preservation of that saving health which has been brought to her by the Spirit of God. Has she yet learned this?

John 15:10. *"If ye keep my commandments, ye shall abide in my love, even as I have kept my Father's commandments, and abide in his love."*

The love of the Lord Jesus Christ is expressed in His commandments as well as in His promises and invitations. To believe in the Lord Jesus Christ is to believe that His commandments are expressive of His love. When He gave to the man with the withered hand the command to stretch forth his hand, it was His love that found utterance. So also when He told the lepers to go and show themselves to the priests. When He told the disciples in the latter part of this very evening, "Watch and pray," it was in order that they might not enter into temptation. They found it more convenient to seek relief from sorrow in sleep, so quickly did they forget His word, "If ye keep my commandments, ye shall abide in my love."

There is not anything that so disastrously retards the progress of the great body of Christians as their unwillingness to accept of the commandments of Christ as expressions of His love. They believe that in order to maintain their peace of mind, they must give their principal attention to the promises. But every great blessing is borne to them by two Cherubim—one a promise and one a command. We would affectionately say to the Christian who has been long feeding upon the promises, "Christian, do you know that, in answer to your prayers, there is in a certain place a large accumulation of blessings waiting to be appropriated?" "No," he says, "I knew nothing of it; where are they, pray?"

These accumulated blessings are in the commandments. As often as you shut your eyes in the presence of a command of the Savior, you shut your eyes to an exquisite gift sent down to you from the Father of mercies. The two Cherubim, of whom I spake, are twin Cherubim—inseparable. They came to Abraham once. The one said, "Get thee out of thy country and from thy kindred unto a land that I will show thee"; and the other said, "I will make of thee a great nation, and I will bless thee." Search and see: from the patriarchs to the apostles, from the apostles to ourselves, there was ever one undivided mission to these twain.

"Keep yourselves in the love of God," says Jude. How may we do this? By keeping the commandments of the Lord Jesus. Let us, then, turn to these commandments with all eagerness of expectation, giving them, instead of the cold looks with which we have too often greeted them, a friendly welcome, a kiss of love.

The first commandment which meets us as we set out in this new search for the treasures of Christ's love is this: "Let not your heart be troubled, neither let it be afraid." We may have been accustomed to view this as a promise. It is nevertheless a command. It is the command of Christ that the heart of the believer be kept free from trouble. "How," you say, "can this commandment be constantly obeyed? I have had some experience as a servant of Christ, and I have not found it possible to keep the heart for ever free from trouble."

The answer is, that you have not given due heed to the commands of Christ, and therefore trouble has from time to time invaded your heart. Had you kept His commands, you would have had His love diffused in your heart, and in the presence of that love, every trouble as it crosses the threshold, no matter how proudly, must quickly be dwarfed and covered with confusion.

We come to another command: "Believe me that I am in the Father, and the Father in me"—believe that there is omnipotence along with Christ's love, and that the love of Christ actuates Him Who sits upon the throne of the universe. Let every act and word and suffering of Him Whose life and death are portrayed in the Gospel be to you an expression of the love of the Father, and let the providential government of God reveal to you the wisdom and the grace of Him Who is Head over all things in the church.

Behold yet another commandment—"That ye love one another." Keeping this, we shall abide in His love. Is there not yet a large remainder of obedience to be rendered to this command? May we not make vast progress in this direction? Let us understand that to be making progress in this is to be advancing in the knowledge of Christ's love to us. There was one who counted all things but loss for the excellency of the knowledge of Christ. You may be sure that he sought this excellent treasure in the observance of Christ's command, That ye love one another.

"That ye should do as I have done to you." Do not dislike this word "do." You cannot exist without doing something, and it were vastly better that your doings should emanate from the will of Christ than that they should simply proceed from your own capricious will. That you may abide in the love of Christ, do according to the example He has left you—wash the feet of His disciples, prefer their interests, their pleasure, their comfort, their honor, to your own; be last of all and servant of all. Oh how much of the love of Christ you have suffered to be locked up from you! How much you might have done for His people that you have not done! The Christian is not more truly constituted a servant of Christ than he is a servant of Christians. "Inasmuch as ye have done it unto one of the least of these my brethren, ye have done it unto me."

"Even as I have kept my Father's commandments, and abide in his love." And on another occasion, "The Father hath not left me alone, for I do always those things that please him." As man, Jesus abode in His Father's love by keeping His commandments. "He learned obedience; and being made perfect, he became the Author of eternal salvation." He took upon Him the nature of a subordinate—our own nature; a finite soul and a human body, like ours, only without sin; He was made under law. He kept His Father's commandments and abode in His love, and He gives us the ability to keep His commandments and abide in His love.

It is a fact that the same blessed Spirit that dwelt in Jesus, leading Him to keep His Father's commandments, dwells in His people now. You will say, perhaps, that the material that He has to do with is very different from that which He operated on in Christ. This objection might have weight if the Spirit of God were not God the Spirit.

When once the idea of omnipotence is presented, the depravity of man's moral nature ceases to be available as a plea for imperfect service. Because we are utterly depraved we are commanded to abide in Christ and to find all our life in Him. "Whoso keepeth his word, in him verily is the love of God perfected" (because the Word of God is the channel by which the perfect love of God is to flow into his soul; the whole Word is that perfect channel; half of the Word avails not); "hereby know we that we are in him."

"Beloved, if our heart condemn us not, then have we confidence toward God: and whatsoever we ask, we receive of him because we keep his commandments, and do those things that are pleasing in his sight."

John 15:11. *"These things have I spoken unto you, that my joy might remain in you, and that your joy might be full."*

As an aid to the understanding of this, let us look at a similar passage contained in the prayer recorded in the seventeenth chapter: "And now come I to thee; and these things I speak in the world, that they might have my joy fulfilled in themselves." The two passages evidently refer to the same solicitude. A retrospective reference to the words, "Peace I leave with you, my peace I give unto you," will also be found useful.

Jesus desired that earth should lose nothing by His departure. He would unload Himself, so to speak, of all the treasures with which He came freighted into this world. He was pre-eminently a Man of sorrows, yet He had experience also of joy. We are not only told that He was "troubled in spirit," but also that He "rejoiced in spirit." He had an abiding consciousness of the Father's love—unbroken communion with the Father. He was without guile, holy, harmless, undefiled. He had that perfect love which casts out fear; the law of the Lord was His delight. His faith, beyond that of all others, substantiated to Him things unseen, and made real the things hoped for. The tendency of all these was to inspire Him with joy. This joy He would have remain with His disciples, found in them after His departure, and carried to a height which the peculiar circumstances of His mission did not allow of in Himself during His earthly pilgrimage.

"These things have I spoken unto you, that my joy might remain in you." What things? Things concerning privilege and concerning duty. "Abide in me and I in you." "If my words abide in you." "That ye bear much fruit." "Keep my commandments." "That ye love one another." These things were spoken that His joy might remain in us. If we desire joy, we are to seek it here.

Christ is willing that we should have His joy—not any other, for every other is a forgery. His is the joy that came down from Heaven. There was no true joy in earth. Jesus came that we might have it, and that we might have it more abundantly. Jesus is the true Vine come down from Heaven, and the fruit of that Vine is the only true fruit to be found on earth. His peace is the only true peace; His love is the only true love; His joy the only true joy; His knowledge of the Father the only true knowledge; His holiness the only true holiness: in Him is found the only true union.

What a sublime mission is this of Jesus! How slow we are to understand it! How slow to enter into His plans! How stupidly do we cling to our own conception of joy, though six thousand years have proved it to be a base fabrication passed off by Satan upon the imbecile credulity of man! The words of Jesus Christ are seeds sent down from Heaven, that plants of heavenly joy, peace, love, knowledge and power may take root in humanity, the first-fruits of the New Jerusalem and of the trees growing upon the banks of the river of the water of life.

These wondrous words are passed from one to another through this world, rejected and despised by men. The universal exclamation of all men is, "Who will show us any good? Who will give us joy?" But they laugh the Savior to scorn when He says, "Joy is come down from Heaven to earth, and is to be found in My words." Alas that they should seem to find a warrant for their incredulity in the conduct of those who are called the people of Christ! If they who are professedly the people of Christ make so little account of the joy that He offers them, and leave neglected so many precious words embosoming this joy, is it a marvel that others should be skeptical? "Who is blind but my servant? Or deaf as my messenger that I sent? Who is blind as he that is perfect, and blind as the Lord's servant?"

There is no blindness so astonishing as that of the enlightened. Their eyes have been opened to see a multitude of precious things, and therefore it is amazing that so much should remain unperceived by them. Were they wholly blind it would not be so surprising. Who is deaf as the Lord's messenger? It is beyond question that many ministers of the Gospel are strangers to the peace, joy and love which are contained in the very words they preach.

"That your joy might be full." This was the desire of Christ, and the means by which this desire may be fulfilled have been pointed out by Him. We are not merely informed of the desire, but of the way in which it may meet fruition. His words were spoken, written, conveyed to us, that by means of them our joy might be full. We are to have our ideas of joy revolutionized, throw away what we call joy, take Christ's joy and make it ours, and then labor to have Christ's desire fulfilled, our joy made full.

Fullness of joy! Are we to take these words in their obvious meaning? Are we really permitted to expect that the loftiest and amplest and intensest aspirations of our souls shall be realized? From what we have seen in our hearts, we are fain to believe that many rivers of happiness might empty themselves into the ocean of our desires without communicating fullness of joy. But the Savior knew what was in man; He knew these hearts, and knowing them, He is not at all reluctant to undertake the task that seems so hopeless—that of satisfying them.

Oh that the Spirit of God would show us the preparations for our fullness of joy made by the Savior in the Gospel! "How great is thy goodness which thou hast laid up for them that fear thee!" O my soul, gaze with reverence upon these words of Christ. You are here in the garden of Eden; you are here in the presence of a fountain of which whosoever drinks, it shall be in him a well of life and of joy. The dreams of your youth that faded away into air, the enchanting illusions which, vanishing, made this earth such a drear and dead Sahara, the aspirations awakened by poetry and music and beauty and eloquence and genius, the presentiments of a higher and diviner life, afterward discarded as having no antitype,—what would you say if all these dreams and longings should present themselves to you embodied in glorious reality? They served the purpose of exalting your conceptions of fullness of joy; but you were angry with them for tormenting you with such treacherous anticipations and showing you no avenues in the universe by which the ideal Elysium [Paradise] of your soul could be reached.

154

But gaze here upon the glorious announcement that there is such an Elysium—nay, something infinitely more satisfying than the realization of your old erring dreams would have constituted. There is for you fullness of joy. It is contained in the words of Jesus. You look at these words, handle them, interrogate them, and cannot discover in them any capacity to create for you an Elysium. They are not given to be looked at; their creative power and beatific energy are only revealed when they are taken into the heart. Let me take them into my heart—take them all, promises, instructions, warnings, behests; let the Spirit guide me into all truth; then, doubtless, shall I enter upon fullness of joy. Let Christ abide in my heart by faith; let His Word dwell in me richly in all wisdom; then shall life, love and fullness of joy be in me and be effluent [flowing] from me.

John 15:12. *"This is my commandment, That ye love one another, as I have loved you."*

As I contemplate the love of the Lord Jesus Christ to me, I am lost in wonder, love and praise. "He loved me and gave Himself for me," said Paul; and what Paul said I am also permitted to say. I am permitted to look at the wonderful descent of the Son of God from Heaven to earth, at all the sublime details of His life in the flesh, at His sufferings in the garden and in the hands of His enemies, and at His death on the cross, as an exhibition of the love of Emmanuel to myself. And what do I now hear? He charges all His people, from the least unto the greatest, to cherish that same love toward me.

Instead of a departure of His love with Him from the earth, my attention is called to the measures taken by Him for the continuance of that love multiplied by as many disciples as there may be. That love has descended from Heaven to earth, not merely to tarry here for a season and then ascend to the throne of God again, but to take its place abidingly in the stream of humanity, and continue to bless the Church till the next coming of the Savior. Having been introduced in the person of Jesus into our common humanity, it refuses to disengage itself, and makes provision for its own perpetuation.

The disciples had seen the love of the Savior exhibited in His life: they already knew that it was incomparable; but they were yet to have their views of it exalted by what they should witness on the coming night and morrow, and afterward, by the outpouring of the Spirit of God, they should discover in it a length and depth, a breadth and height, surpassing all their present conception. Whatever discoveries they might make of the love of Christ, were discoveries of the love which they were required to entertain for one another. They were each commissioned to carry on the loving life of Jesus.

Imagine this command fulfilled, and in the Church of Christ what a glorious scene bursts upon your view! The New Jerusalem is seen descending from Heaven, having the glory of God; her light like unto a stone most precious—even a jasper stone—clear as crystal; prepared as a bride adorned for her husband.

Yes, it now appears Jesus died not merely that He might save you, in any ordinary acceptation of that term, but that He might win for His own love your heart, and having it, He would fill it with His own divine love for the brethren, as plainly appears by this commandment.

But one may say, "This thing is preposterous! In these defiled and shattered hearts, it is impossible that love like that of the Son of God should dwell." And another may reply, "Beware of irreverence." The Son of God weighs His words before He utters them. He knows the capacity of your heart; He knows its incapacity infinitely better than you do. He knows that there is nothing in humanity in the least resembling, but much that is intensely opposed to, His love. Nevertheless He says it: "This is my commandment, that ye love one another, as I have loved you."

And do not believe that these commands of Jesus, like those from Sinai, are given in order to produce a sense of condemnation. There is no condemnation to them that are in Christ Jesus. These commands are not given to torture the disciples of Jesus with a sense of their grievous deficiencies. "These things have I spoken," He says, "that my joy might remain in you and that your joy might be full." No; these commands are given as directions: they indicate the way in which He would have His people to walk. They are to be obeyed. The Savior has a right confidently to expect that we will yield compliance to His wish in this particular.

But how may this thing be? How can we possibly fulfill so lofty a vocation? How can I love the people of Christ with Christ's own love?

Let Christ abide in your heart by faith. It is by virtue of the most blessedly intimate union of the believer to Christ that the heart of the former becomes the depository of the Savior's own love for His people. The question, "Can I love with Christ's love?" resolves itself into the question, "May the Savior's prayer for the union of His people with

Himself be fulfilled?" "Not I, but Christ liveth in me," says Paul. He has redeemed us that He may dwell in us. "That the love wherewith thou hast loved me may be in them and I in them."

He is in His people that He may draw down to them the love of the Father which flowed toward Him when He was separately present in this world, and He is in them that He may perennially exhibit to His people the love He bears them. The vocation of every believer is this: to be a revelator of the love of Christ.

The believer is an epistle of Christ—an epistle of His love. He is the Vine and His people are the branches; and if they stand in this relation to Him, He has surely a right to expect that the love which is in Him should be in them.

"If ye abide in me and my words abide in you, ye shall ask what ye will and it shall be done unto you." Is it difficult to see why the prayers of Christ's people are not more promptly fulfilled? They do not suffer His word to abide in them. They do not practically recognize their obligation to love one another as He has loved them. They do not, in acquainting themselves with the love of Christ, keep distinctly before them the commission to manifest that very love in their own walk and conversation.

We may infer that just in the degree in which we give heed to this responsibility, will there be a glorious fullness of response to our petitions. Christ is intent on one thing and they on another, so that it cannot be said that Christ and they come together before the Father when they pray. There is a union undoubtedly, but it is grievously imperfect: many things that have a prominent place in the regard of Christ are little heeded by them; and can they wonder that much is denied to them?

Who knows how many of our prayers that now climb but a little way to Heaven and then fall to the ground would mount up as on eagles' wings, would fly unweariedly straight to the throne of God and return with branches from the tree of life, if we would take home to our hearts this unbefriended word of Jesus, "Love one another, as I have loved you"? Who knows how many priceless expressions of the

Father's love toward us are effectually repressed by the fact that we are inattentive to the sweet mandate of Jesus, to give each other His love?

We profess at times, doubtless, to have longings for the rest, the joy, the holiness of Heaven, but we are deceiving ourselves, it may be; we are assuredly, if we have no solicitude to do justice to this long-neglected precept of the Savior. We profess to desire earnestly the outpouring of the Holy Spirit, but we shall do well to note that one of the first things which the Holy Spirit will aim to produce in us, will be this Christ-like love to the brethren.

How many brethren in Christ are now effectually separated from you by a high wall of social position—a wall of conventionality that has been reared by human pride? Were Christ's mysterious and unfathomable love to them to find its way perchance into your heart, how would it laugh at the huge hindrance of this wall, and by a breath, cause it to dissolve into the ambient air! This is no hypothesis. In lands where the Spirit of God is poured out, we are told of the sudden and beautiful flowing together of social streams that have been flowing separately on for generations. Love like that which Jesus manifested to the Samaritan woman and to the woman that was a sinner has now found new exhibitions of itself.

My Christian brethren see not the Savior with their bodily eye, but I have been commissioned by the Savior to afford them in some sense a compensation for this deficiency. I am commanded to let the love which found its exhibition in His mortal person, find now its exhibition in my life—a command which would be utterly idle and futile were it not that He, the ever-loving One, is willing to put His own love within me. The command is really no other than to be a branch in the true Vine. I am to cease from my own living and loving, and yield myself to be the expression of Christ's love.

> *"Love divine, all loves excelling...*
> *Fix in us thy humble dwelling,*
> *And thy faithful mercies crown."*

John 15:13-14. *"Greater love hath no man than this, that a man lay down his life for his friends. Ye are my friends if ye do whatsoever I command you."*

"All that a man hath will he give for his life," and the gift of His life includes all possible gifts. It is seldom that a man can do more for us by dying than he could by living. When we need this particular expression of love and receive it, we then receive the highest expression of love that can be given among men.

Between one life and another there is, in respect to value, a great difference. The death of one man is an event unnoticed; the death of another gives a shock to the entire community; millions lament it, and posterity envies the generation that had such a member to lose. Between the best of all the sons of men and the Lord Jesus there is an infinite difference. They all differ in their degrees of unworthiness; He differs from all in the fact of His perfect worthiness. He was holy, harmless, undefiled and separate from sinners. The lives of all men on the face of the earth would unitedly be as nothing in value compared with the life of the Lamb without blemish and without spot.

As an expression of love and devotedness, the surrender of a mere human life is valid. The surrender of the life of Jesus is an unimpeachable testimony to His love. This being granted, the importance of the fact is infinitely enhanced by the consideration of the value of that life. Rightly to understand the fact, it is necessary to consider the dignity of the person of Emmanuel; the unloveliness of man's character; the reception encountered by the Savior; the nature and circumstances of His death.

But it may be said—what will not man, in his thoughtlessness and unbelief, utter against the Gospel?—that to die could only be for Christ a happy exit from a world like this. He breathed here an empoisoned atmosphere. He dwelt here under the shadow of the throne of Satan. He was perpetually wounded by the shafts of malignity. He was a Man of sorrows; Heaven was His home. Could there be to a spotless soul like His any greater punishment than to be compelled to reside in this world? We can answer this by a reference to facts.

When He drew near to the cross, His soul became exceedingly sorrowful even unto death. His sweat was as it were great drops falling down to the ground. He cried out in agony to His heavenly Father to take away the cup from Him. Concerning no other period of His life, have we any characterization at all approaching this in darkness and terribleness. Ah, there was something infinitely more than common in this death. In infinite condescension He speaks of it as death, as a simple laying down of life—uses language that would be appropriate to the act of a common man. "Greater love hath no man than this, that a man lay down his life for his friends."

We inquire what is meant by this laying down of life, and are conducted into a region that has no limit. The highest intelligences of Heaven, after thousands of years spent in contemplating the "Lamb as it had been slain in the midst of the throne," are heard exclaiming, "It is high, we cannot attain unto it."

"Ye are my friends if ye do whatsoever I command you." Jesus laid down His life for His friends, who do whatsoever He commands them. Not for others? Do not let us neutralize the words of the Master. If we say that whether men obey Him or not He laid down His life for them, we virtually cancel what is here written. Imagine one of the eleven disciples whispering to another, "Believe me, it is all one whether we obey Him or not, so far as the laying down of His life for us goes."

Ah, how many such whispered denials there are! How many passages of the Gospels are cancelled by the tacit understanding of the Church that they have no particular significance! Glory to God in the highest for the outpouring of His Spirit!—but we need still mightier influences of the Spirit before there can be a resurrection of the whole Gospel from that state of suspended animation in which so much of it is yet lying.

But are we not expressly told that the Lamb of God takes away the sin of the world? that Jesus was a propitiation not for our sins only,

161

but for those of the whole world? that He was a ransom for all, to be testified in due time? that He tasted death for every man? We are; and we must be careful that we impair in no wise the integrity of these passages. The only orthodoxy is that which does honor to the whole of Scripture. Alas, the orthodoxy that has too long been reputed among men is that which arms itself with some favorite text and with it slays a multitude of other texts.

Christ died for the world in one sense, and in another He died for those who by their obedience show that they are His friends. He died for the world in such a sense that it is now meet for God to pardon whomsoever He will, and meet for all that will, of every nation, tribe and tongue, to come and take of the water of life freely. And He died for believers in this sense, that they alone do actually obtain everlasting life through Him. His death provides for all the means of salvation; it provides for His people salvation. His death takes away the sin of the world, so that the holiness and justice and truth of God interpose no longer a barrier in the way of the salvation of any among the sons of men who may desire to take of the water of life. But God has purposed from the foundation of the world that His Word should not return to Him void—that some should be saved—that the offer of life should not be universally rejected. For these last, in a most blessed sense, Christ laid down His life.

In this connection let us say to the unreconciled sinner, "In the former of the two senses mentioned, Christ laid down His life for you, yet you are not saved. For many days you have heard the word of the Gospel, yet you are where you are. If Christ died not for you in the second sense, you will derive no advantage from His death. It will be as though there had been no Christ, so far as any hope of salvation is concerned. What a tremendous uncertainty hangs over your prospects for the future! Is there no way by which this uncertainty may be dispelled? There is: Believe in the Lord Jesus Christ; become His friend; do His commandments; make your calling and election sure."

Abraham was the friend of God. The Lord Jesus, in Whom is all the fullness of the Godhead bodily, goes about among us, seeking some to be His friends. Nothing could give such an awful idea of the impenitence and alienation of the natural heart as to see how many and how amazing acts of friendship, performed by Christ, fail to win the friendship of that heart. The treasure of wrath accumulated against the day of wrath is simply the treasure of the rejected love of Christ. But we profess to be the friends of Christ.

Many ask, "What is the true Church?" Christ tells us that the true Church consists exclusively of those who keep His commandments. We must come back to this test. He commands us to believe on Him, to abide in Him, to pray through Him, to love Him, to love His people with His own love, to wash the disciples' feet, to let our light shine, to count all things but loss—a right hand or a right eye—that we may be found in Him, to live unto Him, to pray always and not faint.

Have you a friend? Then you have one whom you can confidently ask to do what you desire, though it should interfere with some desire of his own, and you know that he will do it unmurmuringly. Are you a friend of Christ? Then you have one whom Christ can at all times call upon to do His will, with surrender of personal predilections [preferences] and sacrifice of private ends. His word may be, "Sell all that thou hast and give to the poor"; you will comply unhesitatingly, for in fact there was much more than such compliance in any original act of consecration to Him. The name of Christ's friend was given to you because one day you made over to Him all your property, your powers, your pleasures, your aims, recognizing His loving will to be the law of your being. Especially, being Christ's friend, your heart belongs to Him, that He may fill it with His Spirit, His love, His peace, His joy. Being His friend, you are His advocate in the world; and it is everywhere expected among men that you will be ready to speak in His praise, and to urge His claims upon their reverential love.

163

John 15:15. *"Henceforth I call you not servants; for the servant knoweth not what his lord doeth: but I have called you friends; for all things that I have heard of my Father, I have made known unto you."*

We should have thought that the Lord Jesus had all along treated His disciples with great frankness and friendliness and cordiality. His language and demeanor were well fitted to inspire confidence not only on their part, but on the part of publicans and sinners. Yet there were doubtless certain barriers to unreserved communion—not arbitrarily opposed by Him, but arising out of the very nature of the case—arising, especially, out of the imperfection of their views, their inability to comprehend the work and mission of the Savior, their unbelief, their self-regard. And perhaps there is reason to believe that a gradation in intimacy, such as is here set forth, is characteristic of discipleship in general.

He calls us servants so long as we require to be called servants—so long as we require to be influenced by a reference chiefly to His authority. When we have been enabled not theoretically to see, but practically to feel, that His manifested love for us demands the most thorough consecration to His will, that all His requirements are the requirements of love, then we have purchased to ourselves a good degree, better infinitely than any ecclesiastical degrees, any doctorate or episcopate—the degree of a recognized friend of Christ.

The disciples were friends of Christ before. He sometimes called them such (Luke 12:4). But in an important sense they only now entered into that deeper intimacy that was specially expressed by this designation. The sinner that yesterday found peace and joy in believing is most welcome to speak of himself as one whom Christ calls a friend; yet, while rejoicing in the marvelous friendship of Him Who is made higher than the heavens, let him know that he is saved by hope, that there is more in the future—a heaven above the Heaven into which he has been translated. Let him forget the things that are behind and press toward the prize that is before him. Let him never be satisfied until the grace of the Lord Jesus Christ has such an ascendancy over him that every requirement of his Master shall seem the behest [instruction] of a tried and precious friend.

There are some who welcome ardently every statement that recognizes the believer as the friend rather than as the servant of Christ. They see that the Lord Jesus Christ attaches great importance to that confidence which clings invincibly to the persuasion of His love. They are right; but let them take heed that no error intermingle with the blessed truth of which they have been put in possession. It is of the highest importance that they should abide in the assurance of His love, but it is not a matter of little importance whether they do or leave undone some of His requirements.

It is not the characteristic of a friend of Christ that he is less attentive to the doing of Christ's will than a mere servant is, or condemns himself less for any neglect of the Savior's will. On the contrary, the true friend of Christ will give vastly more heed to the will of Christ than a mere servant would, will discover far more of Christ's will than the dull eye of a servant possibly could, and will abhor himself for neglects altogether too slight to affect the conscience of an undergraduate, a mere servant.

But, as the passage before us emphatically teaches, the characteristic of a friend of Christ is this—that he does everything for friendship, honors Christ by believing that friendship dictates all His commands, and by trusting in the power and wisdom of the Savior to guide and strengthen him in the execution of His gracious will. And when his friendly, scrupulous heart condemns him for the imperfection of his service, he does not for a moment permit this feeling of self-condemnation to separate him from his Lord. He hastens with his deficiencies into the presence of his august Friend, and urges these deficiencies as an eloquent reason why the power of Christ should more triumphantly be put forth in him.

There is no condemnation to those that are in Christ Jesus and who walk after the Spirit; but it must not for a moment be supposed that such make light of their own shortcomings. They make the more haste to discover them, and are the more zealous in abhorring them, because their Lord refuses to frown upon them. This is true friendship. All that know anything of this sacred bond, even when it but unites a mortal to his fellow-mortal, know that it renders each most careful of the feelings of the other. There is a process of mutual identification wrought by it, and whatever is dear to the one becomes equally dear to the other. Thus Christ is formed in the believer's heart, the hope of glory. The believer is careful of the feelings of Christ; Christ is careful of the feelings of the believer. Christ is the believer's Friend; the believer is Christ's friend. He writes His law in the hearts of His people; they write their prayers in His heart.

"All things that I have heard of my Father I have made known unto you." How shall we reconcile this with what He says a few verses on?—"I have yet many things to say unto you, but ye cannot bear them now." Ah, if John had been writing this from his own invention, or with as much freedom as Plato or Xenophon used in reporting the words of Socrates, there would have been none of these apparent discrepancies. The spirit of fiction would have carefully eliminated these apparent inconsistencies; the Spirit of truth shows us that the inconsistency is apparent only, having relation merely to the language, and not to the thoughts expressed by it.

"Henceforth I call you friends (says the Savior) because I have laid aside all reserve in speaking to you. If at any time I have kept back anything from want of confidence, this is now no longer the case. I have spoken to you freely of the wonderful union existing between my Father and Myself, and of the equally wonderful union between Myself and My disciples. Language cannot embody more of promise, prerogative or love than is contained in the words now spoken to you." To the end of time, Christians, even those who are most filled with the Spirit of God, will come back to these words as to a repository of incomparably precious and sanctifying truths.

To lay aside all reserve is one thing, and to communicate all information is another. Who could for an instant suppose that Christ had communicated all that He knew to His disciples? They were yet to be His disciples, though they were His friends; and a day was coming when they should be in a position to receive what now they could not.

If Christ, having called us His friends, yet withholds some knowledge from us, let us rest assured that it is not because of reserve or mistrust, but simply because we are not in a position to receive the desired communications. Let us have communion with Him according to the basis now established by Him, and we shall thus be fitted to ascend to a higher level.

"All things that I have heard of my Father." He speaks here of the Man Christ Jesus, Who in early years grew in wisdom, and Whose faculties, however admirable, were limited, because they were the faculties of a creature. God was manifest in the flesh; in Christ we behold the union of the Godhead with humanity—the divinity not destroying the humanity, the humanity remaining in its integrity in order that the divinity might be revealed by it. They that cannot see in Christ the finite as well as the infinite cannot rightly see the glory of God shining in the face of Jesus Christ.

But the special meaning of this passage is, that the believer is brought into the same confidential relation to Christ in which Christ stands to the Father. Christ, the Man, enjoyed the matchless favor of His God— was brought wonderfully near to the Fountain of all wisdom and blessedness; this the Father's own declaration from Heaven and all their observation perfectly attested. They were now informed that as Christ was near and dear to the Father, so the believer was near and dear unto Him; that all which the Father had given Him He gave to the believer, and that in Him they enjoyed the same prerogatives that He Himself enjoyed.

The thought expressed here is, beyond all others, the thought that Jesus labored to express in this parting interview. If He spoke of the inconceivable intimacy between Him and the Father, it was that they might rejoice in the fact that an equal intimacy existed between them and Him. In all things He was our righteous Advocate and Representative—living, dying, ascending, triumphing, that He might obtain gifts for us.

To know our riches, we must know the riches of Christ. Alas that we should be living upon the mere fragment of a Christ!—that we should be content to know simply the feeble pulsations of life in the outskirts of our being!—that the Gospel should have such a poor and beggarly representation in our experience!

John 15:16. *"Ye have not chosen me, but I have chosen you, and ordained you, that ye should go and bring forth fruit, and that your fruit should remain: that whatsoever ye shall ask of the Father in my name, he may give it you."*

"We love him because he first loved us," says John in his Epistle. "Herein is love, not that we loved God, but that he loved us." Christ is the choice of the believer, but would never have been had Christ not previously chosen him. And what is faith in Christ but a recognition of Christ's love already existing and freely proffered? That is a counterfeit of faith which imagines that it creates love in Christ by coming to Him. "We know and have believed the love that God hath toward us."

There is sometimes in the heart a feeling of intense need, a profound sense of misery, an ardent desire for the salvation that Christ bestows, but this state of mind is not in itself saving. There must be the actual coming to Christ, and in order that there may be this coming, it is necessary that the soul should apprehend the encouragement to come held out by Christ Himself.

The invitations of Christ afford this encouragement: "Come," He says, "all ye that labor and are heavy laden, and I will give you rest." The sin-stricken soul objects, perhaps, that it is not aware of any special invitation singling it out from other souls and authorizing it to come. This objection is simply the language of unbelief. Faith says, "He invites all; I am not by name excepted: I am evidently included, for I labor and am heavy laden; I need rest, and I have not come to Christ. The invitation is to *all* such, and therefore to me. I will come." This is the language of faith. Would that all concerned might cease from the subterfuges which nullify the proffered grace of Christ, and no longer ask Him to depart from the principle which He has Himself laid down, no longer ask Him to grant a victory to unbelief!

There are myriads of persons this day seeking the rest which Christ bestows—rather let us say longing for it—who are not making the least approach toward it, because they refuse to exercise that faith which the Gospel demands. They want Christ to treat the Gospel with something of the same contempt that they show to it, and bestow upon them a private gospel with their own name alone in it. He will not do it, though they weep their sight away. He will not deny Himself. He has taken His stand in the midst of humanity, and His proclamation is, "If any man thirst, let him come unto me." He that asks Christ to give him a white stone with a name written in it known to the recipient only, promising as a return for such a gift to believe upon the Savior, asks and promises in vain. This stone cannot possibly be given except to faith. It is faith alone that can discern either the stone or the name written therein. It is not, "Take and believe," but, "Believing, take."

The believer comes to Christ because he recognizes His love to sinners, and knows himself to be one of these sinners. Afterward, it may be, he learns that, having been drawn of the Father, he did not come to Christ, that Christ, besides having invited the multitude to which he belonged, had chosen him individually to everlasting life, and that in fact the entire history of his awakening, repenting, believing, is neither more nor less than the history of the means by which Christ's own choice was carried into effect.

Your choice of Christ is the evidence of Christ's choice of you. You have not to ascend into Heaven, and make your way to the place where a glorified Christ sits enthroned, in order to ascertain what are Christ's desires; your own desires for Christ are the revelation of Christ's desires. Do you wish to know whether He has chosen you? Choose Him.

"I have chosen you, and ordained you, that ye should go and bring forth fruit." Whom He chooses, them He appoints His fruit-bearers. This is that doctrine of election which appears in Scripture. It is not an election to eternal life save as it is an election to fruitfulness. That is not faith which knows Christ in the future only. That is not eternal life which might exist apart from Christ. He that believeth hath eternal life because he hath Christ, and as Christ was when in the world so are we, because we have Christ, consequently the divorcing of

169

salvation and of holiness is an absurdity. If we are the elect of Christ, we are elected to live a Christ-like life upon the earth—elected to be branches in the true Vine and to bring forth fruit.

The disciples were to *go* and bring forth fruit. They were to fill the face of the earth with fruit. Where should they go? Wherever there was sin, misery, death—east, west, north and south, as far in this ruined world as the grace of God would permit them. The grace of God destroyed all limits in the day when Christ said unto His disciples, "Go into all the world, and preach the Gospel to every creature."

How many there are who fail to bring forth fruit because they do not *go* and bring forth fruit! Their fruit is to be found elsewhere. Among the tens of thousands of ministers of the Gospel in Great Britain and America, are there not many who, if ordained of Christ at all, are ordained to go to unevangelized lands? An ordained minister of Christ, let us say, is one who does the work appointed him by Christ, and who would regard as the greatest of calamities that ignorance of Christ's will which springs from the deference accorded to a subtle self-will.

"And that your fruit should remain"; abiding in Christ, their fruit should abide. Is the reference here to the churches to be founded by them? Their permanency would of course depend upon the condition already laid down, "If a man abide not in me he is cast forth as a branch." The seven churches and all the apostolic churches existed upon this condition, yet the apostolic fruit was not altogether swallowed up by Antichrist. It found for itself a wilderness life, a sackcloth condition.

The apostolic fruit is in the Acts and in the Epistles, in the characters of the apostles made deathless by the New Testament, and there are, it may be, millions this day built upon the apostles and prophets, Christ being the chief cornerstone. Like the seed found in the mummy-cases of Egypt, sown in our day after a slumber of three thousand years, and causing our fields to wave with unexpected harvests, the fruit of the apostles survived the death and darkness of the Middle Ages, and is now reproducing itself in many lands.

"I have chosen you, and ordained you, that whatsoever ye shall ask of the Father in my name, he may give it you." It is at the throne of grace that we bring forth fruit to Christ. We are made fruit-bearers by being made suppliants. The Name of Christ believingly presented at the throne of grace is the victory which overcomes the world. Thank God that we are receiving new and precious instructions in the truth brought out in this passage! Blessed election! Hast thou, O Lover of my soul, elected me to bear Thy Name to the Father, and receive in Thy Name the magnificent awards that belong to such a Name? To earthly banks we take the sign-manual of Christ and receive simply a gaze of astonishment; at the treasury of Heaven all the wealth of Heaven is poured forth at the mere whisper of this marvelous Name.

Believer, go to the treasury of Heaven, and report that Christ has chosen you and ordained you to go and bring forth fruit, and ask, with all confidence, that the means of bringing forth that fruit may be given you.

John 15:17. *"These things I command you; that ye love one another."*

For the third time this evening this command falls from the lips of the Lord Jesus. Evidently He is in earnest about this matter. He has it unspeakably at heart that His disciples should understand and be prepared to do His will thus expressed. He knows the material that He has to deal with, and that there are immense difficulties in the way of introducing into their minds the conception of Christian obligation existing in His. Hence this repetition. It is doubtless needed.

At the mention of a commandment the thought that rises most spontaneously to the mind is that of some external and definite service to be rendered to the Master. "These things I command you," says the Lord, speaking in the plural number as though He heard them say, "Will you not give us ten commandments, as God gave to Moses, so that we may distinctly know what we, the apostles of the Messiah, have to do for You?"

In reply, we may suppose Him saying, "The ten things I command you are these: first, you are to love one another. And second? Love one another. And third? Love one another. I will not let you turn away from this expression of My will. There is nothing to alternate with this. You are not to do this, and then do something besides. Do this ever: all things are summed up in this. I am no more in the world, but My disciples are, and I invest each believer with all My claims upon the love of each believer. Love your brother, then, as you love Me; love Me in loving him; consider that you obey all My commandments when you love him."

"Ah, it is one thing to love Christ," you say, "and another thing to love His imperfect disciple. In Him I see perfection, in the believer repulsive imperfections." Faith must come to the aid of your staggering love, and show you how intimately this same defective believer is united to Jesus—show you also the new nature struggling to emancipate itself in your brother from the burdensome remains of the old, and destined to achieve a victory through your love.

172

As you love Christ, come to the help of that new and immature nature. It will be treason to Christ if you turn away because of the evil yet unsubdued in the heart of your brother. Christ has put into your heart love to him that you may come to his aid. Christ sends His love to him through you, and sends it the more because he so needs it; and you, instead of conveying the precious gift of your Master, turn away in disgust. How does it escape your notice that in thus acting, you merely reproduce in yourself the repulsive trait of your defrauded brother? You defraud both him and Christ: nay, you defraud yourself, for Christ has nothing better for you than that love to your brother so repeatedly commanded you.

Let me, then, love the people of God. How love them? As Christ did and does. Did Christ love them by shutting His eyes to their imperfections? No: He extenuated [ignored] their faults in no degree. He practiced no deception upon Himself with regard to their characters. He loved them, not because of what their nature was, but because of His own nature. And their sins, infinitely more formidable and odious in His sight than in yours, indicated to Him their need of His love, and afforded that love the opportunity of new triumphs.

It is time enough for us to turn in disgust from our imperfect fellow-Christians when love in us has done for them all that love can do. Sometimes, indeed, love to the disciples will require us to withdraw all countenance and communion from one whose conduct is an occasion of opprobrium [scandal] to them. He that strengthens the power of an evil example by his countenance is loving with no hallowed love. We are never, in our love of one, to lose sight of the interests of others. But leaving out of view these extreme cases, is it not manifest that Christ's reiterated command meets with very little from us that is worthy of the name of obedience? It is the more manifest because we are in these latter days obtaining a juster view of the obligation to love one another.

Oh let us press forward in this direction! There will be un-thought of revelations of the glory of Christ to our souls, when we make it our chief study to promote the welfare of our brethren in Christ. When we shall have so far remounted to the Pentecostal level as that none of us shall deem aught that he has his own, then shall it be made clear to us as it never was before, that all things are ours and that we are Christ's.

All things are ours; there is a climax beyond this amazing height: we are Christ's. When we love the brethren with Christ's own love, then will it be beyond all controversy that we are Christ's. His Name will be seen upon us, and the name of the city of my God, which is New Jerusalem. Jehovah Shammah will be written upon us.

After all, the great difficulty in the way of fulfilling this command of Christ is our self-preference. Men are so much taken up with a vain ideal of their own goodness, so much absorbed in the sad work of covering the blotches made continually by sin in this ideal, so carried away by the idea that they can subdue and expel the leprosy of the soul, viewed by them as a mere superficial blemish, that there remains neither time nor capacity to entertain an unselfish love.

And it is with a view to the subjugation of this disease of selfishness that the Savior so insists upon brotherly love. Oh, if we would only look upon each fellow-Christian as an embodied opportunity of inflicting another wound upon our great enemy, Self, and as a medicine-bearer from Christ! For in giving to him our affection, we save our affection from diseased action. Kept in our own hearts, it is like the air at the bottom of empty wells, mephitic [putrid], fatal.

We are being educated for Heaven by means of this law of brotherly love. Have we aspirations for the joy, the peace, the glory, the power, of the heavenly life? Let us show these aspirations to be genuine by giving heed to this law. Christ prepares His people for the place which He has gone to prepare for them by teaching them to love. Our prayers to be brought triumphantly through the battle of life into the place of victory before the throne of God, if answered at all, are answered by the creation and augmentation in us of a disposition to look less upon ourselves and more upon our brethren, to live for them rather than for ourselves.

There is nothing we need to be on our guard against so much as the disguises of selfishness. It too often manages to pass itself off for love. Whatever errors enter into our conception of Christ will equally enter into our love of the brethren. If we know Christ as the Christ of a sect, selfishness will reign only the more supreme in us because it permits us to rejoice in those who are like-minded with ourselves. A true love of the true Christ will effectually bring the axe to bear upon the root of our selfishness.

How many are proclaiming this day, by the most unequivocal conduct, that they know not Him Who is the Head of the Church, but only a spectral Christ, the deification of their selfishness and prejudice!— not Him Who holdeth in His right hand the seven stars, but One Who holds in His hand a single star!

What a glorious body of divinity is given in the epistles to the seven churches! What hallowed and potent instruction as to the largeness of the mind of Christ! Not merely does the church of Ephesus receive light concerning its own deficiencies and interests, but it is taught by the other epistles to look with love and interest upon the sister churches. One Christ is over all. Philadelphia is not permitted to repudiate even Laodicea. What right has she to spew out of her mouth that which Christ hath not yet spewed out of His mouth? Behold, He stands at the door even of Laodicea and knocks.

Ah, if this glorious Being Who walks in the midst of the golden candlesticks should write seven letters unto seven churches now existing, how would some of us not be rebuked? We should find the Master recognizing what some of us coldly ignore. "It is a mere bruised reed," say these—"let it break." "Nay," says the Savior, "I will not break it, nor let it be broken." Our modern Thyatira would be covered with confusion by the mention of the woman Jezebel so treacherously allowed to maintain a connection with the church, and also by the fact that some despised Philadelphia receives a more unqualified commendation. Such letters would exalt that which is now humble and abase that which is now exalted. Such missives shall yet be read. "My word shall judge them in the last day." The Spirit of God, now coming forth in His glory, will not rest until He has emancipated the Word of Christ from the bonds in which unbelief has hitherto held it, and made it quick and sharper than any two-edged sword.

John 15:18-19. *"If the world hate you, ye know that it hated me before it hated you. If ye were of the world, the world would love his own; but because ye are not of the world, but I have chosen you out of the world, therefore the world hateth you."*

Love suggests hate. God is love; love was incarnate in Christ; Christ was despised and rejected of men. "These things I command you," He says to His disciples, "that ye love one another." And immediately He proceeds to speak of the hatred of the world, which they might assuredly expect to encounter if the love that was in Him should abide in them.

We have here the statement of a fact: "The world hateth you." The reason of that fact: "Because ye are not of the world, but I have chosen you out of the world." And a ground of consolation: "It hated me before it hated you."

Light is come into the world; men love darkness rather than light; you are the light of the world. So long as men love darkness rather than light, and so long as Christians are the light of the world, so long may they expect to be, like their Master, despised and rejected.

Christians are the sons of peace; they are commanded to follow peace with all men; their vocation is that of peacemakers. They are meek, long-suffering, forgiving; they give no place to wrath; they are kind, benevolent, self-sacrificing. How comes it to pass, then, that they are hated of men? Men do not ordinarily hate those that love them, bless them, pray for them; they hate those that injure them, that take from them, that oppose them.

Consider this: the mission of Christians is to take from men something that is unutterably dear to them, to reduce them to a condition that seems to them worse than slavery, to carry them away into perpetual exile, to foil them in every enterprise that they have at heart, in fact— we may as well say it—to kill them. Do you start back in horror? Hear me to the end.

There is not anything so dear to the man of this world as the idea of his own unblamableness. Every day of his life he has been engaged in rearing, in his inner thought-world, a lofty edifice—a tower of Babel—to answer at once the purpose of a monument in his own praise, and to enable him, when the time shall come, to step from its pinnacle into Heaven. Every day he has been busy carving to some answerable shape the stones of his daily experience. He has diligently, all his life long, done battle with the insolent voices of a miscreant conscience, establishing by successive victories the difficult fact that he is, take him for all in all, one whom God must look down upon with benignity, if not with admiration.

You come to him in the Name of Christ for the very purpose of depriving him of this idea of his own goodness. Your aim is to do what that tormenting conscience of his, with all its advantages of time and place, failed to do. Do you think that he has fought with the Goliath of his own conscience so many times, and so successfully, to be now discomfited by you? Will he allow you to be victorious over him, and take from him the idea of his own integrity in the sight of God, after he has gone through a thousand fights to obtain that pearl of price?

You tell him that he is a mere rebel against the most high God, that he has never been anything else, that all his righteousnesses are contemptible in the sight of Heaven, that he deserves the wrath of God, and you ask him to take this same view of himself. You ask him to adjudge himself to be worthy of everlasting punishment. How easy were it for him in comparison to surrender all his worldly substance! Self-esteem permeates his whole nature like the fibers of a cancer, and to bid him part with it is like bidding him surrender life.

Well, but need a Christian come to his fellow-sinner in just such a way as this? He may come in what way he will. He may come with a thousand tokens of love in act and word, but if he is indeed a Christian, a light in the world, he must in some way testify to the condition of the impenitent in the sight of God. He must make known to them that there is a new birth, and that upon all who have not experienced it, the

177

wrath of God abideth. No man is saved by his own goodness: the blood of Christ alone cleanseth from sin. His mission is to awaken men to these discoveries, to bring home to their inmost convictions these tremendous truths. The light that he communicates is the light which they hate; consequently they hate him.

He invites them to come with him, but, to their apprehensions, the region in which he dwells is a vast, howling wilderness. They cannot conceive of the least approach to happiness in a life such as is proposed to them. It were like going into the direst captivity. Their joys are his sorrows, his joys are their sorrows; his gains are in their eyes, loss, even as their gains are loss in his estimation. The sun, of whose glorious and soul-refreshing beams he boasts to them, is in their regard a sun perpetually eclipsed, and the sun of their life is darkness to him. How little way, then, will suavity, kindness, the most unlimited generosity even, go in reconciling the world to the presence of a set of men whose business is to convince them of sin and danger, and lead them to forsake all that they may follow One in Whom they see nothing attractive! Kindness and generosity had their highest embodiment in Christ, yet He was hated of men unto the end. And just as surely as His disciples are such will they be hated.

"I have chosen you out of the world." The world has discovered that its truest policy is to induce them to come to a compromise. It has brought all the resources of its wisdom to bear upon this problem: how to hinder the separation of Christians from the world, and at the same time allow them to regard themselves as Christians. It says to Christians: "We, after all, think very much as you do; there is a great deal that is excellent in what you say; you have probably in some things misapprehended the Master's meaning. We must calmly and deliberately investigate these matters; let us avoid anything like a rupture. Some of your positions we do not yet see our way to adopt; some of our views are unpalatable to you; but so far as we have attained, let us walk together. We must bear with one another. You are surely too enlightened and too philosophic to break away rashly and put a great gulf betwixt yourself and us. You would never be able to do us any good after any such fanatical procedure. In the mean time it must be encouraging to you that we adopt Christian phraseology to so great an extent. Take you 'hope' for your motto, and we will take 'peace' for ours." Such is the strategy of the world in these days, and it has been amazingly successful.

One of the great ends for which we need the outpouring of the Holy Spirit is that Christians may be chosen out of the world—that they may yield to the choice of Christ and come fairly out of the world. If they are the elect, then are they elected out of the world. Remaining in the world, they cut themselves off from the number of the elect.

Lot was elected unto life by being elected to quit Sodom; and it would not have been more absurd in him to remain in Sodom, flattering himself that he was nevertheless elected unto life, than for Christians to remain in the world and yet buoy themselves with the hope of everlasting life.

If there is ground for believing that there are Christians, more or less, seeking earnestly at this time to come out from the world and be separate from everything that is defiling, if we can obtain anywhere a glimpse of a body of believers, few it may be, and yet described as an hundred, forty and four thousand, standing with the Lamb upon Mount Zion, redeemed from the earth—then do we have an occasion of rejoicing beyond what the mere fact of the conversion of myriads or hundreds of thousands would furnish us with. If we cannot discern such a body anywhere, would it not be well to set about raising up one, and, as a first step, to seek ourselves to reach that blessed summit?

If an individual grows up in a Christian community, with a law very deeply imprinted on his moral sense forbidding him to give any offence to society, then you may suppose that such an individual, even though a church member, will instinctively, as it were, shrink back from every path in which he will be likely to meet the frown of men. He knows nothing of the hatred of society. Why? Because he makes it his constant study not to transgress the tacit requirements of society.

The dread of giving a shock to the common sentiment of what is fitting, influences him even in his interpretation of Scripture. He is hindered by the mighty and perhaps unsuspected power which the world has over him, from even discovering that it is his duty to enter a path in which he will encounter the hatred of the world. The fact that there is now so little persecution compared with what there once was, is best explained by the circumstances that the world begins farther back, and, instead of waiting till the individual presents himself with the whole armor of God upon him, imposes upon him a law not to pay the least attention to requirements which would cause him to give offence to society.

This is a formidable impeachment to make of the church of these days. Ah, there is too much ground for it. *Society* is the Protestant Antichrist, calling itself the vicar of Christ, forbidding men to interpret the Scriptures except in consonance with the laws of society. When the time of sifting shall come, it will be found that, even in what we call the true church of Christ, Christ is the Master that receives least reverence, and Christians will acknowledge with unspeakable shame, that many lords have had dominion over them.

"The world cannot hate you," said Jesus to some of His earthly relatives. Nothing more terribly suggestive of soul-ruin could be uttered than these words, and yet it is to be feared that the same utterance would fitly be addressed to the great body of professing Christians in our day. The world cannot hate them because it cannot hate itself. These Christians have too often put a singular honor upon the world, by receiving it into the church and compelling the acknowledged servants of Christ to pay all respect to the laws, the usages, the preferences of society.

John 15:20. *"Remember the word that I said unto you, The servant is not greater than his Lord. If they have persecuted me, they will also persecute you: if they have kept my saying, they will keep yours also."*

It is one path that is trodden by Christ and by the people of Christ. He that sets out to follow Christ is distinctly informed of the ruggednesses of the path in which he is to walk. It should be a source of satisfaction to him, as he pursues his heavenward journey, to see ever and anon a monumental pillar with the inscription, "I, Jesus, passed this way." It would be a strange thing indeed if he found fault with these indications that he is in the right way. No language can be more unequivocal than that in which Christ informs all who would follow Him what it is they must expect.

The same character and the same principles that were embodied in Christ, will, wherever embodied, and according to the degree in which they are so, meet with repulsion from men as long as men are what they are. Does the Christian expect that God, simply with a view to his comfort, will control the feelings and passions of ungodly men along the pathway of his life, and cause them to act unnaturally—that is, Christianly—merely that he may escape persecution? It was not done for the Master; why should it be done for the servant? If we ask why it should not be done, important reasons will readily present themselves.

To suffer with Christ is the law of Christian discipleship. Millions are hindered from becoming professedly disciples of Christ, because in the circumstances in which they are placed, even the feeblest profession of Christianity will involve a certain measure of obloquy [scorn]. This it is that hinders myriads of professed disciples from becoming out and out, the followers of Christ. But the profession is a lie before God and man unless it be accompanied with a readiness to suffer for His Name's sake.

If Christ Himself may be allowed to define the law of discipleship, the believer is a cross-bearer, hated of men. It were a much simpler matter to take the Christian to Heaven than to secure for him an untroubled path through this world. The same reasons that exist for his continuance in this world for a season, require that God should not, in His ordinary providence, change the character of this world so as to make the path of the Christian peaceful.

The servant is not greater than his Lord. The Lord Jesus was accompanied with the credentials of Heaven. He did the works of Him Who had sent Him: He was manifestly the Son of God. The winds and the waves obeyed Him; devils trembled at His presence and fled at His command; angels waited upon Him. As though it were a little thing that He Himself should have power to heal diseases, cast out devils and raise the dead, He invested His disciples with similar authority. Holiness, in this endeavor to obtain for itself a footing in the world, did not come in utter weakness and with an entire privation of all that usually has power to awe men, but it was allied with superhuman perfections and the evidences of a divine majesty.

It is evident, then, that if, under these circumstances, and in despite of all that was so fitted to hinder the outbreak of human animosity, the wrath of man broke forth and the Savior had to bear the brunt of fierce opposition, it would be in vain to expect for His followers a serene path through life. If they persecuted the Master, unrestrained by the power and majesty with which He was invested, how much more will they be likely to persecute the disciples, accompanied with far inferior evidence of super-human dignity!

The principal trial in connection with the opposition that the Christian has to endure, arises from the silence of God, and from the apparent assent which the proceedings of the persecutors meet with from Him. He Who has all power does not for a long time, it may be, interfere in behalf of His servant and to the confusion of His enemies.

Relying upon the promises of God, the believer goes forth, and his conception of those promises leads him to expect that, immediately upon the proof given of his devotedness, God will speak from Heaven, saying, "Touch not my anointed one." He is disappointed, and perhaps he is tempted to doubt the faithfulness of God. Then let him remember that the servant is not greater than his Lord. The Lord Jesus was not exempt from even such trials; He had to drink this very cup to the dregs; the last hours of His life were embittered by the presence of this same temptation.

Remembering this, the believer will gain a victory over the tempter, and the very pillar on which he wearily leans, weeping tears of despondency, discloses to him the inscribed words of Jesus, "I, your Master, passed this way. He that follows Me shall have the light of life. I was thus tempted in all points that I might succor you."

The servant of Christ is not greater than his Lord, yet no other servant stands in such relations to his master as the Christian does to his. Christ is identified with His people, and they are His representatives upon the earth, and the same thing which exposes them to the unfriendliness of the many gives them a passport to the sympathies and fervid affections of those who have been taught of God. The servant of Christ is the bearer to them of that which they esteem above thousands of gold and silver. There is nothing in the wide world of which they have so keen and joyous an appreciation as of the words of Christ; and if I am the servant of Christ, freighted with His message, my coming will be to them like the morning star.

Some people glory in the mere fact that they are hated. If they fail to enlist the sympathies of Christians, they still, and perhaps the more persistently, affirm that it is because they are the servants of Him Who was despised and rejected. But it is not impossible that they may be deceiving themselves. If we are truly Christ's, we shall not merely be disowned by the many; we shall be welcomed, embraced and loved, by the people of Christ. That which secures us opposition will also secure us affection—the affectionate regard of those who are called the salt of the earth. Because the Christian encounters opposition, it does not follow that everyone who encounters opposition, is a Christian.

The Christian does his utmost to conciliate men; to be indifferent to those feelings would be to show that he is not the servant of Christ; his

183

mission is one of love. "They hated me *without a cause,*" said Jesus. Causes of love there were, tens of thousands, in the life of Christ, and therefore the hatred which He encountered was odious beyond degree. The Christian aims so to live that if he should encounter similar hate, he may be able similarly to say, "They hated me without a cause." The apostle tells us that ministers of God approve themselves such "by kindness, by long-suffering, by love unfeigned." If, after all this, they are repulsed, they avail themselves of the consolation that Christ offers them.

But there are some who meet with opposition, not so much because of the truth which they declare, as of the austere or truculent way in which they declare it. He that winneth souls is wise, but these are neither wise nor loving. Paul became all things to all that he might save some; these will not unbend in the least, or make the least allowance for the prejudices and ignorance of others. The opposition they encounter is not a proof that they are Christ's. In the case supposed, it is simply a proof that they have failed to use those means of engaging the good-will of their fellow-men which Christ has given to His people.

John 15:21. *"But all these things will they do unto you for my name's sake, because they know not Him that sent me."*

The martyrology of the Christian Church, written and unwritten, more unwritten than written, is comprehended under the words, "all these things." With malevolence, man combines the wisdom of the serpent; and the glorious intellect which, if consecrated to God, would make him the companion of God, spends itself on the invention of ways and means for the gratification of his hostility to all that reflects the image of God. Rude expressions of malignity may do for a rude age, but for a refined age like this, something very different is demanded.

There is nothing in such general ill-odor at present as the word *persecution*. The enlightened men of this day are astonished at the violent proceedings of their ancestors. They are ready to join with Christians in doing honor to the martyrs; and it is universally agreed that the spirit which manifested itself in the persecution of sincere men, was an erring and an odious spirit. The age is quite sure that it has outgrown persecution, and will never more return to those childish ebullitions [fits] of passion.

In the days when our Lord was upon the earth, the Jews had a similar conviction of their own superiority to the error of their forefathers, and said, "If we had lived in their days, we would not have done their deeds." But they knew not their own spirit. Our Lord knew it, and told them distinctly that they were capable of all that their fathers had done and much more. We concede, however, that this is not a sanguinary age. It has a standard of morality which condemns everything like a violent outburst of vindictiveness against unresisting men. Its great aim is to show, to itself and to others, that it is so good as not to need regeneration; and were it to sin very much against its own standard, it would lose the comfortable feeling of its own righteousness. In many respects, it is a matter of congratulation that we have come to such a century as this; in other respects, the change works adversely. The gloss thrown over the face of society disarms the Gospel of its power,

185

somewhat; Christians are silent, nine times in ten, when they should speak.

It is true, however, that the strait gate is still strait, the narrow road is still narrow. If any man set out to live godly in Christ Jesus, let him abandon the thought that he will find all favorable to him. First, he will find the world against him—not with stones or instruments of torture, but with weapons that are perhaps more difficult to combat. The world will smile kindly upon him, and congratulate him upon the generous desire he exhibits, to rise above the dead level of an ineffective humanity, and with blandest ratiocinations [reasonings] will seek to make him understand that the saints are mere Pietists, and that the true type of a manly piety is to be found in the outer court of the church.

If he succeeds in vanquishing this temptation, identifies himself with the people of God, and then resolves to go beyond their standard of godliness, he will meet with opposition from them. They will misapprehend him, and he will find it perhaps more difficult to resist these suggestions and insinuations than he formerly did to force his way into the church. And the very fact that he is bound to them by so many and such sacred sympathies, will make it a severer task to penetrate the barriers set up by their limited conceptions of Christian duty.

"All these things will they do unto you for my name's sake." It is because of the erroneous conceptions of Christ, too greatly prevalent in the church, that the godly follower of Christ is spoken against in the church, and it is because the world knows not Christ, that it disfavors Christians. And the fact that men know not Christ shows that they know not God. The advent of Christ established the fact so angrily denied by men, that the world knows not God, and the advent of the sanctified follower of Christ establishes the same fact in the particular age and place in which he makes his appearance.

Let me come to men in the likeness of Christ; if they reject me and my words, then what have we but a verification of the Scripture assertion that men know not God? It is because they know not God, that they

186

need the Gospel, and the fact that they despise and reject him who bears the Gospel message, so far from being a discouragement to the messenger, should only the more deeply impress him with a sense of their need. Did they gladly receive him, there might be room to discredit the statement of the Gospel that they know not God.

It is therefore expedient for the messenger to use the various forms that opposition takes as arguments to awaken his own sensibilities for those whose sad condition is so plainly revealed, and also as arguments at a throne of grace that He Who sent His Gospel should send with it His Holy Spirit.

"They know not Him that sent me"; this is the reason that I was sent; they were without that knowledge that is essential to everlasting life, and I am sent that they may have it.

If the inhabitants of India had from the very beginning of the preaching of the Gospel among them, hailed it with acclamation, and made haste to cast themselves at the feet of Jesus, that would have exposed the Gospel to doubt and suspicion. How could they hail with joy the divine character made known in the Gospel unless they had previously learnt to love it? If already acquainted with God, whence the need of such a plan of salvation for them? No; they were utterly ignorant of the true God, and accordingly they could not but greet with indignation and hate, the revelations of the Gospel. It is important that there should be full proof given of this great fact that they know not God, and hence they are permitted to reject for so many years, the Word of Christ.

When, at length, by the power of the Spirit of God, the knowledge of the true God is made to triumph over those abominable conceptions of deity that occupy their minds, then and thenceforward they will recognize that they have been saved by grace. The truth found in them nothing responsive. With all the force of their nature they fought against it, and Omnipotence alone brought them into the glorious liberty of the children of God.

The Gospel is the power of God, but, like the Lord Jesus Himself, it seems to come in weakness first; and the heathen, for many a long and cruel year, are permitted to mock it, buffet it, crown it with thorns. They say unto it, "Are you come to save, and cannot save yourself? You cannot conquer the very meanest of our innumerable gods. They one and all laugh you to scorn."

The life of the Gospel is a living crucifixion. Christ died upon the cross. It lives upon the cross. But it will yet prove itself "the power of God." It will save those that mock it; it will deliver them from the horrible darkness and grinding captivity in which they are. The knowledge of the true God, of Him Whose Name is love, will shine into their wonder-stricken minds, and the Name of Jesus will awaken their rapturous hosannas.

John 15:22-24. *"If I had not come and spoken unto them, they had not had sin: but now they have no cloak for their sin. He that hateth me, hateth my Father also. If I had not done among them the works which none other man did, they had not had sin: but now have they both seen, and hated both me and my Father."*

"If I had not come and spoken unto them; if I had not done among them the works which none other man did"—in other words, if there had not been such a bright and glorious revelation of the character of God in My life—their sin, especially this all-comprehending sin of hating the Father, would not have been made manifested as it now is. This sin they had before, but it was cloaked. It was disguised to themselves and to others and it pleased them to think that they were doing God service in thousands of things which really proved that they were without God in the world.

The presence of Jesus in the community was like the presence of a great light, revealing undreamt-of chambers of imagery in the very temple. By the teachings of Christ, attested as they were by signs and wonders, the common conception of religion received a great shock. The Pharisees, the elders and the scribes, had hitherto enjoyed a high degree of religious popularity. They were looked upon as the oracles of men in all that related to the worship and service of God. The Scriptures were only known to the mass of men through the glosses [lenses] of these interested [biased] interpreters. Men looked upon them as the impersonation of true piety. No one thought of imputing sin to them.

But a mighty change was witnessed when Christ made His appearance with heavenly credentials and poured the light of day upon the Scriptures, and upon the falsifications of God's Word which had so long passed current. No sooner did He open His mouth to declare that the poor in spirit, the meek, the pure in heart, were blessed, than men began to see with new eyes; the cloak began to be taken away from the long-denied sin of the Pharisees. Those who claimed to be the religious guides and models of the people, took up an attitude of hostility toward Christ; and as it was evident to every unbiased mind—evident even to the consciences of the biased—that the truth of God was expressed in the words and in the ways of Christ, it followed that all who denounced and resisted Him, were the enemies of God.

The intensity of their opposition to Christ indicated the depth of their hatred of the true God. They had formed for themselves an idea of God—formed for themselves a god, let us say. To him they had sworn fealty, and stood ready to transgress every commandment of the true God as an expression of their devotedness. By pride and ambition and avarice and extortion, by devouring widows' houses, and counting all but loss for the honor that comes from man, they had gradually prepared themselves to commit the most heinous of all enormities and put to death the Son of God.

They were determined to give such proof of their hatred of Christ that it would be impossible for men ever to doubt it; and in doing this, they also placed forever beyond the reach of doubt, the fact of their hatred of the Father. "Now they have both seen and hated both me and my Father." "He that hath seen me hath seen the Father"—a truth full of unspeakable blessing to him that sees believingly, lovingly—a truth that places him who sees and rejects in the position of an avowed rebel against the Most High.

The Gospel has come upon the most gracious of all errands; yet we see that it has come to do what men are unwilling to have done, what men would rather die than have done. It has come to take away the cloak from their sins. They have spent many a long year in contriving this cloak. They have employed the best artificers to execute it. The greatest geniuses of the day have spent their strength in giving to mankind, books designed to aid them in the work of cloaking their sins.

Every man is aided in the matter by thousands and tens of thousands and all the marvelous gifts which God is bestowing on society through

190

the instrumentality of man's inventive powers, these, and in fact every success of the age, and the great majority of all the influences that visit us, are combinedly at work to provide the sin of man with a cloak.

It would seem as though the nearer the Gospel came to them, and the more industriously it let fly its arrows upon this cloak, the greater are the efforts by which they seek to maintain it in its integrity. But, as we are ever repeating, it is only by bribing those who are commissioned to reveal the Gospel, only by inducing them to fling their javelins wide of the mark, that men are able to retain this cloak of their own righteousness. Christians know that it is the livery by which the god of this world declares men to be his own—the badge of a frightful captivity, the shroud of perdition, and they are recreant [disloyal] to the eternal interests of their fellow-men when they shrink from wounding them and from making war upon this destructive delusion.

The words of the Lord Jesus Christ, rejected by us, go to the throne of God and tell the recording angel how great our sin is. The question is not so much, "Have I lied? Have I stolen? Have I murdered?" as, "What have I done with the words of Christ? What reception have I given them? How have I been affected by *His* mighty works and mightier sufferings?"

There is but one sin in the world, properly speaking, and that is, the sin of not loving God. The sins that we commonly speak of are but different manifestations of this one sin. They are different in degree, diverse in various respects, diverse in enormity, but the enormity is chiefly to be determined by the measure of the revelation made of the character of God unto us. God becomes manifest in Christ; and lo! this unknown God is found to be a Being of most amazing love, humbling Himself to the meanest of mankind, bearing all things, suffering long, seeking not His own, answering the insults and contradictions of sinners with words and acts of incredible blessing.

Thus does the glorious Being Who upholds all things by the word of His power draw near to you with papers of manumission [emancipation] whereby you may escape the captivity of sin and Satan, the liability to death and hell, with hands pierced in the conflict with him who has the power of death, winning for you a path to life and glory. Now the universe looks on to see how you will receive the words of this Redeemer. It is possible for you to commit a sin of greater magnitude than you conceive of by simply neglecting the words of Christ. You are on your trial whenever you are in the presence of the words of Christ. As you treat those words you show your feelings for God. How fearful the alienation of the heart from God when such a surpassing embodiment of divine love fails to overcome the indifference of the heart!

John 15:25. *"But this cometh to pass, that the word might be fulfilled that is written in their law, They hated me without a cause."*

This word has never wanted a fulfillment. The people of God of every age have been hated without a cause. To declare one's self unequivocally on the Lord's side has always had the effect of bringing an individual into collision with the world. Men are in a state or rebellion against the Most High. They keep such of His commands as they choose to keep, break such as they are disposed to break. They break all in a sense, seeing that it is not out of regard to the authority of God that they keep any. They dislike—all rebels do—the epithet "rebellious," and spurn it from them. Nevertheless, the fact remains— they are conspirators against the majesty of Heaven; and, of course, it is a great sin against them to come out on the Lord's side, and show one's self zealous for the authority of the Lord of hosts.

Their commandment is, "Thou shalt love the world with all thy heart and with all thy soul and with all thy mind, and thou shalt love God only so far as thy duty to the world may permit." The greatest of crimes is that of treason against the world. They pursue with their hatred those who are guilty of it. They never fail to find justificatory causes of their hatred, for they are careful to consult only the authority of their own perverted judgments.

David, however, and other Old Testament saints, knew that there was no just ground for their hatred. Not that these hated ones were sinless. Far from it! They found in themselves much cause of self-loathing. It was not their sins that exposed them to the wrath of men. On the contrary, these sins would have gone far to propitiate the world with them had it not been for their very decided adherence to God, and for the great prominence given by them to the claims of God.

But surely there was never anyone who could use this language with more emphasis than Christ. He had come into the world, clothed with extraordinary power; and whereas He might have used this power to crush His enemies, and violently to trample down all obstacles, He,

193

on the contrary, used it to communicate sight to the blind, hearing to the deaf, health to the sick, motion to the paralyzed, sanity to the possessed. His words subdued the winds and the waves, and sent legions of evil spirits howling to their place.

These same omnipotent words might have sent equal confusion into the ranks of His human adversaries had such been His will. He could have called down lightning from Heaven and anticipated Titus in the work of hurling Jerusalem from her foundations. But how did He employ His power? He went about doing good. He gave heed to every tale of woe, and hastened, with heartfelt sympathy, to communicate the alleviation, the deliverance, that men demanded.

If He indignantly denounced the sins of those who were systematically working out the destruction of the community, it was not until He had many, many times knocked friendlily at their door, and sought to persuade them to receive His words of wisdom and of life. They not only hated Him without a cause, but they hated Him in the presence of ten thousand arguments for love. In every street and in every lane these arguments were to be found—men and women and children who had received from Christ such favors as no other man could have bestowed. The man who saves another from death is in many communities deemed worthy of the highest civic honors. Even on this low ground, what unparalleled claims had Christ on the reverence and gratitude of men!

What has Christ done that men who have grown up from infancy within sight of the Gospel, and who are not content that the designation of Christians should be withheld from them—what has He done that these should show such an unwillingness to hear of Him, to read of Him, to speak of Him? What has He done that there should be such elaborate arrangements made to keep the subject of His acts and sufferings, His glory, His words, His cross, separate from the ordinary channels of thought and speech?

What has He done that men should studiously restrict the liberty to utter Christ's truth to a particular body of men, and this body to particular times and places? Why is it that there should be, as often as men come together, a wall of reserve with reference to this one theme, all others being considered allowable? And why should a violent effort be necessary in order to break down this wall and permit Christ also to appear in the midst? This is aversion; it is not reverence.

What has Christ done that He should be so carefully excluded from the ordinary society of men professedly Christian? One would think that He were the harshest, austerest, bitterest of men, from the studied neglect with which He meets, instead of being, what His Gospel declares Him, ineffably kind, condescending, long-suffering, patient, forgiving, conciliatory, gentle, refined, wise—a physician, a shepherd, a teacher, a brother, an advocate, an ally, a light, a sun, a shield, One Who washes the feet of His disciples and sheds His blood as a propitiation for their sins and ever lives to make intercession for them.

To the question, "What think ye of Christ?" the great majority of even church-going men would reply, "We never think of Him; why should we think of Him? The things that interest us do not interest Him; the things that interest Him do not us." Ah! this is a sad confession to make! Do you expect Christ to change? Do you expect that the angels of Heaven will be brought over to your view of things? Do you calculate that Heaven will be secularized in order that you may feel at home there?

Evidently there is a great gulf between Christ and you. Christ will not throw into the depths of the sea, His treasures of wisdom and knowledge, to live upon your thoughts and be shriveled to your mental and moral dimensions. Christ is in the Word of God. Heaven is in the Word of God. Go to the Word and look upon the only Heaven that exists in the universe of God for redeemed sinners, and see whether you have a nature that will permit you to find happiness in it. Take this Gospel into your heart and let it revolutionize your thoughts and your lives, your speech and your aims, your associations and your imaginations. Without such a revolution you will only be proclaiming, by the Christ-ignoring tenor of your speech and of your life, that you hate Christ without a cause, and that you are dead in trespasses and sins.

195

John 15:26-27. *"But when the Comforter is come, whom I will send unto you from the Father, even the Spirit of truth, which proceedeth from the Father, he shall testify of me: And ye also shall bear witness, because ye have been with me from the beginning."*

The Savior, in His previous reference to the Comforter, had expressed Himself thus: "I will pray the Father, and he shall give you another Comforter, that he may abide with you for ever, even the Spirit of truth." He now says, "I will *send* unto you from the Father." There is a style of language suitable to Jesus as "one with the Father," and another style that accords with the relation in which He stands to us as set forth in the words, "My Father is greater than I."

He that enters the school of Christ enters upon the study of these two glorious relations of Christ—His relation to the believer and His relation to the Father. As first apprehended, these relations, perhaps, may be expressed by two greatly extended cords connecting Christ with God and Christ with man. As the believer advances in the knowledge of Christ he sees these cords contract, sees Christ come nearer and nearer to himself, sees Christ come nearer and nearer to God, and himself brought correspondingly nearer and nearer to God.

In order to reconcile two truths, seemingly opposed, we must master those truths. So long as we stand outside of them, we cannot discover the law of their harmony. Many persons look upon the doctrine of Christ, and see, as they suppose, invincible contradictions in it. They condemn it and pass by on the other side. They have no right to condemn it. There are thousands of truths held by them which would seem to them equally repugnant to each other, were it not that they have mastered them; they have entered into them, and are able to see that they are the complement of each other. There is evidence before you that Jesus has the words of eternal life. Come then, sit at His feet and learn of Him. Drink in with joy the assurance that He is One Who can be touched with the feeling of our infirmities, and accept with equal joy the revelation of His divine power and Godhead.

It imports us to know that through Jesus only, can men entertain the hope of obtaining the gift of the Holy Ghost. Our prayer is a nullity without His prayer. It imports us all to know that after the sacrifice offered by Christ for the sins of men there remains no difficulty on the part of God to be overcome by Him. Therefore He says, "I will pray," and "I will send."

When Jesus was on the earth, it depended on Him whether He would communicate the blessings that men asked of Him. They asked and He gave—always gave. He ascended that He might give a greater gift—greater by all that height to which He ascended. He stopped not at any of the grades set forth by the expression, "Principalities, powers, might, dominion." Not from any such elevation could He give a sufficient gift unto men. Legions of angels would have helped us little. He ascended far above the highest of Heaven's hierarchy. In fact, it was to give Himself to us that He ascended on high, having previously descended to give Himself for us.

Without the Holy Ghost we have no Christ. Christ, with all His infinite resources, with all His love, all His glory, is brought nigh to the individual believer and made a part of his being by the gift of the indwelling Christ.

"The Spirit of truth." The Spirit of God and the truth of God are not to be divorced. Without the Spirit there is no saving truth for us; without the truth there is no Holy Ghost for us. The truth and our own natures are in necessary and violent enmity, without the conciliating Spirit. The truth lives and our own nature lives when the life-giving Spirit comes to us in the Word. Our own spirit is not a divine spirit of truth until permeated by the divine Spirit.

"He shall testify of me." The Spirit testifies of Jesus to the believer, and teaches the believer to testify of Jesus. The Spirit in the believer testifies of Jesus. His presence in the believer is a powerful testimony to the world that Jesus has ascended on high, and that He is the Mediator between God and man—powerful just according to the degree in which the believer yields himself to His influences and makes way for Him in his affection, in his intellect and in his life.

Oh, that we might take these perishing sinners who compass us about in such countless numbers to the very sea of glass before the throne where Jesus sits in glory, and give them just one view of the majesty and grace of Him Whom all the heavenly hosts adore, that they might hasten to believe upon Him and submit themselves to Him!

Well, Jesus has appointed you to something like this very office you so much desire. Be filled with the Spirit, and let the mighty Spirit in you testify to Jesus and convince the multitude around of the glory and unspeakable beauty of Him Whose promises they have so long disdained. Oh, is there none who will resolve to sound the utmost depth of the grace of the Savior, in the endeavor to body forth the evidence of the glory and majesty of Him Who was dead and is alive again? Is there none who will seek to satisfy the aspiration of Jesus expressed in these words? Are not Heaven and earth waiting, groaning, travailing for such a testimony to the crucified and risen Savior as has not yet been given in the Church on earth? To reveal Christ, the believer is in the world and the Spirit is in the world.

"That the world may know that thou hast sent me," said the Savior, looking forward to a time when He should not be personally in the world, and anticipating more glorious results from the operation of the Spirit in believers than had been accomplished by His personal ministry on earth. Am I thus revealing Christ? Does the world learn from my life that Jesus is the Sent of God, the Savior of the world?

The Spirit in me and my spirit, do these bear witness to the condescension, the purity, the love, the unworldliness, the long-suffering, the meekness, the power, the all-sufficiency, the unchangeableness, of the Redeemer? Is every part and parcel of my life made to bear witness to Christ? Are my talents, my tastes, my opportunities, made over to Christ to witness for Him?

The apostles had been with Jesus from the beginning. They knew ten thousand particulars of His life. The materials of thousands of discourses on this ever-blessed subject were stored up in their understandings; yet we see that they remained speechless when the hour came for them to testify of Him. Even the very night in which these words of Christ were spoken, saw them take flight with all their treasury of precious information concerning the Savior. It saw one of them explicitly deny Him, bear witness against Him. It saw one who, even when brought to a sense of his sin, was still incapable of overcoming it, and went out to weep, lest his tears should bear witness against him and for Christ.

Only when the witnessing Spirit came down were they able to testify to Christ. On the day of Pentecost they became witnesses indeed. We, in like manner, have the materials of thousands of discourses concerning Christ in our minds, but our lips are sealed and our lives ineloquent until the Spirit of Pentecost comes upon us, and makes Christ's truth to live in us and shine through our transfigured lives.

Chapter 16

John 16:1-3. *"These things have I spoken unto you, that ye should not be offended. They shall put you out of the synagogues: yea, the time cometh, that whosoever killeth you, will think that he doeth God service. And these things will they do unto you, because they have not known the Father, nor me."*

Christ had spoken to His disciples of the persecution which they would encounter, in order that when the evil day came, they might not be confounded and paralyzed as in the presence of some unexpected event. They had gradually obtained a lofty conception of the power and of the love of Christ. Knowing that He took the profoundest interest in their welfare, what could they expect but that He would so reveal His power in their behalf as to awe their enemies and make them shrink from lifting up a finger against them?

Slowly and with great difficulty, Christ had conquered for Himself, a royal place in their confidence. He had convinced them of His boundless power and His surpassing love. The hour was coming when this confidence should be severely tested, when Providence should seem to say unto them, "Give up your conviction of His power, or give up your conviction of His love." Why should they put us out of the synagogues? Why should they kill us? Though we are weak, is not our Shepherd mighty to save? Will He not acknowledge us before His enemies, and teach them that whosoever touches us, touches the apple of His eye? If He do it not, what are we to think of His power to save, His readiness to befriend?

Think thus, that along with His power and love there is a third—even wisdom—and that these three are one. Were He to acknowledge you in such wise that all men should realize the connection between your weakness and His omnipotence, and feel instinctively that in dealing wrathfully with you they were rushing upon the thick bosses of His buckler, there would be no scope for the development of your faith. You are being trained for great things—for an endless destiny, for the companionship of angels, the celestial service of God. It is needful that your nascent [budding] faculties should be subjected to a suitable discipline.

You must learn by degrees to go invested with the power of God. While your powers are yet immature, while there is still such a large unvanquished remainder of pride, wrath, selfishness, ambition, you cannot be trusted with more than a very little of the power of God. The unestablished mind is immediately carried away by the vainglorious idea of flaunting abroad in a garment of Heaven. In the work of educating us for Heaven, it is meet that the guiding Spirit should thoroughly exercise us in meekness, humility, long-suffering, contrition. As we cease from ourselves, we shall be fitted to have the more public attestations of Heaven.

Or let us say that the power of God is communicated to the believer, not stintedly, but in methods that elude the gross discernment of men. The power of God is not put forth in fire from Heaven to consume your enemies, but in that spirit of patience, humility and self-denial by which you are enabled in a Christ-like manner to confront their rage.

Perhaps, after all, the sublimest exhibition of the power of God was that which was made by Jesus when He was as a lamb led to the slaughter, when He, being reviled, threatened not, and when He continued, amid the taunts of His persecutors, to hang upon the cross. Let us look for power where the world does not dream of looking for it—in the depths of our own sanctified experience, in the patience, meekness and long-suffering by which we endure as seeing Him Who is invisible. This is to put on Christ.

Some would be very glad to put on that power of Christ by which He wrought mighty signs and wonders—that glory which beamed from Him on the Mount of Transfiguration; but they never dream of putting on His humility and long-suffering, His condescension and contentedness, His gentleness and prayerfulness. This is the reason why they make so little progress. The Holy Spirit is holding out to them one part of the apparel of Christ, and they have their eye on a different part.

"These things have I spoken unto you, that ye should not be offended." Though I ascend up on high and clothe Myself, on your behalf, with unlimited power, yet do not suppose that I will bind in chains of awe the faculties of men along the pathway of your life. Be not confounded when you see that men are permitted to molest you and make havoc of you. To you is indeed committed a treasure of treasures, the everlasting Gospel. Think not, however, that this commission will be equivalent to an immunity from all human violence. Enough to know that the Gospel shall live on, however they who bear it may be mowed down by the enemy.

"They shall put you out of the synagogues." The element of special bitterness in the sufferings here predicted is that they were to be inflicted by religious men. The disciples were to encounter the open denunciations of those by whom the religious portion of the community were accustomed to be guided. It were a very small thing to be persecuted by an infidel and licentious rabble; the respectable, the devout, the interpreters of God's ways to man, were to hold them up to public execration as men guilty of teaching heresy and of subverting the institutes of religion.

The persecutors of Christians are often sincere. They believe that they are serving God and promoting the interest of religion. This sincerity is the ground for their more severe condemnation. They have dethroned the true God and put another in His place. Allow men to have a false god, and they will be very faithful to him. "They know not Him that sent me," said Christ, and added, "They have no cloak for their sin." Men take to themselves a false conception of God, love it with all their heart and soul and strength, offer to it sacrifices of the best blood of humanity, and then demand our praise for their sincerity.

The conviction that one is right in doing what is odiously wrong, so far from meriting an apology, demands a more severe condemnation than mere wrong-doing, for it is the consecration of wrong-doing. In order that a man may do evil upon a grand scale, and with comfort to himself, it is convenient that he should obtain a conviction that the thing is good and not evil. He asks at Satan's warehouse for such a conviction, and does not ask in vain.

"And these things will they do unto you, because they have not known the Father nor me." Christians are known by their resemblance to Christ. They that know them not, and persecute them, show that they know not Christ, and write their own condemnation in the irrevocable acts by which they utter their hatred of the true Church. There are many Christs in these days, and every Christ has his church; and every one who comes into the church chooses among these Christs the one that he likes best. Instead of openly persecuting the people of Christ, he joins himself to a body whose Christ is different, and indirectly makes war upon the true Christ by the zeal with which he upholds his fiction of a Savior.

As our views of Christ become rectified, so our views of the Church will undergo a change. We shall find it where once we would not have thought of looking for it. Men that did not know Christ rightly have attempted to write the history of the Church, and they did not even succeed in identifying the Church. They have given us the history of something very different.

John 16:4-6. *"But these things have I told you, that when the time shall come, ye may remember that I told you of them. And these things I said not unto you at the beginning because I was with you. But now I go my way to him that sent me, and none of you asketh me, Whither goest thou? But because I have said these things unto you, sorrow hath filled your heart."*

About to be delivered into the hands of sinners, and to bow for a brief and agonizing season beneath a storm of unexampled sorrow, Jesus occupied Himself rather with the more distant storm of persecution that would burst upon the heads of His disciples. He was the good Shepherd, about to give His life for the sheep, yet in this momentous hour He is chiefly solicitous to provide for His disciples a means of resisting the adversary when he should come against them in a future day. The Savior loved His own unto the end. Let us sit at His feet that we may learn what love is. Let us not think anything enough in the way of devotedness to the welfare of His Church, so long as there remains ought that we can do. If we have the opportunity of making great sacrifices, let us not be content with this, but let us seek to arm weak believers with Christ's truth against a day of unexpected trial.

The Savior teaches us things that are intended for present use, and other things that have reference to a future day of use. We take these up as curiosities, wonder at them, and when we interrogate them as to their deeper significance, they bid us wait for the light of a day to come. So we put them in a chamber of memory, and walk softly before God, knowing that the future has something strange for us.

"These things have I spoken unto you, that ye should not be offended, that, when the time shall come, ye may remember that I told you of them." In Christ the believer gets a glimpse of common things. The Savior makes him sit with Him in the chariot of a white cloud, whence a view of the pilgrim's far-winding path is enjoyed. There seated, the believer, with anointed eye, perceives the adversary and his instruments in a most distant glen; sees the arrangements made to ensnare him, to surprise, overwhelm and destroy him, the instant he shall set foot in that glen, sees the towers built from whence javelins shall be thrown at him, sees a bottomless chasm covered with deceitful twigs and leaves, sees the coverts in which ferocious animals are taught to wait for their opportunity, sees the tree thrown across the path of safety that winds aloft along the mountain side.

In due time the instructed disciple, after many intermediate vicissitudes, finds himself at the entrance of the glen. "He is come; he is come," whisper his foes one to another. They are sure of their prey. But the moment his eye falls upon the scene before him he recognizes it in all its details. "Ah," he says, "this is the dangerous spot on which I looked down from the white cloud." He knows at once how to proceed. To the astonishment and confusion of his enemies, he pursues the path of safety and looks triumphantly down upon their vain machinery.

Ah, Lord! Let me not refuse to come up and sit with You in that chariot of Yours. You will show me dreamlike things, as some might deem them, but not dreamlike; for in a future hour I must stand face to face with them. I must conquer these future enemies now, in a most important sense, for their power is in their unsuspectedness. He is sure to fall before them who comes upon them unprepared. They can only be defeated by being foreknown.

O my soul, beware how you slight any invitation of the Savior. You cannot say what mighty things are at stake when the Spirit is whispering to you, "Come, the Master calls you." To be spiritually minded is to have it inwrought in our nature, as a law inviolable, to give heed to every suggestion of the Spirit, every call of Christ.

"The Master calls you." If the blind man of Jericho had not obeyed that summons, he would have died in his blindness, perhaps in his sins. It was only a little instant, but how much was depending on it! John, James and Peter were once invited to accompany Christ, they knew not well whither or wherefore. They soon found themselves on what they thought a mountain top, a bleak place, with night and comfortlessness about them. They disposed themselves to sleep; but, lo! they suddenly found that the place lighted up with more than the glory of seven suns, saw the Son of man brought near to the Ancient of Days, to receive dominion and glory and a kingdom, that all people, nations and languages should serve Him. They stood in the presence of a magnificent future toward which we are hastening.

"These things I said not unto you at the beginning, because I was with you." He had intimated them, but had not insisted much upon them. The important thing for them was to know Christ, and be united to Him by an unyielding faith. It is the revelation of Jesus to the soul that prepares it to encounter earthly loss and opposition. The pearl of great price must be seen, and then it becomes an easy matter to part with all that one has in lieu of it.

"But now I go my way to him that sent me, and none of you asketh me, Whither goest thou? But because I have said these things unto you, sorrow hath filled your heart." Having accomplished My embassy, and being about to return, I am careful to notify you of the days of trial which you will have to encounter after My departure. The announcement of My departure and the intimation of sufferings to be undergone by you fill you with sorrow.

But why do you not ask Me whither I am going? Is it not just possible that there may be something in the reply to such a question that will dissipate your sorrow and abundantly strengthen you for the scenes that are before you? Is it not possible that My departure may be the complement of that love which began to be expressed in My advent? Would you not naturally gather, from all that you have seen of Me, that nothing less would ever induce Me to depart from you than a full conviction that I could serve you better by going to My Father than by remaining longer on the earth?

Consider, therefore, whither I am going. You need a friend at the throne of God, ever living, to intercede for you. Will it not be a blessed discovery when you grasp the wonderful fact that the omnipotent One in Whom you live and move and have your being is, by the power of My sacrifice, so reconciled to you and so drawn to you that you may count upon the same fervent friendliness of feeling in Him toward you as you have been accustomed to recognize in Me? If I depart, it is that I may bear you and all your interests with Me to the throne of the Ever-blessed. Instead of being orphans you shall be heirs—heirs of God, joint heirs with Me.

John 16:7. *"Nevertheless, I tell you the truth: It is expedient for you that I go away: for if I go not away, the Comforter will not come unto you; but if I depart, I will send him unto you."*

Strange and scarcely credible though the announcement may appear to you, I nevertheless tell you but the simple truth when I say that it will be for your advantage that I ascend unto the Father and send to you the Holy Ghost, the Comforter, to be your perpetual guide. And when I say that it will be for your advantage, I do not mean that the Holy Spirit is greater than I am, or that He will prove a truer Friend to you. In fact, the special office of the Spirit will be to bring you and Myself into a more intimate and a more blessed union than has yet been revealed to your consciousness.

Though you have journeyed with Me during these latter years of My earthly pilgrimage, yet there is no use in disguising the fact that a moral chasm yawns between us. You yourselves must often have felt the deepest pain in reflecting upon the very feeble amount of influence exerted upon you by One Who is manifestly God in the likeness of men. You have mourned that the words and acts of One Who was proclaimed the only-begotten of the Father, Who was transfigured before you, Who was served by angels, Who spoke unto the winds and waves and they obeyed Him—you have mourned that the discourse and the acts of such a One should have wrought so feebly in your hearts.

The desire for sanctification exists in you, but the new and elevated conception of holiness which has been introduced into your minds only makes you the more sensible of your great moral deficiencies. If miracles could have given you the victory over your sins, you would now be the holiest of men. Since that hour when one of you fell at My feet, exclaiming, "Depart from me, for I am a sinful man," how many glorious displays of My power have you witnessed! Yet are you still sadly aware that pride, ambition, worldliness, have authority over you.

Surely you must have admitted to yourselves that if three and a half years of such stupendous exhibitions of power have left you the unsanctified men you are, ten years of such displays would not give you the victory over your evil nature. For three and a half years you have listened to a greater than Solomon—to One Who spoke as never man spoke, to the Wisdom of God. You have enjoyed such opportunities as never before were enjoyed by mortal man to know the mind of God concerning the way in which He would be served, and what is the result? You yourselves are constrained to admit that the result is very unsatisfactory.

Ah, if all that man needed were to have a teacher, were to have lessons of divine wisdom set before him in the most intelligible and most impressive forms, then would you now be incomparably the holiest of men, proof against all temptation, superior to all earthly influences. But what is the fact? Was it not necessary that I should this very evening begin the work of instruction over again, as it were, by washing your feet? Have you not this very evening been disputing among yourselves who shall be greatest? Are you not this very night to make even the unprofessing world astonished by deserting Me in My hour of trial?

Why do I now dwell upon these things? Simply that you may be assisted to recognize that My life on earth, however marvelous and glorious as part of the divine system by which God is bringing you to Himself, is yet of itself unable to effect your spiritual redemption. It is one thing that the image of God should have been placed before you; it is a very different thing that you should be changed into that image.

Man foolishly asserts that he only needs to know the true, the good, the beautiful, to be himself the embodiment of truth and goodness and beauty. Heaven has come down to earth; the very King of Heaven has tabernacled among men. He Whom Isaiah saw in the temple, high and lifted up, adored by seraphim, has come down from His throne, dismissed the seraphim to Heaven and dwelt with the people of Isaiah year after year, yet it is not seen that the men so amazingly distinguished have been rendered seraphic in holiness and love. Something else, then, is necessary that men may not only be made acquainted with the image of God, but changed into the same.

Not only have the words which I have uttered in your hearing during these years been unfruitful in your minds; you have not even remembered them. Thousands of words of infinite account in the sublime work of bringing a lost world to God—words destined to convey life to men of innumerable tongues and tribes now enslaved to heathenism—have been uttered in your hearing, and have been forgotten by you. They have been given to you that you might give them to mankind, and that by means of them myriads of souls might be plucked as brands from the burning, and yet these words have passed from your memory. What you cannot recover from the depths of your dark minds the Holy Spirit can.

It is expedient for you, therefore, that I depart and that He come unto you. Then will you hear again the words already heard, and they will be brought home to you with a power that you dream not of. He will show you My acts with such richness of interpretation that you will stand awestruck in presence of the works which made but a feeble impression on you when viewed merely through the medium of your senses and your native powers.

But not only must you be sensible that you have little remembered, little learned, little obeyed, of all that I have told you and shown you; you must be keenly cognizant of the fact that your influence as My servants and the expounders of My Gospel is all but nothing. In presence of a perverse and rebellious race your hearts sink within you, and you ask yourselves, "How shall we ever be able to bring men over to our views of Christ?" You feel your need of some unknown power by which the minds of men may be rendered obedient to the truth. You find yourselves utterly at a loss to communicate your deepest convictions.

You are ready to ask, "Is there not something beyond miracles, even?—something beyond the power of a holy life? Is there not in the resources of God some means of reaching the hearts of men, and subduing that hostility by which they are hindered from receiving the testimony of a holy life and of a blessed Gospel?" There is. I die that you may have life, and that you may have it more abundantly. I ascend on high that the Comforter may come unto you. Then shall you be strengthened with a strength of which you have hitherto had no consciousness. Rivers of living water—even of the water of life—shall flow forth from you. Then the wilderness shall be glad, the desert shall rejoice and blossom as the rose.

John 16:8. *"And when he is come, he will reprove the world of sin, and of righteousness, and of judgment."*

"When he!" "He," in the original, is emphatic. It might be rendered "that One." He it is Who, coming, will convince mankind of sin. His very advent will revolutionize their ideas of sin, being a testimony from Heaven more striking than that of the voice from Heaven at the baptism of Jesus to the fact that Jesus the crucified is none other than Christ the glorified. By the simple fact that the world has placed itself in opposition to Jesus' testimony to Jesus will be testimony against the world. Observe that the promise of the Spirit was unto the disciples, "I will send him unto you"; and the change here intimated as to be wrought in the sentiments of men generally, was to be in consequence of the descent of the Spirit of God upon the disciples.

The Gospel is preached to convince men of sin, of righteousness and of judgment. The disciples of Christ are in the world that they may make known the sin of men, the judgment of God and the way of escaping that judgment by means of the righteousness of Christ. But here we are told that the work of introducing the new convictions on these subjects into the minds of men is to be accomplished by the Spirit of God. Accordingly, the apostles speak of themselves as having preached the Gospel with the Holy Ghost sent down from Heaven.

What is here promised, then, is such an outpouring of the Spirit of God as shall not only reveal itself in the consciousness of the disciples, but substantiate itself as an undeniable and wonderful fact to the apprehensions of the onlooking world. And such was the advent of the Spirit on the day of Pentecost. "He hath shed forth this which ye now see and hear," said Peter to the multitude. That which they saw and heard did what all the miracles, the incomparable words, the irreproachable life of Jesus, had failed to do.

Let us say that these miracles began now to be seen, those divine words began now to be heard, for the first time. By the outpouring of the Holy Spirit upon the disciples, the people of Jerusalem began to look upward and see Jesus at the right hand of the majesty on high. They saw their own sin, heinous beyond all conception, saw the righteousness of Him Whom they had put to death, the Prince of life—saw it to be such a righteousness that in comparison the entire race of man stood forth appareled in darkest iniquity. They saw the judgment of God, inevitable and dire, against all who should be found in opposition to Christ. It was as though they had been taken up into Heaven, and had seen the judgment-seat, the books opened and their own deeds manifested in the unerring light of that tremendous scene. Sublime arrangements of Him Whose wisdom is unsearchable!

Are the people of God at all awake to all that is implied in the promise of the Spirit? Is it enough that they languidly recognize their obligation to make known the Gospel to their fellow-men, and take various steps to have it preached? Is not the great thing wanted this—that the Spirit of God should be so poured out upon Christ's people that men should be made aware of His presence with them, and of the presence of Christ at the right hand of God, so poured out that there should be a coming together, in some sense, of the blessed God and of that world which has separated itself from Him, that the powers of the world to come should take hold upon men and constrain them to cry out, "Men and brethren, what must we do?"

The Greek is wonderfully felicitous in that it does not represent the Spirit of God as coming once for all, but as persistently coming. He it is Who, coming, shall convince. He comes as the rain from Heaven, that must still come and come again, as the wind, that must still blow and blow again. We are not to look back for our Pentecost. The Pentecost of the Acts is simply given to make the Church of Christ acquainted with the privileges belonging to this dispensation. It is only the first step in a ladder of Pentecosts by which the world and the kingdom of Christ are to be brought together. It is the specimen to accompany the promise, that we may be stirred up to plead the promise with the greatest fervency.

The Spirit of God inundates the minds of men with truths that had previously no entrance to them. Now, it occurs to us that an observation of no little importance may here be made. Truths which the Holy Ghost has taught us may be retained in the mind by the mere natural power of memory. Are we not in danger of deceiving ourselves in this way as to the measure of spiritual influence enjoyed by us? We might have as scanty a measure of the Spirit's influence as the disciples had in the days preceding the death of Christ, and yet be immensely in advance of them in respect to the amount of our knowledge of the way of life.

Is it not to be feared that, in those portions of the Church which have not yet been visited by a true revival, Christians are to be compared with the first disciples, not as they were on the day of Pentecost, but as they were previously—compared, we mean, as regards the actual amount of divine influence enjoyed by them? Because they have the truth, they imagine they have the Spirit of truth. Perhaps the word of Christ to them is, "Tarry ye in Jerusalem until endued with power from on high."

We are baffled, bewildered, confounded, by our utter unfitness to convince men of sin, of righteousness and of the judgment to come. Is it not that we fail to realize how absolute is our need of the mighty and manifest advent of the Spirit? It is possible for Christ so to cause the Holy Spirit to be seen descending upon us that the world around shall discover, by this fact alone, the Heavens opened and the Son of God standing at the right hand of God.

Oh, it were unpardonable if, in a day when God is doing so much to inspire us with lofty conceptions of the power of the Holy Spirit, we should still refuse to apprehend the glorious illimitableness of this promise. Consider it. We are to look at the work here assigned to the Holy Spirit, in order that we may entertain a just view of His power.

Look abroad upon the earth, and see the nations, tribes and tongues refusing to be convinced by all that God in His providence has taught them during thousands of years, by all that missionaries are teaching them at this eleventh hour, of sin, of righteousness and of judgment. Form an estimate of the wickedness which envelops the earth like a dense and deadly atmosphere, scarce suffering any of the rays of the Sun of righteousness to penetrate it. Then consider that the Spirit of God, for Whose effusion we are taught to pray, is pledged to rain conviction upon the world, and anticipate for a most sublime and blessed end the final judgment, by leading men to look to the righteousness of Christ, the desire of all nations.

John 16:9-11. *"Of sin, because they believe not on me; Of righteousness, because I go to my Father, and ye see me no more; Of judgment, because the prince of this world is judged."*

The sin of not believing on Christ is to be estimated by the character of Christ; the glory renounced by Him; His labors for the good of man; the brightness of the evidence that accompanied Him; the things that He suffered; the reason for which He suffered; His present exaltation; the glory of His mediatorial reign; His long-suffering toward the unbeliever; the disastrous influence of unbelief; the unspeakable blessing called down upon the world by faith.

Rightly ponder any of these considerations, and the sin of unbelief will be seen to be infinite.

And yet there is no sin that so lightly burdens the consciences of men as the sin of not having believed in Christ. Men condemn themselves bitterly for other sins—for a lie, for instance, into which they may have been surprised; and yet there is not in their heart a whisper of self-reproach for having made Christ a liar. This is that one sin which gives all other sins a perpetuity of damning power. If you owed ten thousand talents and had naught to pay, would you stand quarreling about some item of three or thirteen talents, and refuse to hear the voice of a third party offering to pay the whole debt? If you were condemned to prison for myriads of years, would you spend your strength in contesting some item of six months, when there stood by you a Deliverer offering you eternal life?

And do you not see that the sin of unbelief is altogether a peculiar sin? It is this, and this alone, that shuts the gate of the kingdom of Heaven against you. This it is that cancels all the gracious words contained in the Scriptures, leaving the Bible a mere book of wrath. Unbelief seizes the Lord Jesus as He is about to ascend from the Mount of Olives, and compels Him to give you back the sins which He bore for you on Calvary.

The terrible thing about this sin is that its life is a life of slumber. It makes no noise in the heart. It has no visible shape. An angry word that falls from your lips has a reverberation in the depth of your heart,

213

but unbelief is simply a state, and does not ordinarily reveal itself by any overt symptom. It is the atmosphere in which you move; and as you never moved in any other, it does not shock you. But it is the sin of sins, and until you learn to hate it above all sins there is little hope of your deliverance from sin. The true way of showing your hatred against all sins, not only yours, but those of all men, is to hate this sin, and by the grace of God to have nothing more to do with it. The way to war with all other sins is to war with unbelief, for the life of every sin is hid in unbelief, and if you slay this last you slay all.

The office of the Holy Ghost is to teach us this. He teaches us the sin of not believing in Christ by showing us the infinite righteousness and worthiness of Him Who died upon the cross and ascended on high to the right hand of the Father, there to exercise all power in Heaven and in earth. The reason why we see not Christ is that we have rejected and crucified Him, and the Father has exalted Him, giving Him a Name above every name. The Spirit of God poured upon the disciples is God's demonstration to the world of the righteousness of His Son. Every word uttered by Jesus, every act performed by Him, receives thus the attestation of God. The Holy Spirit convinces us of the sin of unbelief, by teaching us to recognize righteousness in Christ, not in ourselves.

The great quarrel between the unbeliever and Christ is on this ground: the unbeliever says that he is righteous and denies that Christ is. Unbelief in Christ is an affirmation of one's own righteousness. The unbeliever claims to be his own savior and his own intercessor. The affirmations of Christ and those of the unbeliever are utterly contrary the one to the other.

"No man cometh unto the Father but by me," says Christ. "False," says the unbeliever. "Will God reject His own children?" "I am the true Vine," says Christ; "if a man abide not in me he is cast forth and is withered." "Not at all," says the unbeliever; "God's mercy is over all His works." "Turn ye, turn ye, why will ye die?" "We will not turn, and we shall not die." "If ye believe not that I am he, ye shall die in your sins." "Though we believe not, yet we shall not die, for we have goodnesses that will buoy us up in the sea of demerit." "He that heareth my words and doeth them, is like a man that built his house upon a rock." "Nay, without being governed by Thy words, I am safe."

The great question is, "Shall the sinner's pretensions be sustained, or shall the assertions of Christ be ratified?"

This question is answered by the outpouring of the Spirit of God. He makes known the righteousness of Christ, and the fact of His righteousness overwhelms, with the deep confusion of a manifested and gigantic unrighteousness, the miserable sinner who so long rejected the Savior.

"The Prince of this world cometh and hath nothing in me," said Jesus, when the time drew near for His arrest and condemnation. He looked upon the rulers of the Jews and the Gentile governor, with their soldiers and servants and the populace swayed by them, as simply the agency by which the god of this world expressed his wrath against the Holy One Who had invaded his dominions. But by His resurrection and by the baptism of the Holy Spirit given His disciples, He wrote, as it were, upon the walls of the palace of the prince of this world, "Mene, Mene." Men saw that the prince of this world, who had ventured to sit in judgment upon the Son of God, was now himself arraigned in judgment and condemned. And as the same Spirit Who bore testimony to a risen Savior bore testimony also to the future advent of that Savior in glory as the Judge of all, men became cognizant of the absolute ruin destined to overtake the earthly kingdom of the prince of the power of the air.

Oh, the infinite grace of the loving Spirit, Who comes to the heart of the sinner, there to set up by anticipation the great white throne and exhibit the doom that is to go forth against all that belongs to that kingdom of darkness! In these days of skepticism and of an accommodated Bible, what thanks can we render to the God of all grace that He is pleased to pour out His Spirit in such a way on Christendom as to give authority to the awful truths of the final judgment, and thus, by convincing men of the inevitable day of wrath, of the triumphant righteousness of Christ, of that all-comprehending sin of unbelief, to dispose them to look unto the crucified One Whose blood cleanseth from all sin?

John 16:12-13. *"I have yet many things to say unto you, but ye cannot bear them now. Howbeit, when he, the Spirit of truth, is come, he will guide you into all truth."*

A seemingly different statement, "All things that I have heard of my Father I have made known unto you" (John 15:15), is explained by its context, "I call you not servants, for the servant knoweth not what his Lord doeth." He was not hindered by any reserve from communicating divine truth to them. There was an entire readiness on His part to unfold to them the treasures of wisdom and knowledge that were in Him. He treated them as friends, and desired nothing more than that they should continue to stand upon the most confidential footing with Him.

From the passage now to be noticed it appears that there was a hindrance to the larger and freer communication of His treasures of thought to them, and that this hindrance was in them, not in Him. They could not bear it. They were not in a position to profit by it. The avenue of their minds was blocked up by many undisposed-of and unheeded treasures. They had not mastered the things already revealed. A great many important, nay, sublime communications, made with utmost impressiveness and earnestness, were still uncomprehended by them. It was absolutely necessary that they should grapple with these things, and assimilate them to their moral constitution, and put on the strength they were commissioned to bestow, before they could profit by the remaining instructions of their Master.

How many there are to whom this language may be applied! A mass of precious truth is lying before their door unused, and they are clamorous with Christ to give them something better. They wonder that soul-refreshing views of Christ should be withheld from them, while they have just touched and forgotten many words laden with a mint of wealth. Many are asking for increase of faith, and expecting it, if at all, in some surprising and supernatural way, whereas the most faith augmenting promises and indications of the power of which they have had some experience, are treated as exhausted, empty husks.

It may be that Christ has many precious things to say to us, and cannot say them because we cannot bear them. We are waiting for Him, as though the delay were on the part of the Master, but He is waiting for His supine and foolish scholars to return to the glorious things He has revealed to them, and see how slight a taste they have of the celestial truth showered upon their path from trees of paradise. How treacherous a part we are acting toward ourselves if we reject what Christ would gladly bestow, by neglecting to avail ourselves of the means of sanctification long since brought to our notice! Let us understand that in appropriating a blessing we do something more than enrich our minds with that blessing: we make way for another and higher to follow.

The reason why some Christians cannot bear certain doctrines of Scripture is because they neglect other doctrines that naturally come before them and open the door for them. They should go deeper into the things that Christ has already set before them, and let these have larger sway over them, and they will then be strengthened to bear what now seems so onerous.

One that is strictly guided by the Spirit applies himself to just the lessons that the Spirit of God brings before him. We cannot dictate to the Spirit of God what things He shall teach us and what not. He will perhaps bring before us something that was supposed we had long ago completely conned and mastered, but we shall find it good to sit down to it with all the freshness and zest of a first attack. Some unnoticed diamond, richer than all we had yet taken out of the casket, will be detected by us, and will flash light along a multitude of consecutive truths.

"Howbeit, when he, the Spirit of truth, is come, he will guide you into all truth." The Savior seeks to give His disciples a most exalted conception of the dispensation of the Spirit to be introduced by His ascension on high. Christ had many things to say to them; the hour had come when He was about to depart out of the world; were these precious untold things to depart with Him and be lost to the Church for ever? Far from it! The Spirit of truth should come and guide the

217

disciples into all truth. The Spirit of truth would rapidly demolish in their minds the lumbering and elaborate framework of old opinions and hereditary misconceptions which, in the place where they now stood, could not possibly be overthrown without bringing in a chaos of religious ideas.

Christ was the truth; and none but the Spirit of truth could guide them into anything like a worthy apprehension of His character and work, His sufferings, His death, His will, His help. He teaches His disciples to look forward to the advent of the Spirit as to the moment of deliverance from a humiliating bondage. He promises them the highest, noblest form of liberty—the liberty of moving unimpeded through the domain of truth.

Guidance is essential to this liberty. He that sits down to read the Word of God, unconcerned about the guidance of the Spirit, and exulting in the delusive sense of liberty, will be none the less guided by a spirit, namely, by his own erring, undisciplined and biased spirit—a spirit much more at home in falsehood than in truth. Guided by this spirit, he can never know true freedom. Where the Spirit of the Lord is, there is liberty, there alone.

We put on freedom just in the measure that we bring to the study of the Word of God the sense of our absolute dependence upon the Spirit of God to guide us into the truth. Without His guidance, it will prove a mere labyrinth to us. He that gave the truth gave the Spirit of truth. Christ referred His disciples to the influences of the Spirit as affording the only means of really availing themselves of the words He had spoken, the truth He had exhibited. To suppose that the truth is enough, the guidance of the Spirit unnecessary, is to say that Christ knew not the need of man. It is a virtual dismissal of Him Whom you profess to call your Physician.

"All truth." "We have an unction from the holy One, and know all things." There is nothing in this language that speaks of a limit to religious belief, a gate over which is written, "Thus far you may come, and no farther." Without the guidance of the Holy Spirit, the unction of the

218

holy One, we find ourselves in the presence of mere dead words, and we rush in every direction against the barriers of thought. Christ is the image of the invisible God, when brought before us by the Spirit of truth; and we are changed into that image. The Spirit of God is omnipotent with respect to minds like ours and circumstances like ours. He is able to make God known unto us.

We cannot know all that God is—we cannot know all that any creature is. We can, in fact, know God better than we can know any creature, for there are elements of uncertainty in creature character that are not present with the ever-blessed Creator of all. We know in Whom we have believed, and we show that we know Him by earnestly pressing forward after further and more particular knowledge, and thus will we do, if God permit, to all eternity. Those that we know most we delight most to know; we seek their society, and note their ways and words with an avidity that nothing else awakens.

John 16:13. *"He shall not speak of himself; but whatsoever he shall hear, that shall he speak: and he will show you things to come."*

We learn from the Gospel of John that Jesus frequently sought to impress upon His disciples that He spoke not of Himself: "He shall know whether I speak of myself." "I am not come of myself." "I do nothing of myself." "I have not spoken of myself." "The words that I speak, I speak not of myself." He was found in fashion as a man. He came in the likeness of sinful flesh. He had to work out for Himself, by the exhibition of His holy and superior nature, a position far elevated above that of a mere man. At the same time, He was to be recognized as the legate of God, commissioned and inspired not only with regard to all His works, but with regard to His every word; so that God should be manifest in Him, and that there should be nothing in Him which did not manifest God.

And as it was of vital importance to the success of Christ's mission that His works and words should be received as works and words revealing the mind of God, and that the Father should be seen in Him, so it was necessary that the Holy Spirit should be understood as uttering the mind of the Father and of the Son, Who is one in Him. He shall not speak of Himself; He shall not speak independently. He will be simply a more perfect medium of communication between you and Me. What I have left unsaid, because ye cannot bear it now, I will unfold to you by the agency of the Holy Spirit. Language could not be more express as to the great and blessed truth that, under the dispensation of the Spirit, Jesus comes nearer to His people, and makes more intimate and enriching communications to them, than was possible in the days when He dwelt upon the earth.

"He will show you things to come." This He did by guiding the disciples into all that truth concerning future things which had been so copiously given through the ancient prophets, and concerning which they and all others had such defective, such erroneous views. Under this dispensation, the people of God are taught to grasp the true idea concerning the future of Messiah's kingdom. After the outpouring of the Pentecostal Spirit, the apostles were able to unfold the spiritual sense of the prophecies which had been so wrongly and mischievously interpreted by the Jews. A multitude of the promises and predictions of the Old Testament are brought forward in the New, with inspired interpretations, so that we may possess the true clue to future things.

Ah, if in all our studies of the prophecies we had ever kept in mind that it is the province of the Spirit of God to show us things to come, and that only He Who is under the guidance of the Spirit of truth is under the guidance of the Spirit of prophecy and the Spirit of interpretation! He does not begin by showing us things to come, except so far as they bear specially upon our own present duty. He may show us the coming terrors of the Lord, or the future blessedness of the saints, to strengthen us for the fight of faith. His teaching will relate pre-eminently to our obligations, and to the claims of Christ upon us, and to the excellency of the Gospel. According to the earnestness with which we follow Him through these instructions will be the freedom and clearness of His communications concerning the things of the future.

The proper understanding of the present, our present, is the only stand-point from which we can look out rightly upon the future. In vain, however, we ask the Spirit of God to give us an insight into the scenes of days unborn if we give not heed to the indications of His will in our daily and hourly walk. Other things being equal, the man who has enjoyed the richest and fullest experience of the operations of the Spirit in his own heart will be most competent to interpret the prophecies to his fellow-men. These prophecies were originally given by the medium of holy men of old, the holiest of their generation, who spake as they were moved by the Holy Ghost. The key to them will be placed by the same Spirit in the hands of him who yields himself heartily, fearlessly and unflinchingly to the guidance of the Spirit.

"He shall not speak of himself." Neither will he that is born of the Spirit speak of himself. As the Spirit of God honors Christ by seeking to give exhibition to the wishes, aims and feelings of Christ, so the believer should know himself but as a medium for the manifestation of the mind of Christ. Can it be said of us—yet it ought to be—that we speak not of ourselves, not independently, not aside from Christ, and that for us to live is to reveal, not ourselves, but Him?

John 16:14-15. *"He shall glorify me: for he shall receive of mine, and shall show it unto you. All things that the Father hath are mine: therefore said I, that he shall take of mine, and shall show it unto you."*

The Holy Spirit glorifies Christ by revealing His glory to His disciples upon the earth. Glory in the realms of glory, Christ hath never wanted. The soul of every believer is a kingdom where the Redeemer is seen ascending the steps of the palace so long usurped and degraded, penetrating in more or less rapid succession to its chambers, and in due time mounting, in undisputed authority, its throne.

The soul is the chaos of a universe, and the work of Christ is to recreate this shattered and blasted immensity, and compel everything to circulate in harmony around the central sun. He will create in every believer's heart a heaven, and to all eternity reign there a sovereign Redeemer. Round about the throne were many thrones, and all were for the glory of Christ. "I dwell in the high and holy place, with him also that is of a contrite and humble spirit." Much more they which receive abundance of grace and of the gift of righteousness shall reign in life by One, Jesus Christ. The Father glorified Christ by raising Him from the dead and from the earth, exalting Him above principalities and powers, and placing Him at His own right hand. The Holy Spirit glorifies Christ by making Him known as glorious to the believer.

If we profess to have our eye fixed upon the glory of Christ as upon a luminary which is destined to make glad the face of universal nature, let us show that we are under the influence of faith and not of imagination, by ardently laboring that the great aim of the Spirit of God in our hearts may be speedily accomplished. Let us fall in with this blessed project of the Spirit, and command all the faculties of our nature to yield to His control, that Christ may be glorified in us.

It is as the Spirit of truth that the Holy Spirit glorifies Christ. That which particularly exhibits the omnipotence of the Spirit and the sublime nature of His operations is the fact that in the *written Word*, with which we are familiar, He is able to reveal unto us what eye has not seen, nor ear heard, nor heart conceived. Whether it was in the body or by the

Spirit that Paul was caught up into Heaven and heard unutterable things, I cannot tell, but it is evident that Paul attached no extraordinary value to this vision, while he constantly magnifies the work of the Spirit in making Christ known unto him by the Word. It is with reference to this influence of the Spirit of truth that he says, "We have our conversation in Heaven, where Christ is": "God hath blessed us with all spiritual blessings in heavenly places in Christ"; "He hath made us sit together in heavenly places in Christ Jesus."

The god of this world has blinded the minds of them that believe not, lest the light of the glorious Gospel of Christ, Who is the image of God, should shine unto them. It is therefore by the removal of unbelief that the Holy Spirit makes it possible for the glory of Christ to be poured in upon the mind.

The Holy Ghost is Christ's advocate in the heart, pleading His cause, urging His claims, vindicating Him from the unworthy representations made by that which is earthly in our nature, rebuking the noisy advocate of the world, bringing to memory the sufferings of Christ and the resultant glory, and showing the vanity of those things whose paltry attractions still threaten to shake the soul from its steadfastness. In order that we may be taught to see Christ glorious, it is necessary that the Spirit of God should liberate us from all those false ideas of glory which so universally obtain among men. If we are intent upon our own glory and pine inwardly for the admiration of men, if we desire to have our faults ignored and our virtues magnified by men, if we are cultivating a spirit of self-complacency, it is impossible that we should advance in the knowledge of the glory of Christ. We must decrease that He may increase.

Just here is the great difficulty with many. It is to be feared that there are very few who are not cutting themselves off from important discoveries of Christ's glory by the habit of secret self-laudation, and by a desire for the plauditory regards of men. There is not anything more utterly opposed to the mind of the Spirit. While these self-complacent thoughts prevail, the Spirit of God is vanquished. "The flesh lusteth against the Spirit and the Spirit against the flesh; and these are contrary the one to the other." It is intended of God that no flesh should glory in His presence. If we still connect the idea of glory with anything that belongs to our miserable natures, it is clear that our ideas of glory are flagrantly erroneous. The mission of the Spirit is to correct this error, and cause us to discover all glory in Christ, and count all things but loss for the excellency of the knowledge of Him Who gave Himself for us.

"All things that the Father hath are mine; therefore said I, that he shall take of mine and shall show it unto you." The believer is taught to recognize the Father in Christ and Christ in the Father. The glory of Christ is the glory of the Father, and the glory of the Father is that of Christ. But the Father is not glorified if the Son be not glorified, for where there is depreciation of Christ there is not the true knowledge of God, and there the Spirit of God is not. The language here used by the Savior is that of One Who is conscious that in Him dwells all the fullness of the Godhead bodily. When the believer has been brought a good way into the paradise of the Gospel, everything in nature will speak to him of Christ, even of Him Who was in Christ reconciling the world unto Himself. "All things were made by him and for him." And all things are ours because they are Christ's and because we are Christ's.

The things shown to us are not things in which we are slightly interested, but things in which we are intensely interested. All that tremendous interval, by which the consciousness of sin naturally separates us from the blessed Godhead, is annihilated by the Spirit's exhibition of the love of God in Christ Jesus. The Spirit of God alone knows how to introduce us to the holiness and justice and truth of God. He solves this perilous problem by taking us to Gethsemane, and disclosing to us there the Son of God, the Man of sorrows, drinking the cup that we should have drunk through eternity, and purchasing for us a perpetual interest in the love of Him Whose Name is Love.

John 16:16-19. *"A little while, and ye shall not see me: and again, a little while, and ye shall see me, because I go to the Father. Then said some of his disciples among themselves, What is this that he saith unto us, A little while, and ye shall not see me: and again, A little while, and ye shall see me: and, Because I go to the Father? They said therefore, What is this that he saith, A little while? we cannot tell what he saith. Now Jesus knew that they were desirous to ask him, and said unto them, Do ye inquire among yourselves of that I said, A little while, and ye shall not see me: and again, a little while, and ye shall see me?"*

Christ had previously said, "Yet a little while and the world seeth me no more; but ye see me." Though He should disappear from the world's view, yet He would be manifest unto His disciples. Here another fact is stated, namely, that there was to be an interruption in their perception of His presence. There was to be a period the like of which had never been seen and should never be seen—a period when the believer was without his Christ, when Christ was buried and with Him all the promises by which we have access to the Father. Darkness then brooded over the face of the Church. The Son of God, in taking unto Him the sin of the world, had also taken unto Him all its most sacred interests. All these went down with Him into the night of the grave; and we may conceive of the guardian angels of humanity standing on the edge of this gulf, trembling, wondering if from such a profound abyss there should be a resurrection of those precious interests, a return of the self-sacrificing One.

The disciples are assured that though that dark and critical hour should shortly come, yet it would not be of long duration: "Again a little while and ye shall see me." For the elect's sake that time was shortened. It might have been three full days and nights, but every hour told terribly upon the faith and hope of the apostles and of the multitude of others— disciples and inquirers—"who trusted that it had been He which should have redeemed Israel"; and therefore the Lord diminished the interval to the narrowest possible limits consistent with the Jewish definition of the period of time mentioned, reducing it, in fact, to about thirty-six hours.

In chapter 14:16 we have the words of Christ, "I go away and come again unto you; if ye loved me ye would rejoice because I said, I go unto the Father." In this and in the verse under consideration, the idea does not seem to be that He would go to the Father, and then, leaving the Father, would come again unto them. They were to console themselves in the dark interval of His absence with the reflection that, after a brief interval, He would appear to them again. At the same time the language used finds its solution only in the revelation of Christ made on the day of Pentecost and since. By the power of the Holy Spirit believers are brought near to the risen and glorified Redeemer. "I came forth from the Father and am come into the world; again I leave the world and go to the Father."

The representation is nowhere made that He will again leave the Father. "Sit thou on my right hand until I make thine enemies thy footstool." "He hath sat down for ever at the right hand of God, from henceforth expecting till his enemies be made his footstool." The great, the inexpressible gain of the disciples, shadowed forth in the words we are considering, is this: Christ has ascended on high without being removed from them; they have more intimate communion with Him than ever; by the Holy Spirit they are made to sit together in heavenly places. Their actual knowledge of Him and enjoyment of His love are frightfully curtailed, it is true, by their imperfect faith and consecration, but we are to contemplate what God has provided rather than what man appropriates.

There are many who read the words of Christ without ever saying, "What is this that He is saying?" If they were called upon to give an explanation of this and that word of the Master, they would be utterly at a loss. It is truly amazing, the amount of ignorance that exists even among those who have been familiar with the Scriptures from their youth. The reason is that they do not inquire. The meaning of the passage does not strike them at once, and they are deterred by mental and spiritual sloth from searching into the Scriptures.

Now, the blessings of Scripture are particularly connected with that effort of mind which is implied in the words, "Search the Scriptures." One of the best evidences of the presence of the Spirit of truth is the readiness of the mind to give itself reverently, patiently, perseveringly, to the searching out of the meaning of the Word of God. Familiarity with the word of truth often hinders men from becoming aware of their lack of comprehension of it. It were well, therefore, that we continually called ourselves to account concerning what we read, and ascertained whether we have an understanding of it or not.

They said among themselves, "What is this?" But none of them could enlighten the other. Their mutual interrogatories only made manifest their common ignorance. It was right in them to consult with each other concerning the meaning of Christ's Word. The disciples of Christ should more often employ their seasons of reunion in this way. "Then they that feared the Lord spake often one to another." If Christ has given a blessing to one, it is that he may communicate it to his brethren. It is ever the Master Who must teach us. He may do it through another. It does not become us to despise prophesyings, written or spoken. But the Lord is willing to teach us directly. In fact, we should receive everything from Him, whether it come to us directly or indirectly.

If we are desirous of asking Christ the meaning of His words, if such is the character of our desires, we need not fear to approach Him with them. Such desires are, in fact, the promptings of the Holy Spirit Whom He has sent to draw us unto Himself. These are certainly not the desires that we need to be ashamed to bring to Christ. The disciples were bold enough to come to their Lord with a desire that He would give them places of honor at His right hand and left, when He should take to Himself His royalty.

"Blessed are they that hunger and thirst after righteousness." Only let them come with their hunger to the Bread of Life, Who came down from Heaven to give life unto the world. "If any man lack wisdom, let him ask of God, who giveth to all liberally and upbraideth not." We need not fear that Christ will upbraid us with our folly if we bring it to Him. But we must be content to receive the answer that He shall give us.

Often, perhaps, it will seem to us unwisdom, simply because we have not mastered the previous communications, constituting the avenue to the present truth. Christ's answer may be very different from our expectation. Then we are put upon our trial with reference to this, whether we surrender our own conception and believe Christ's statement to be the true one, or the contrary. Thus Nicodemus came to hear some glowing and surprising descriptions of the heavenly world, and was sadly disappointed at having his attention drawn to the lowest round of the ladder which reaches to Heaven: "Except a man be born again, he cannot see the kingdom of God."

John 16:20-22. *"Verily, verily, I say unto you, That ye shall weep and lament, but the world shall rejoice: and ye shall be sorrowful, but your sorrow shall be turned into joy. A woman when she is in travail hath sorrow, because her hour is come: but as soon as she is delivered of the child, she remembereth no more the anguish, for joy that a man is born into the world. And ye now therefore have sorrow: but I will see you again, and your heart shall rejoice, and your joy no man taketh from you."*

"Ye now have sorrow"—through the words which Christ had spoken unto them. He had spoken to them of treachery, denial, flight, danger, on their part; of triumph on the part of the Jews; of humiliation, suffering, death, on His own part. It was difficult for them to receive this testimony; it seemed to them that He was speaking in parables; still, they were constrained to believe that some dread calamity was impending.

"Ye shall weep and lament." Their present sorrow was to be greatly increased, and that soon. When they should see their adorable Master in the hands of His enemies, led captive by them, subjected to all manner of indignities, treated as the filth and off-scouring of all things, struck upon His face by servants and soldiers, crowned with thorns and crucified between thieves, how intense would be their anguish! They would weep and lament, and their enemies would taunt them with having put their trust in One Who, so far from being able to save others, was not able to save Himself.

How terrible was the calamity when the ark of God was taken by the Philistines, and led away into their own territory! This climax of woes broke the heart of Eli. The death of his sons, the defeat of his countrymen, these sorrows were dwarfed by this gigantic and unequalled disaster. But Christ was infinitely greater than the ark of God. In Him was all the fullness of the Godhead bodily. The tabernacle, the ark, the temple, were mere foreshadowings of this glorious incarnation of Deity. The Son of God was to be treated as a worm and no man—a reproach of men and despised of the people. They, His followers, were to stand by and see Him subjected to these indignities, these sufferings, without any other privilege than that of weeping and lamenting, in the midst of a rejoicing world.

We may take note that the apostles tell us nothing of their own feelings during the passion of their Lord. Had they been mere uninspired writers, how largely would they have dilated upon their feelings of sorrow, amazement, despair, at the cross of Christ! Every painter who has attempted to treat this subject has placed prominently in the foreground the group of weeping disciples, but in the Scriptures we have their sorrow presented to us only in the words of Christ.

But their sorrow was to be turned into joy. The bitterness of that hour was introductory to a day of jubilee. The pains of childbirth are acute, but there is alleviation in the thought that they are introductory to the existence of an immortal creature in whom the image and glory of God may be revealed throughout eternity. How unutterably more sublime the considerations—had they been in a position to entertain them—connected with the return from death of the Savior of the world, made perfect through sufferings, leading captivity captive and having the keys of death and hell! The Sons of God who shouted for joy when God brought this world out of its pristine chaos had now an immeasurably more exalted occasion of joy.

How many of our sorrows there are, the means of triumphing over which have been placed in our hands by our tender-hearted Redeemer—placed there in vain because of our unbelief! Had the apostles only embraced with an adequate faith the assurance now given, how would they have been armed against the mighty sorrow that came upon them at the time of the crucifixion! Faith in these words would have enabled them to say to each other, "Courage, brethren; this day of darkness is simply the door closing upon a dispensation of sorrow and great imperfection, and a door will immediately open to introduce us to a dispensation of glory such as eye hath not seen, nor heart conceived."

The marvelous and blessed things of which the prophets have spoken are now to receive their fulfillment.

It is not death we behold, but the communication of an indestructible life. Yes, the Savior had given them hundreds of blessed words to keep them from despair in that hour, and to cause them to behold with thrilling interest the sublime process of a world's redemption. Yet we have the best reason to believe that only in the faintest degree possible did they avail themselves of these amulets [protections].

Thus it is constantly happening with many Christians. They are overwhelmed with sorrow and stupefaction at the things that happen unto them. They express unbounded astonishment at the dispensations of God, as though it were a very difficult thing to justify them; and it never once dawns upon their consciousness that the Savior had not only forewarned them of those hours of danger, but had even given them a shield, so that not a single fiery dart of the adversary should reach their persons.

How idle, how sinful, to cry out against ills, the means of averting which have long been with us! Have we not, placed at our disposal, the very armor of God, by the favor of which the apostles were enabled to pass through such multiplied difficulties and dangers and privations, always rejoicing, always triumphing? Will it not be early enough for us to talk of the severity and mysteriousness of God's dealings with us when we avail ourselves to the uttermost of God's promises and gracious declarations?

"I will see you again, and your heart shall rejoice, and your joy no man taketh from you." Christ would see them again, and they would then, in some sense, see Him for the first time, for they would see in Him a glory and a beauty that they had never been able to discover in Him before. They would then rightly begin to understand the nature of His mission. All His past acts and words—nay, all the words of the ancient prophets—would then begin to be intelligible to them. They would see from what a horrible pit He had delivered them, by what an amazing sacrifice their sins had been atoned for, and how glorious and beneficent the mission to which they had been appointed by Him.

The joy that Christ's presence had hitherto imparted to them was a joy that might be taken from them—it was to be taken away from them; but it should be soon succeeded by a joy that no man could take from them. With the risen Savior their buried hopes should rise and mount on high, never more to fade. Jesus, having all power in Heaven and in earth, would be with them always, even unto the end of the world. Therefore it could be said of their joy that no man could take it from them.

If we have a genuine and an adequate faith, we may laugh to scorn the efforts of men to rob us of this our joy. They make take from us our earthly possessions; they may deprive us of health and liberty and the society of those we love; but they cannot take away our Christ, and so they cannot take away our joy.

Do Christians understand that they have a joy that no man has power to take from them, save as they basely surrender it? Is this culpable surrender the only adequate explanation of the fact that they are without this joy unspeakable and full of glory?

John 16:23-24. *"And in that day ye shall ask me nothing. Verily, verily, I say unto you, Whatsoever ye shall ask the Father in my name, he will give it you. Hitherto have ye asked nothing in my name: ask, and ye shall receive, that your joy may be full."*

The English word "ask" is here made to do service for two different Greek words. "In that day ye shall *ask* me nothing." This looks back to the nineteenth verse: "Jesus knew that they were desirous to *ask* him." They wished an explanation of what He had previously said. He tells them that under the dispensation about to be introduced they would not be thus embarrassed in apprehending the meaning of His words. They would be in a position to understand a great deal that was now obscure to them. This idea is again dwelt upon in the twenty-fifth verse.

Let it suffice now to call attention to the fact that the two "askings" mentioned in the present verse are very different. The meaning is not that the disciples were to ask Christ nothing because the Father would give them everything. "Ye shall be so taught of the Spirit of God that the mystery which now invests much that I say unto you will be dispelled; My remembered words will be intelligible to you. You see, then, that beyond the sorrow and the anguish of the hour which is now at hand there is a compensatory period of light and liberty and heavenly privilege. It is impossible that you should form too glowing a conception of the glorious privileges of that day. Verily, verily, I say unto you, 'Whatsoever ye shall ask the Father in my name, he will give it you.' What more would you have? What more could I give? What more could God bestow?"

"Whatsoever ye shall ask." You are permitted to draw nigh to Him Who has all power, all treasure and you are assured that "whatever you ask in my name, he will give it you." Is it possible for the heart of man to crave any ampler or sublimer privilege than this?

Were I to give you a power by virtue of which you would be able to discover the exact locality of all gold mines, were I to anoint your eyes with an eye-salve that should guide you infallibly to all the deep-hidden diamonds of earth, were I to clothe you with a mysterious influence that should compel all men to place themselves at your disposal, I would not thereby bestow upon you gifts worthy for a moment to be put in comparison with that which is communicated in the promise, "Whatsoever ye shall ask of the Father in my name, he will give it you." Material treasures, or treasures of human influence, how inconsiderable a part of God's property do these constitute! Your range is throughout the unending and ever-multiplying corridors of God's treasury.

Nothing could be more independent of limits than this promise. "Is there no limit? May I ask what I will?" Yes, you may ask what you will, for you are a believer in Christ, and faith in Christ means that Christ is precious to you—above all things precious; that you have adopted His views of things, that you are crucified unto the world and the world unto you. He that is not a believer in Christ is a believer in this world—in its treasures, its honors. To give him such a promise as this would simply be to dash him with a mightier impetus down the broad incline that conducts to death.

He in whose heart the fiat of God has descended, saying, "Let there be light," and who has thus been made to discern the glory of God in the face of Jesus Christ, has such desires that you may, with the most unquestioning confidence, give him this promise and send him to a throne of grace. The very faith that makes the promise available is a faith that renders his desires harmonious with those of God. As the plant is sure to ask nothing but a nutritive soil and moisture and light and heat and day and night and an uncorrupted atmosphere, so the believer in Christ will ask of God nothing save what will conduce to his spiritual growth, his usefulness and the welfare of others.

You still cherish a doubt, perhaps, if anything human can be trusted with such an unlimited promise. This promise places all wealth and honor within his reach, and is it likely that he will exercise such an unfaltering control over himself as never to stretch out his hand and take, for instance, a crown? Can he be trusted? He can be trusted just so far as he trusts; it is only as a believer that the promise is given him.

Observe, the asking must be in Christ's Name. The supplicant is one whose interests are closely intertwined with those of Christ. Anything that will be to the prejudice of Christ's kingdom, or anything that will tend in any way to mar the union between the believer and Christ, God will not grant. There is a story of one who asked for the power of converting everything that he touched to gold, and who, having obtained what he desired, died of famine. God is not our enemy that He should grant us such malignant benedictions as these.

Does this promise seem to you to lose something of its magnificence in consequence of what I have now said? I counsel you then, to let go of everything you have in the world, to take this very promise and go to God with it, asking Him for this one thing—that you may see Christ to be the chiefest among ten thousand, the sum and symbol of all preciousness.

"Hitherto have ye asked nothing in my name; ask, and ye shall receive, that your joy may be full." It was in the Name of Christ that all, even from the beginning, had been bestowed, but the recipients of grace knew not that they were indebted to Him for all. Now that Christ was about to consummate His propitiatory work, it was suitable that they should be informed of the virtue that would be found in His Name. His Name would be to them, at the throne of His grace, more even than His visible presence with them so many months and years had been.

At the cross of Christ the believer learns to transfer to Christ all the confidence that he ever had in himself. "You have seen," says Christ, "how great the love of the Father to Me; you have heard the voice from Heaven, proclaiming Me His well-beloved; you remember the Mount of Transfiguration; you know that He heareth Me always. Would it not be a blessed thing if I could clothe you with My own sonship, so that the Father would receive you as Me, love you as Me, love Me in you? Well, that is the very thing I am doing in giving you this promise,

'Ask in my name.' It will be as though I asked; the Father will hear you always, because He heareth Me always."

"That your joy may be full." "In thy presence is fullness of joy." What is there more than fullness of joy? This again shows how unlimited is the promise. Has anyone ever measured the length and breadth, the depth and height, of the human heart? That must be done before you can tell all that is meant by fullness of joy. "My people shall be satisfied with my goodness," saith the Lord. Fullness of joy, then, is to be obtained by asking in the Name of Christ, and receiving from the Father. There must be fullness of prayer, fullness of faith, in order to have fullness of joy.

The believer cannot be made completely happy by any merely private blessing, even though that blessing be spiritual. The soul of the believer is sometimes gloriously overflowed by the tide of God's love. But, after a season, it becomes evident to him that even the mightiest and fullest and most constant stream of divine love cannot make him permanently happy, if he be not permitted to communicate happiness to others. His soul is oppressed with the love of God when that love stops there.

The love of God transforms him into the likeness of God, and the likeness of God makes it the law of his being that he should largely find his happiness in communicating happiness. As surely as we feast upon the love of God, we find it impossible to continue alone at that feast. We rise up, saying, "We do not well; this is a day of good tidings, and we hold our peace." The branch drinks in the fullness of the vine, but can only continue to do it in the measure that it prepares itself for fruitfulness. The clusters are the glory of the branch. Conceive of a branch that would say, "I will drink abundantly of the tide of life proceeding from the vine, and I will treasure it all within myself; wherefore should I engage in laborious fruit-giving?" Pent-up happiness! It turns to misery.

John 16:25. *"These things have I spoken unto you in proverbs: but the time cometh, when I shall no more speak unto you in proverbs, but I shall show you plainly of the Father."*

When figures are made use of in speech, there is an outside meaning and an interior meaning. As the shell conceals and yet protects the kernel, so a truth conveyed topically may be unperceived at first; afterward, when additional light is given, it becomes manifest, and the saying ceases to be a riddle. The Gospel is full of parables that could very little be understood until Christ had suffered and entered into His glory.

When the Spirit of God was poured out upon His disciples, the veil which had been over the words of Jesus disappeared, and the interior truths flashed forth upon them in all their luster. Christ Himself was such a proverb. Once His divine glory had flashed forth upon their astonished gaze, but that was by way of anticipation; it very little dissipated the confusion of their minds. Nothing about Christ could produce its legitimate and full effect upon them until they had been brought out of the restricted and depressed valley of Judaism, and placed upon the elevated platform of the new dispensation.

Many in these days occupy no worthier position than that first inferior one of the apostles. The apostles were not absolutely without the influence of the Spirit during the time that Jesus tabernacled among them, but those influences did little more than make the present darkness visible, and show them in the dim distance the light of the future.

Without knowing it, there are thousands of Christians who have that feeble and equivocal [dubious] measure of spiritual influence which belongs to a different dispensation from this, and shows them to be two thousand years behind their privileges. We have said it and without shame we say it again. They have, of course, knowledge such as the ante-pentecostal church had not. It is the consciousness of this superior knowledge that tends to keep them ignorant of their spiritual destitution. Their condition is appalling, for they are familiar with the inspiring promises, and have no faculty to catch a glimpse of the glorious things proffered in these promises. They actually suppose that these promises have no more exalted interpretation than that which their own emotionless and inglorious experience affords.

Blessed be God! we are not limited to one Pentecost under this dispensation. Let us but become aware of the abnormal state in which we are, and take knowledge of the lofty experiences to which God is inviting us. Pentecost was not so much a mountain summit as a mountain-high path or table-land, along which the church should have traveled to the New Jerusalem. Let us look steadfastly up above and see among the clouds this highway of holiness, and prove the power of the Savior to bring us to it.

"I shall show you plainly of the Father." Christ is God manifest. "No man knoweth the Father save the Son, and he to whom the Son shall reveal him." The disciples were perhaps disposed to entertain a feeling of disappointment that they had not become more intimately acquainted with the Father through Christ. Untaught of the Spirit, we form extraordinary opinions of what it is to know the Father.

A man may take the Gospel and read it carefully through, and wonder that he should still be so little acquainted with God. Some came rushing to Jesus with great enthusiasm when He was on the earth, and went away sorrowing, knowing no more of the Father than before. "Show us the Father," said Philip, after Jesus had been so long time with them. But there comes a moment when the scales fall from our eyes, and looking at the least word of the Gospel, we cry *Eureka*! in somewhat of ecstasy.

"What man knoweth the things of a man save the spirit of man which is in him; even so the things of God knoweth no man, but the Spirit of God." It is the Spirit of God Who reveals unto us these things in Christ, shows us the glory of God in the face of Jesus Christ. The veil is taken away. Where the Spirit of God is, there is *liberty.*

"I shall show you *plainly* of the Father." This word "plainly" has great significance, and well deserves that we should ponder its testimony. Is there a good deal of obscurity in your views of the Father? Is there a sense of vagueness and uncertainty underlying your address to Him?

Does it seem to you as though He were remote rather than near? This is not as it should be. Christ is willing to show you plainly of the Father. It is your privilege to know God and to feel that you know Him.

You may know Him better than you can know your fellow-man. For the human heart is wanting in simplicity; it has great depths, even bottomless abysses; it is deceitful above all things, changeable exceedingly; yesterday's knowledge of it will not serve for today. But it is otherwise with God. Today's knowledge of Him will serve to all eternity. Not but that you will know Him better tomorrow. You have the tiny plant of the knowledge of God, perfect in its degree, but destined to expand from one degree of volume and of beauty to another to all eternity. "No man shall need to say unto his brother, Know the Lord; for all shall know him." "This is life eternal, that they might know thee, the only true God, and Jesus Christ whom thou hast sent."

"God was in Christ, reconciling the world unto himself." Is it so to you? Is such your Christ? Is your Gospel a marvelous glass in which you behold the steps of the Omnipotent amid the unconscious crowd of His rebellious creatures. Ah! is there not room for one transfiguration after another, each higher in glory, taking the too slighted Gospel up to the throne of God? There are millions of gospels in the world; I speak of the Gospel as it lies in the apprehensions of men. According to the faith of men it is unto them. Oh that we might have, you and I, that blessed and whole-souled faith which will cause the entire Gospel to start into its proper glory and beauty and power and divinity!

A person desires to know God. He is told, on the authority of the Gospel, that God is much more desirous of granting him that knowledge. Ah! if God be willing, how can there be any difficulty, why should there be any delay? It is for you to answer that. God is in the Gospel; the Gospel tells you that He gives His Spirit to them that ask Him. The Spirit of God is ready to show you in the Gospel, plainly, the glory of the Father as it shines in the face of Jesus Christ, the image of the invisible God. How idle, how reprehensible, for you to profess a desire to know God and yet to make so little account of the Gospel! Your ignorance of God is simply the measure of your unbelief.

239

John 16:26-27. *"At that day ye shall ask in my name: and I say not unto you, that I will pray the Father for you: For the Father himself loveth you, because ye have loved me, and have believed that I came out from God."*

A sovereign, for the sake of the love that he bears to his son, bestows favors upon persons for whom his son intercedes. It is not that he takes any special interest in these persons—he does not even direct his attention to them; he only knows that his son asked him to bestow the gifts. Should these favored ones have need of further bounties, they must obtain them in the same way: the son must make request in their behalf. Now, imagine another sovereign who is led, by the love he bears his son, to love those who love his son, to regard them as his own friends, to take the same pleasure in doing good to them that he would in honoring his son.

The case between the believer and God resembles this last case and not the former. The believer is not to feel that the great and awful distance between him and the Father is only temporarily neutralized by the representations of Christ, or that the royal largess [bounty] granted once at the Savior's instance is simply the expression of a momentary feeling of good-will. The believer is united to Christ and identified with Christ; and as one would never think of the vine without including in that thought the branch, so the Father will never think of the Lamb of God without thinking of those who belong to Him. This passage is intended to arm us against that inconstancy of faith which makes a Christian hesitate to ask anew for blessings after great blessings received.

"I say not unto you that I will pray the Father for you." He says not that He will; He says not that He will not. What He means is that He will not need to pray for them as though they were strangers, as though they were unreconciled to God.

"For the Father himself loveth you because ye have loved me." Christ is love divine—love become incarnate for the purpose of revealing itself unto us. Becoming acquainted with this love divine in the crucified One, we love Him, we believe on Him. In doing this we, as it were, complete the circuit, so that the love of God may fully, freely and forever flow into our bosom.

"The Father himself loveth you because ye have loved me." How wonderful that the Savior, Who had such an ineffable intelligence of the true nature of love, could have found it in Him to speak of the crude and dubious sentiment so ominously flickering in the hearts of the disciples as love! But the mother is taught, by her very heart of intensest love, to recognize, with rapture, the least dawnings of love responsive in her child. It matters little how minute the love may be, if it only be germinant; unloving man may make light of it, but supreme love watches it with a profound interest. You and I, and tens of millions, owe our present happiness and our sublimer prospects to the fact that Christ was pleased to regard as love that immature and trembling sentiment which bound the eleven to Him.

Alas for those who love not Christ! The Father loves them not. Christ, the Christ of the Gospel—He Who sat by the well and talked with the Samaritan woman, Who ate with publicans and sinners, Who uttered such terrible denunciations against hypocrisy, Who was led like a lamb to the slaughter,—do you love Him? Do His words and ways delight you? If not, then there is no love for you at the mercy-seat. Ten thousand mighty merits will go for naught if you have no love of Christ to show. The very mention of such merits would prove that you have not the love of Christ in you. To see the excellency of Christ, a man must renounce the thought of personal excellence and clothe himself in a garment of conscious unworthiness.

"Ye have loved me, and have believed that I came out from God." "We love God too much," say some, "to believe that Christ came out from God. With all desire to speak well of Christ, we must confess that we find it an impossibility to dwarf our ideas of the omnipotent One by regarding Christ as the embodiment and revelation of deity." Then you love a god whom you have invented for yourselves, and whom you glorify with the omnipotence of the true God.

Christ is come that you may be made aware of your error, your perilous idolatry, and that you may give back to nonentity the ten thousand and one deities that you have formed for yourselves. Christ is God manifest in the flesh. It does not become you to speak of imperfection in this manifestation until you have mastered the manifestation, and that you are not likely to do in ages of ages. The angels of Heaven feel that this exhibition of deity soars immeasurably away beyond their intelligence, above, beneath, around.

Doubtless the disciples found some difficulty in admitting that Christ had come out from God, but they found infinitely greater in rejecting it. They remembered a multitude of glorious acts, each one of which sufficiently attested that He was the Representative of deity; His holy and unimpeachable life attested it. They *knew* that He could not speak an untruth, and His words bore testimony to the fact of His oneness with God. Yet there were a number of things that were different from what they would have expected in the Messiah. Marvel not, O disciples, at that; the marvel would have been had there been no such difficulties. Marvel not, but wait; and now the Spirit of God will make those very difficulties the means of discovering to you unimagined depths of love and wisdom in the incarnate One.

"Loved and believed." That is not love which does not believe. The love extolled in 1 Cor. 13 "believeth all things." Love to God believes all the things uttered by God. He that loves Christ believes that He is the expression of the divine nature. Love sees; everything else is blind rather than love. Without love it is impossible to see anything aright, much less Him Who has in all things the pre-eminence. It is love that will enable us to discover wondrous things in the Gospel. Love alone can understand love. They who, with lack-luster eyes and unloving hearts, read the words of Christ find nothing in them to gladden or sanctify. Love finds a feast in the least crumb that falls from the table of the Master. We love Christ when we open the door for Him to come in and bless us. He is willing to receive this as an initiatory proof of our love, that we allow Him to come in and begin to be a Savior to us.

Lord, I can give You this proof of love; I can let You love me. I can open the door for You to come in and sup with me. Opening it, I see a long train of angel servants reaching to the heavens, each having some blessed burden for me. How I wonder, then, that I should have kept You waiting!

John 16: 28-30. *"I came forth from the Father, and am come into the world: again, I leave the world, and go to the Father. His disciples said unto him, Lo, now speakest thou plainly, and speakest no proverb. Now are we sure that thou knowest all things, and needest not that any man should ask thee: by this we believe that thou camest forth from God."*

"I came forth from the Father, and am come into the world: again, I leave the world, and go to the Father." The fact that comes most prominently to notice in these expressions is that the world and the Father are, in some sense, apart from each other. The world is without God; it lies in wickedness; it has apostatized from truth and righteousness; it has its own god, its own heaven, its own religion; the standard of a rebellious independence waves over it; a broad gulf stretches between it and the place where God's honor dwells.

This language may appear to some to be extravagant or conventional; yet nothing can be more clearly shown to an unbiased inquirer than the correspondence of this description with man's condition. Nor are we speaking of humanity in some strange development. The world to which Christ specially had reference was that which included the most enlightened and religious portion of mankind. It was in a state of apostasy from God, and the same may be said of the most enlightened of modern nations.

Look, for instance, at the picture which the world gives of itself in the greater part of the modern English literature, in some points of view so decorous and so commendable, but put it alongside of the standard of God's Word, and how manifest and irreconcilable the discrepancy! "Whatsoever ye do, in word or in deed, do all for the glory of God." "One thing is needful." "If any man love not the Lord Jesus Christ, let him be anathema maranatha." "Without faith it is impossible to please God." Apply these tests to the world as it looks forth upon you from the greater part of the literature of our day, and how conclusive will be the evidence of its apostasy!

243

God has laid down a track, and men are off the track—so far from it that it cannot even be seen. They are busily throwing up roads to help them forward in their chosen direction. They point out the excellent features of these roads, urging them as justificatory of their presence there. Nevertheless, God's track remains where it is, and shall remain, though not a soul pass over it. The Gospel is the everlasting Gospel, following men into their remote places of activity, and offering to bring them to the track of God, where alone they may find means of journeying to the pearly gates of the New Jerusalem. A great deal of what is lauded as progress in these days has its origin in the world's desperate resolves to make wrong appear right, to justify itself in its alienation from God and to fulfill the first prophecy of its god, "Ye shall not surely die."

The words now under comment show, we have said, that the world and the Father are apart. They also show that there is a communication between them. Christ appears, coming and going, between the two. He makes His appearance in the rebel camp, and returns to the palace of the Sovereign. Christ is the image of the invisible God. In Him was all the fullness of the Godhead bodily. God was manifest in the flesh. The Father came forth in Him. How, then, can it be said that He came forth from the Father? Christ is with His people always, even unto the end of the world; and yet we are told that to be absent from the body is to be present with the Lord. There is a place where the full manifestation of the glory of God and of the Lamb meets with not even a mote of opposition. God is of purer eyes than to behold evil; and when a world withdraws from Him, He withdraws from it.

"His disciples said unto him, Lo, now speakest thou plainly, and speakest no proverb. Now are we sure that thou knowest all things, and needest not that any man should ask thee; by this we believe that thou camest forth from God."

"Needest not that any man should ask thee," referring to the fact mentioned in verse 19: "Now Jesus knew that they were desirous to

244

ask him, and said. . ." He knew what was in their minds without any express communication on their part. He first stated the difficulty which they hesitated to express, and then answered it. They seem to have been much impressed with this. The fact that they were so is, however, somewhat of a reproach to them, and we are reminded of the words used by Jesus on a former occasion, when, referring to His miracles, mighty, yet little heeded, He said, "Perceive ye not yet, neither understand? Have ye your heart yet hardened?"

Repeatedly they had heard Him giving utterance to the unexpressed sentiment of His adversaries. It was late in the day for them to learn that He knew what was in man. Do not let us, however, press this too far. Jesus might have so manifested His acquaintance with the secrets of all hearts as to render His presence utterly unbearable to unsanctified men of little faith; and as we know that His great concern was to inspire men with confidence, it is evident that He would make no frequent display of His power to read the hearts of men.

The original is not, "Now we are *sure*," but simply, "Now we *know* that thou knowest all things."

"Now speakest thou plainly, and speakest no proverb." One would be ready to infer from that that they were now fully prepared for the departure of Christ, and that there was no longer anything mysterious to them in the fact that He was to be betrayed, scourged, crucified and buried. "Now we understand," they exclaim delightedly; "all is clear to us. You are going, but then you are going to the Father."

Is it all clear? Would that it were! The great solicitude of your Master has been, this evening, to forearm you by forewarning you of what is about to be. Therefore He said, "None of you asketh me, Whither goest thou?" Oh if you would indeed, with all your heart, lay hold of the great truth that Christ is going to the Father, and keep an unflinching hold of it when you see Him seized, bound, mocked, scourged and pierced, then would you escape much anguish and a frightful pit of unbelief.

Christ greatly desires to go to the Father; but He refuses to go to Him in any other than that way in which He can bring His people with Him. He has made Himself one with them, and He will not ascend to Heaven without them. Hence the necessity of going to Heaven in that marvelous way, the way of Calvary. Something must be done with their sins, else it were easier for a camel to go through the eye of a needle than for even Christ Himself to conduct His people to the place of His Father's glory. In fact it was only the prospect of Calvary that ever permitted Him to entertain the idea of making them His people.

The disciples chose to think of the departure of Christ for Heaven as characterized by peace and blessedness and glory. So they dismissed the innumerable statements that He had made concerning the treatment He was to receive at the hands of Jews and Gentiles, and exclaimed, "Now speakest thou plainly." They commended Him so warmly for this word as to make it appear that they had been much dissatisfied with His references to a violent and humiliating doom. Much there is of this faith which is simply disguised unbelief. Men toss aside all those utterances of the Word that do not chime in with their own preconceived theories, and ardently lay hold of something which, they imagine, well expresses what they wish to believe.

John 16:31-32. *"Jesus answered them, Do ye now believe? Behold, the hour cometh, yea, is now come, that ye shall be scattered, every man to his own, and shall leave me alone: and yet I am not alone, because the Father is with me."*

"Do ye now believe?" Very many of our professions of faith would probably encounter such an interrogative as this if we had faith to hear Christ uttering it. True faith in Christ is that which will let Him say what He will, and we will receive it; do what He will, and rejoice in it; go where He will, and we will follow Him. To receive certain utterances of His, or to receive Him in certain aspects that happen to be agreeable to our sentiments, is not to have faith in Him. This is just making a Christ for ourselves.

We sometimes fall in with a person very sensible on may topics, but a monomaniac with respect to one class of subjects. When he converses on ordinary topics we listen with respect to what he says; but when the current of his discourse flows among the exceptional subjects, we just listen with patience and wait for the mood to pass by.

Is not this the kind of faith that some have in Christ? They hearken with a measure of deference to many things that fall from Him; but there are certain doctrines of His that fall upon their ears like the idle wind. "Much learning has made you mad," said Festus to Paul; "much devotion has set you beside yourself, so that you overlook the great essential links by which society is bound together," say many that would scorn to class themselves with Festus. And to whom do they say it?— to Him Whom they profess to call their divine Master.

"Do ye now believe?" Do you claim to be regarded as believers? Can you drink of the cup whereof I am to drink, and be baptized with the baptism wherewith I shall be baptized? Have you a faith in My power that will abide steadfast when everything shall seem to say that My power is annihilated? Have you a faith in My divine mission that will remain unshaken when the Father shall leave Me in the hands of My enemies without a single token of recognition? Have you a faith in

My power to save that will retain its tenure of your souls even when I shall appear to men without so much as the power to save Myself from the cross?

Ah, this were faith indeed. When I speak to you of faith, this is what I intend, this is what I demand. How then can I admit that you now have faith? You have vastly more of unbelief than of faith. The hour is at hand when you will abandon Me, scattered like a flock of sheep whose shepherd is smitten. You will leave Me in the hands of My enemies and flee to your several homes, putting your confidence in them, in flight, in absence from Me, no longer in Me.

"The hour cometh, yea, is now come." *Now*—immediately following the hours of sweet and serene companionship with Christ, in which He had washed their feet, and in which He had cleansed their hearts by His gracious words, and given them so many emphatic and precious, but disregarded, indications of the hour of trial on which they were about to enter.

"And yet I am not alone, because the Father is with me." They forsook One Whom the Father would not forsake; that Elect One in Whom the Father's soul delighted; with Whom the Father was as He never had been with man before; with Whom was infinite power, wisdom, honor, holiness and glory; with Whom were life and light and hope and Heaven and all angelic hosts. In forsaking Christ they forsook all this, and found only their own miserable hearts of fear, their own poverty-stricken natures, their own imbecility, helplessness and sinfulness.

Thus do all who forsake Him. They are free to do so; but they might as well understand what it is they do. The fate of Judas shows us what it is to forsake Christ. The other disciples entered the same path, and if they had been left to themselves they would have accompanied him to the fire that is not quenched, where the worm dieth not. But Jesus had prayed for them. Though they left Him alone, yet would He not leave them alone. His love would nor forsake them; and the tremendous trial of that hour was not suffered to overwhelm them.

They were bound to Christ by an unseen cord of love—not theirs to Him, but His love to them—which suffered them to go only so far away and no farther. It all but broke, and afterwards they were horrified to think that one step more would probably have severed it for ever. They were ever thenceforward careful how they tried any bold and perilous experiments with that connecting bond.

"I am not alone." How are we to reconcile this with the cry that went up from Calvary, "My God, my God, why hast thou forsaken me?" It certainly agrees well with the dying exclamation, "Father, into thy hands I commit my spirit." But Christ was not left alone in that hour of darkness, though the sin of the world forbade that there should then be any sensible manifestation of His Father's presence.

The believer may learn from this that the absence of such manifestation does not necessarily imply the interruption of the divine favor. The Father did not leave His servant Job alone when the adversary was permitted to make such havoc of all that was dear to him on earth. In fact this much-loved man was never more loved than at the time when there was a total privation of all those manifestations of the divine good-will, which had formerly so gladdened and transported him. The Savior was tempted in all points like as we are, yet without sin; and hath left us an example that we should follow in His footsteps, hoping against hope, and believing the Word of God, though ten thousand providences may seem to frown upon that Word.

Who shall separate us from the love of God in Christ Jesus? Nothing in the shape of external dispensations; for it is by the Word we are united to Him, and that Word is the same yesterday, today and for ever. If God should send and recover His Word piecemeal from us, so that great gaps should appear in all Bibles, and all memories be at a loss, then indeed we might be alarmed, and believe that Christ was taken from us. But this cannot be; and it matters little what the providence of God may take away from us. The Word is nigh you, even in your heart and in your mouth; made a part of your very life; made your very life; for it is no more I, says the believer, but Christ that lives in me.

John 16:33. *"These things I have spoken unto you, that in me ye might have peace. In the world ye shall have tribulation: but be of good cheer; I have overcome the world."*

"These things." That is, all the remarks that Christ had addressed to His disciples that evening; the words contained in these four chapters; those precious words that we have been permitted to make the subject of our meditations: they were all spoken that His disciples might have peace in Him.

When Christ said, "I have given you an example, that you should do as I have done to you"; when He commanded His servants to love one another as He had loved them; when He spoke to them about the necessity of keeping His words, of bringing forth much fruit, of enduring persecution, His object was still that they might have peace in Him. And they who seek this peace should understand that unless they receive all the testimony of Christ, they will come short of this peace. A peace they will have, perhaps; but it will not be peace in Christ.

Peace in Christ supposes that we are reconciled to all His words; and that we can follow them all up with this Amen, "Even so, Lord, for so it seems good in Your sight, and You are the Prince of peace. No soul can be so intent upon its own peace, as You are upon the peace of all Your disciples. This is to You an ever present object of solicitude, and not a word falls from Your lips that is not commissioned to bear peace. Your words are all intended to bind the believer unto Yourself; to engraft him as it were upon Yourself, so that Your peace may flow like a river of life from You to him, unceasingly."

Some wonder, perhaps, that they have so little of that peace which Christ has promised to give unto His people; and deep down in their hearts there may be found some hard thoughts of Christ on this score. It is so distinctly promised; it is so easy for Him to give; it would be such a blessed and beautiful expression of His love. Ah! you wicked, unbelieving heart, I will confound you. Have you given admission to all the words of Christ? His peace is in His words; and these very words are complaining at the throne of God that you will not harbor them.

Your pursuit of peace is thus conducted: you gather out a few of the words of Christ whose looks you like best, and separate them from the rest, insulting Christ in the great majority of His words, while professing to honor Him in the reception of a few. It is in vain; these few refuse to bless you apart from the company to which they belong.

One would think that Christ were generally of an austere and unsympathizing temper, and that only by chance there could fall from Him a pacific word. One would think so from the way in which you daintily cull out a sentence here and there for the solace and restoration of your nature. It is false. He is our peace. He Himself is the embodiment of our peace. Before we enter upon the realization of it, it looks upon us in Him; it comes to us from Him, just so far as we will let it, in all His looks, in all His words, in all His acts. We show that we know it and that we know Him when we act habitually upon the conviction that all His words are peace-breathing.

"In the world ye shall have tribulation; but be of good cheer: I have overcome the world." It is only faith that can understand these words. What has Christ's overcoming of the world to do with our struggle? If in the world we are to have tribulation, how does it mend matters to tell us that Christ has overcome? The tribulation is inevitable; why, then, bid us be of good cheer? All incomprehensible, except to faith. As a matter of fact the people of Christ have experienced tribulation; as a matter of fact they have been of good cheer, and have even rejoiced with joy unspeakable and full of glory to lay down their lives for the Name of the Lord Jesus.

It was for the salvation of His people that Christ battled with the world. The prince of this world was determined, with his two tremendous hosts, to hinder the accomplishment of His purpose, but he was effectively baffled. He indeed killed the Prince of life, put Him in a sepulcher, sealed it, placed a guard over it, and amid the acclamations of his legions sat down upon his throne.

At that very instant Christ rose from the dead, leading captivity captive. He ascended up on high, giving to the hopes of His people at once the exaltation and the stability of the throne of God. They now know that the Christ to Whom they are united has all power in Heaven and in earth, and this is the victory which overcomes the world, even their faith. Without tribulation there could be no trial of their faith and no perfecting of it. They are of good cheer, because they are dead unto the world and alive unto Christ. Their conversation is in Heaven; their hopes are there, their treasure there; the frown of the world is the frown of one whom they respect not and fear not.

Christ overcomes the world in the heart of the believer. The world says, "My wrath is terrible; a God invisible is scarce a God; I am the God visible; if once my indignation be kindled, woe unto you; all hope of happiness will be at an end; your only hope is in my favor; my favor is life." But Christ says, "The world passeth away and the fashion thereof; what is man, whose breath is in his nostrils? Who is he that will harm you, if ye be followers of that which is good? Fear Him who hath power to cast both soul and body into hell, and who delighteth in mercy. I am he that liveth and was dead; and behold I am alive for evermore, and have the keys of hell and of death." Thus Christ overcomes the world in the heart of the believer. Christ wins the victory, and the believer wins the victory. He wins it by His Word and by His Spirit; we win it by our faith. And these three are one. The Word accomplishes nothing without faith. The Spirit of God does nothing apart from the truth. The whole is the gift of God. Unbelief is the rejection of this divine threefold gift. Whoso will, let him take.

It is for me to show, in my measure, that Christ has overcome the world. If the world overcomes me, then, so far as I am concerned, there is no testimony given to men of the sublime fact that Christ has overcome the world and opened up a way out of it for all who believe. Christ must abide in my heart, and victoriously say to the world, "Get thee behind me."

The outpouring of the Spirit of God is the great evidence that Christ has come off conqueror over the world. On the day of Pentecost, Satan awoke to the consciousness of the terrible defeat he had sustained.

The presence of Christ upon the earth did not so alarm him as this evidence of the presence of the omnipotent Spirit. At first, perhaps, he thought that all was lost, for what could resist the Gospel, the Spirit and Faith, going forth in one, conquering and to conquer? But when he had fled a little way, he turned and took heart, for it was evident that the Church of Christ could be shaken from its faith, and fail to reap those splendid results of the victory of Christ which might have been anticipated. For eighteen hundred years the Church has remained frightfully insensible to the significance of this announcement, "I have overcome the world."

The flag of our General is seen waving on the battlements of the enemy's citadel, yet the army of this victorious Commander fails to give heed to this signal, and instead of taking possession of the conquered city remains supine in the plain. Perhaps we are now awaking to the significance of this declaration. Christ having overcome, we ask why we should not overcome.

Chapter 17

John 17:1. *"These words spake Jesus, and lifted up his eyes to heaven, and said, Father, the hour is come; glorify thy Son, that thy Son also may glorify thee."*

"These words spake Jesus"—the words on which we have been meditating. What a different world would this be if those words had never been spoken by the Son of God! What an incalculable amount of blessing have they been flinging upon the troubled face of human society during these eighteen hundred years!

The amount of gold in the hands of men has, they say, been more than doubled during the last twelve years. How utterly insignificant this accession to the world's wealth in comparison with the riches of grace imparted by the words in these chapters! Into what unimagined treasuries of peace, joy, confidence, love, strength, hope, patience and holiness has many a soul been conducted by these words! How much of Heaven has been brought by them into how many souls! But how little the measure of blessing appropriated, in comparison with that which still lies neglected and unnoticed!

What unsearchable riches are there for you, dear reader! How high might you climb toward Heaven if you would avail yourself of this ladder let down from Heaven! You have pitched your tent among these words and gathered largely of the manna that fell around, but the immaturity of your faith has deprived you of richer and more glorious feasts than have yet been dreamed of by you.

But it is still our privilege to hear the words that fall from the lips of Christ. He does not now address His brethren, but His Father. And it is not unworthy of observation that He addresses the Father as freely, quietly, familiarly, as He had addressed the disciples. There is the same realization, apparently, of the Father's presence as there is of theirs. No new attitude is assumed, no new intonations are used; He simply lifts His eyes to Heaven and goes on speaking. He had been talking with the brethren; He now talks with the Father.

254

"Father!" And we too address God by this appellation. Christ stands at the throne of grace and says, *Father*; then you come to the same throne and say, *Father*; and some of them who stand by say, "The First was the elder Brother; the other was lost and is found; the First-begotten found him, ransomed him, and brought him to the Father." "Behold what manner of love the Father hath bestowed upon us, that we should be called the Sons of God." It is an amazing thing when a rebel is suffered to appear in the audience-chamber of the king, to look upon the face of him whom he has wronged, and live, but who would dream of such a token of regard as the recognition of the rebel by the sovereign as his own son?

"The hour is come"—the hour of which God spoke in the garden of Eden; the hour that Abel dimly anticipated; the hour for the sake of which Noah was preserved when the world was swept away by a deluge; the hour that Abraham saw when the knife was raised above his son Isaac; that was shadowed by the serpent lifted up in the wilderness, by the tabernacle, the temple, the daily lamb; the hour that kings and prophets mused about; the hour for the sake of which the whole creation has for sixty centuries been made subject to the vanity of sin; the hour of which Moses and Elijah spoke on the Mount of Transfiguration; the hour that was to behold the sublimest manifestation of the Godhead, upon which hung the everlasting destiny of the redeemed; an hour infinitely greater than that in which the morning stars sang together and all the sons of God shouted for joy.

To every child of Adam upon the face of the earth we may say, "The hour of which Jesus spoke in His prayer demands your attention unspeakably more than anything that ever yet commanded it. It is not merely an hour in the life of Jesus, but an hour that may and should be added to your life, and when so added will be found to be an hour of unending blessedness—an hour that includes all eternity to come, and all glory and all felicity. Fling away what you now call your life and take this hour. Time, in its evil sense, is no more, when the soul enters into this hour."

"Glorify thy Son, that thy Son also may glorify thee." We see here the thorough oneness of the Father and the Son. The Son is to be glorified that the Father may be glorified. They that fear to give glory to the Son cannot give glory to the Father. But what is here the meaning of the word, "glorified"?

On a previous occasion we were told that the Spirit was not yet given because that Jesus was not yet glorified. Again, "Whatsoever ye shall ask in my name, that will I do, that the Father may be glorified in the Son." Also, when Judas went out, "Now is the Son of man glorified and God is glorified in him." And there was the Father's voice from Heaven, saying, "I have glorified my name, and will glorify it again." Thus it behoved the Son of man to suffer and to enter into His glory. In the same chapter of Philippians and in a multitude of other passages we trace the path of the deepening humiliations of Christ to the grave, and then we see Him ascending by a path of glory to the right hand of the Father.

This is true enough in many important respects, but the sinner who has fled for refuge to the cross of Christ will tell you that there is no glory in the universe like that which breaks upon his soul from the marred countenance of the crucified One. While some of us, it may be, are straining our eyes to behold the glory of the ascended Savior, the inhabitants of Heaven are gazing with rapture and with strong desire on the Gospel. From no place does the perfection of Him Whose Name is Love shine so resplendently upon them as from the cross.

What, then, is the meaning of this prayer, "Glorify thy Son"? It refers doubtless to the exaltation of Christ, because, without His exaltation, His humiliation is a fact that has no special eloquence of meaning. It is the discovery of Christ ascending that sends us to the cross to look aright upon the enigmatic scene. "Glorify thy Son, that thy Son also may glorify thee." Exalt Him to Your right hand, that He may send the Spirit and cause the scales to fall from the eyes of men and enable them to discover the unmatched glory of Calvary. Give Him celestial glory in the eyes of men that He may give You terrestrial glory in the eyes of the universe.

Again we say, apart from Christ there is no path whereby the glory of God may flow to the hearts of our apostate race. He is the Way, the Truth and the Life.

John 17:2. *"As thou hast given him power over all flesh, that he should give eternal life to as many as thou hast given him."*

This is not a petition, but the mention of a fact, the recognition of a gift—a gift so great that all other gifts connected with the salvation of mankind are comprehended in it; a fact that lays the groundwork and supplies the material of all true prayer ascending to God from human lips. He that is about to be delivered into the hands of sinners, and to be gazed upon as the personification of human weakness, is heard calmly discoursing with the omnipotent Father concerning the omnipotence with which He has been Himself invested, and by virtue of which He purposes to give eternal life to men of all ages, of all nations, tribes and tongues. In the presence of an inevitable and ignominious death, He is seen poising in His hand the everlasting destiny of millions on millions.

Two gifts of the Father are mentioned—one, by which the Son is invested with the government of this world throughout the period in which it is tenanted by the race of Adam; the other, the gift of that elect multitude that shall be saved by Him. Another gift is mentioned—the gift of eternal life from the Son to those that are given Him. It is in order that this last gift may be communicated that Christ is clothed with universal power. He must be Sovereign in this world Sovereign of all seas and lands: Sovereign of subjects and rulers; Sovereign of all influences, human and natural; Sovereign of the angels who minister unto them that shall be heirs of salvation; Sovereign of the grave; Sovereign of time and of eternity—in order that He may redeem from the earth and crown with everlasting life those whom the Father hath given unto Him.

One would be ready to think that, after the Son of God had received an authority extending over all creatures and to the utmost limits of the universe, it would be impossible to bestow upon Him the gift of anything additional. But the Son of God is the Savior; salvation is the very element of His being; a sun does not more imperatively demand liberty to shine than Christ demands liberty to save. The mere offer of the

257

universe could never satisfy Him. Seated upon the throne of Heaven, there is nothing in the illimitable expanse beneath and around Him, glorious as it is, that can at all satisfy the yearning of His heart. "Give Me souls," He cries.

The Father gives the highest possible expression of love to His Son when He gives Him the corrupt, debased, ruined soul of man. For this soul the Savior died. You wonder. Know you not that God is love, and that the cross of Christ is just the door by which Divine love fought its way into this world from which sin had driven it? Sin stood aghast at the spectacle of Divine love re-entering this world, for it had fully supposed that nothing could enter here without paying the tribute of sin and putting on the livery of sin.

The soul that you have so effectually ruined, O adversary, and in which you love to contemplate your own detested image, is only rendered the more meet to reveal, in its marvelous restoration through grace, the infinite resources of Divine love. What the nature of angels could not furnish, in that it was weak through holiness, that the sin-smitten soul of man furnished—namely, an opportunity for the mercy of God to manifest itself, and to enhance immeasurably the entire glory of the Godhead.

In order that it might be seen what the riches of the goodness and wisdom of God are, it was expedient that God should begin lower down than nothing. The angels were exalted from nothing to the thrones which they occupy in the presence of the throne of God, but sinners are found at a depth infinitely below nothing, and the ladder of light, by which the love and strength of God descend to them, and by which they ascend to the regions of celestial purity, illuminates the entire universe with a radiance not known before.

Do you habitually, O my soul, regard yourself as a gift of the Father to the Son? as given to the Son to be rendered by Him a monument of what the love of God is capable of in the way of triumphing over difficulties? You are precious to Him because by means of you the preciousness of your Redeemer God may be revealed unto the universe.

Does not this thought give you a wonderful boldness in the conflict with sin? Do you not perceive how inevitably One Who has all power in Heaven and in earth and in your heart must sympathize with your desire for sanctification? How can you but offer fervent, effectual and prevailing prayer in view of the glorious fact that you have been given by the Father to the Son, in order that the Son might give you eternal life?

The fact that the Savior has power over all flesh constitutes the warrant of the Church in the great enterprise of the world's evangelization. Without an adequate faith in this great truth, there will be little heart to prosecute this enterprise. We need to have a greatly augmented faith in the truth that He Who shed His blood for all has power over all. God, our Savior, Who gave Himself a ransom for all, will have all men to be saved and to come unto the knowledge of the truth. Between this blessed will of God and its consummation stands the Church with the Gospel; and if she stands unbelieving, fearful, inactive, unpitying, worldly, how terrible the responsibility, how dire the consequences!

How ready has the Savior been to notice the slightest germinancy of faith on the part of His people, and to open wide the brazen gates of heathen nations as soon as Christians evinced a readiness to convey to them the Gospel! The world imagines that it has broken down so many barriers in this nineteenth century, little dreaming that Christ has done it in answer to the prayers of His little flock. Believers see everywhere the displays of His cosmopolitan power, now that they are lifting on high a cosmopolitan Gospel.

Christ gives eternal life to men by the instrumentality of those who are themselves participators in this life. He is the Vine and His people are the branches. To them is committed the Gospel which is the word of life. Paul labored as he did that he might by all means save some. He did not think that it would be an honoring of God for him to say, "Whatever my faithfulness or unfaithfulness, the gifts of God will reach those for whom they are intended." Christ came with gifts to the

Nazarenes, but could not communicate them because of their unbelief. "Oh that thou hadst hearkened to my commandments! then had thy peace been as a river, thy seed also had been as the sand." "Oh that my people had hearkened unto me! I should soon have subdued their enemies; the haters of the Lord should have submitted themselves unto Him."

God foresaw, from all eternity, this terrible delinquency of the evangelized with respect to the unevangelized. His plans were formed in perfect concurrence with His perfect knowledge; but that foreknowledge of God leaves the sin of man and its sad consequences exactly what they would have been if they had not been foreseen.

John 17:3. *"And this is life eternal, that they might know thee, the only true God, and Jesus Christ whom thou hast sent."*

In the day that Adam and Eve ate of the forbidden fruit they surely died. They lost something that is called life in Heaven, though on earth the name may be given to something vastly inferior. "In thy favor is life." The very act of their transgression created a rupture of the bond by which they had been previously united to God. Their will ceased to be a minister of the Divine thought. Not merely were they in a way that led to death; death was enthroned in their hearts, for sin is death. Viewed from the standpoint of celestial holiness, sin is not only death, it is hell, for they who are in Heaven estimate the misery of alienation from God by the ineffable happiness which they experience in communion with Him.

When Adam sinned, he fell from Heaven to a curse-smitten earth. A moment before, he was in Paradise. There all spoke of God. God Himself walked there. It was a mansion of God. The leaves of the trees could not rustle without loading the air with divine promises; the streams murmured assurances of the love of God which passes knowledge; the winds too had a mission not limited to the refreshing of the body. There was in them a still, small voice conveying thoughts of beauty and of joy from the soul of God Himself. But the moment of transgression witnessed a fearful change. Adam and his companion were no longer in Paradise. The trees, the streams, the winds, spoke to them no more of the love of God. Sin had stretched its blighting wand over everything. Their former condition was life, their present was death.

"This is life eternal, that they might know thee." Adam ceased to know God when he sinned. Before, God was on the throne of the universe; God was his God. But, by the act of transgression, he placed another on the throne; he constituted himself his own sovereign; took away the law of God that he might substitute his own will. Before, he knew the only true God, Whose Name is love, Whose service is

261

blessedness. Now, there was no more, to him, such a Being in the universe. Satan whispered another god into his knowledge.

Eternal life is the recovery of the true knowledge of God. This is an amazing thought. To know if we have eternal life we are to look into our intellect. Here let it be observed that the intellect is restored to its true place by the knowledge of God. It is not to be looked at apart from the will and the affections. When the knowledge of God was forfeited by sin, then disorganization took possession of man's nature; his heart and mind and will were thrown asunder. The restoration of the knowledge of God is the restoration of life to our nature, and the will, affection, emotions, actions, are determined by the glorious truths that are present to the intellect.

We are saved by faith. But do you suppose that faith has nothing to do with the intellect? The intellect of fallen man is an intellect that is self-excluded from the instructions of God. Faith simply brings it back into the rays that flow from the throne of the Father of lights. Faith is just the reception of certain truths; it simply lets God be true; it is an opening of the door that light and life may come in. "Hear, and your soul shall live."

"Thee, the only true God, and Jesus Christ." The previous verse informed us that Christ had power over all that He might give eternal life to some. It is He that giveth eternal life; it is He that giveth the knowledge of the only true God, which is eternal life. Yes, say some, the knowledge of God; that is life; it is of little consequence what we think of Christ. But, observe, it is Christ that gives this knowledge. That only is the true knowledge of God which Christ gives; there is nothing that tends to life in the knowledge you have apart from Him.

This declaration that knowledge is life is flanked on either side by the statement of our dependence on Christ for this knowledge. Christ came to give us this knowledge and how gave He it? Not by telling us certain things of God, but simply by living among us, and then telling us that he who had seen Him had seen the Father. This is eternal life, that we should see the glory of God in the face of Jesus Christ. He that has the least indisposition to do honor to Christ, knows not the only true God. To break this verse in two is to break in two our only hope of everlasting life.

"This is eternal life." May we not lose this knowledge? No, for this knowledge is life; it recreates the soul; it translates us beyond the reach of death. It is because it is invincible that this life is entitled to be called life. A mere liability to death would be, in some sense, death. The knowledge which Christ gives His people is one that animates them with zeal, holy desire, vigilance, patience, with a spirit of prayer, of perseverance, of charity and of a sound mind, with purity and docility and humility. It clothes them with the armor of God, and enables them to fight the good fight of faith. It is the life of a moral being, and it is secured to us by moral means.

Let us look at the nature and condition of physical life. The heart beats, the lungs respire, without our volition. The blood is sent regularly through the veins, the process of respiration is constantly maintained, digestion goes duly on, without our observation. Our mind is left free to avail itself of the results of these processes. Yet every volition tells in some way upon the life. Our thoughts, feelings and acts are constantly marring or favoring the processes on which our life depends. Our comfort, health and existence even are dependent, mediately or immediately, on our voluntary nature.

In every individual there is supernatural life and a natural life. Processes are wrought out, moment by moment, that could not advance in the least degree without the impulsion [impulse] of a mind infinitely greater than that of the individual, and essentially different from it. Yet these processes are so subordinated to his own most limited mind as that he may direct, control, mar and utterly thwart them. Suppose the body actuated by a thoroughly well-constituted mind, [then] there will be the harmonious, constant expression of the finite and of the infinite mind in all the movements and operations of the organism.

Translate this idea into the moral world. In the renewed man there is the life that Christ has given, and the result of that gift is that in all moral acts there are (sin excluded) the concordant expressions of the divine mind and of the created mind. There is perfect liberty on the part of the creature, but there is a tendency to use that liberty in the ways that please God. There is liberty in the steam-carriage to move, but the tendency is to move upon the line of railway. There is liberty to go off the track, but it is known that there is destruction in that exercise of liberty, and the tendency is just to move forward. Ah! if this were the only tendency! But we are now looking simply at the new man—at Christ's gift of eternal life.

John 17:4. *"I have glorified thee on the earth: I have finished the work which thou gavest me to do."*

Let us take another parting look at the previous verse: "This is eternal life, that they might know thee, the only true God, and Jesus Christ whom thou hast sent." Christ here speaks of Himself in the third person. He often spoke of Himself as the Son of man, sometimes as the Son of God; here, and here only, as Jesus Christ. This name Jesus Christ only occurs twice in the Gospels. But the entire testimony of the Gospels relates to this, that Jesus is the Christ. He is the anointed One—anointed to be a Prince and Savior. God gave not unto Him the Spirit by measure—gave not merely the Spirit to dwell in Him personally, and to be manifest in His ministry, but to dwell in His body, the Church. All outpourings of the Spirit of God, from the foundation of the world, belong to the anointing of Christ; they are all attestations that Jesus is the Christ.

Having spoken of Himself in the third person as the Son and as Jesus Christ, the Savior now speaks of Himself in the first person: "I have glorified thee on the earth." This comes in like a comment on what went before. "To know You and Jesus Christ is life, because in Christ You have been glorified upon the earth, where before You were not glorified. You were ever glorified in Heaven; You have now been glorified on earth." The glory of God was manifested by the Son, so that now all that was needed was the gift of the Spirit in connection with the Gospel, that the true and saving knowledge of God might be brought home to the apprehensions of men.

What a sublime simplicity of confidence betrays itself in this language! What an amazing contrast between every prayer of a believer and this prayer of Christ! He speaks of having done that which no man from Adam downward had ever done—of having glorified God in the absolute sense of the word, of having perfectly and irreproachably accomplished the work given Him to do; yet may no one discern the least trace of undue assumption or of self-laudation in the language.

For the words are not addressed to men, but to God, and not in a vehement appeal, but in a calm and dignified simplicity of statement. If a man can overhear the Savior, with the tomb of Lazarus behind Him and the cross before Him, addressing thus His righteous Father, and not perceive how triumphant in every sentence is the evidence of His divinity, it remains for us only to pity his obtuseness and to pray that the veil may be taken from his mind.

"I have glorified thee on the earth"—not Myself. "I can of mine own self do nothing," He once said. He did nothing apart from God, and we see Him aright only when we see God in all He did, in all He said. Every man stands in the way of the glory of God, of that glory which to reveal is the proper end of his being. He lives not to give expression to the will of God, the thoughts of God; the web of his life is woven of his own will. The believer, as his faith is increased, is overwhelmed with confusion at the discovery of the stupendous wrong which he is constantly doing to his loved Lord by the interposition of his own will and his own character.

The unbeliever refuses to come to the knowledge of this, affirming that man is too insignificant to produce such a result as the obscuration of the glory of God. But in the life of Christ we see that glory of God which we were each and all created to show forth. We have but to put our life and our character beside His to know what sin can do. As sinners we are not insignificant; we are not dwarfs, but demigods.

It is calculated that the light of the sun is equal to more than fifty thousand times that of the moon, yet in a certain position the moon extinguishes all the light of the sun, in a particular field of vision, extinguishing her own light at the same time. As we were suffered to put Christ into the grave, so we are suffered to put the glory of God into a grave—it is what almost every individual is doing; but there shall be a resurrection, a terrible one. The believer is one that knows this, and stands in awe of his own power to sin, rejoices that there is one greater than that all but omnipotent principle, and flees to Christ to save him from himself. Yet he is often grieved to find himself thrust forward in the place of Christ. Oh, to be a living sacrifice—living only in the abnegation of self and the exhibition of Christ!

Let us not suppose that the glory of God demands rare opportunities, great deeds. If we look to the life of Christ, we see that it comprehended a thousand petty details that are commonly regarded as essentially and hopelessly lusterless, if not ignoble. Yet Christ glorified God in all these details. This lesson we need to learn from His life, and to impart into our own life its benedictions. We shall meet with a delightful cordiality on the part of the Spirit of God when we seek His guidance and hallowing influence in the doing of those innumerable little acts that make up the sum of life.

Does your conception of goodness and of greatness correspond with that of God? Were your aspirations, your dreams of grandeur, suddenly reduced to writing and submitted for your own tranquil inspection, would they resemble the life of Christ? This is God's conception of all that is exalted in humanity. You perhaps indulge some dream of heroism on the battlefield; God rejects that and substitutes the temptation of Christ in the wilderness. Blessed is the man whose air-castles are in the New Jerusalem! We are told of a day when the earth shall be filled with the knowledge of the glory of God. That day is just one in which men will have parted with all those ideas of glory and of grandeur which now make such havoc of society, and will have embraced with all their heart God's ideal of humanity.

The temple of fame is to be emptied of those statues that now occupy its pedestals; its various inscriptions are to give way to some of a very different character. Above every name therein shall be exalted the Name of the Lord Jesus, and no name shall have any honor save that which He gives it. When, in that day of the restitution of all things, you and I shall stand within the threshold of that fane, we will look up to the dome and be surprised to see it lifting itself above the stars. Its pillars shall resolve themselves into the everlasting hills; the sun shall arise within its portal and there shall be no night there. Ten thousand times ten thousand living and lustrous monuments of the grace of the Lord Jesus Christ, bearing His Name upon their foreheads, shall walk there in love and beauty, gathering fruit from the tree of life.

In the meantime how is it with that temple of fame—your own heart? Who is exalted there? Have the heroes of this world fallen from the pedestals whereon you placed them? Has that chief of heroes, Self, abandoned his lofty throne? Has the verse we are now considering any authoritative place there? Christ glorified God in Judea of old: have you suffered Him to show unto you the glory of God? He finished a work in Judea, but that was only by way of external preparation for a work in your heart which can only proceed with your consent. Shall a day come when Christ, presenting you blameless and unreproveable before the throne of His Father, shall be able to say, "I have finished the work which You gave me to do, in the heart of this recovered sinner"?

John 17:5-6. *"And now, O Father, glorify thou me with thine own self, with the glory which I had with thee before the world was. I have manifested thy name unto the men which thou gavest me out of the world: thine they were, and thou gavest them me; and they have kept thy word."*

Upon the earth, in humiliation and privation, Christ had glorified God. He had finished the work given Him to do, and He now asks that He may be glorified with God's own Self. He speaks not here of inheriting a glory that He had never known, but simply of entering into that glory which He had ever had with the Father before the world was. Should we not naturally have expected Him to refer to a more modern date? Why go back to times before the world for that pristine glory? Was it not at His incarnation that He laid it aside? Does He mean, "before the world was, in respect to Him present in it?" The words do not seem naturally to bear that construction.

May we, then, understand that the humiliation of Christ in some sense dates from the beginning of the world? His advent was from the beginning the subject of prediction; His sufferings were shadowed forth by the lamb daily slain; He bore the responsibility of the sins of all whose sins were pardoned during those forty centuries; their burden rested upon Him, increasingly from age to age, till it was done away at the cross. The reproach that Moses endured is said to have been "the reproach of Christ." As the promises relating to Him were treated, so was He Himself treated. When those promises met with disregard or scorn or denial, it was Christ Himself that met with these things. When the prophets that came in His Name were evil-entreated and put to shame, it was He that was insulted and rejected. "The reproaches of them that reproached thee fell on me"; the reproaches that fell upon His servants were really aimed at Him. In all their affliction He was afflicted.

But is not this equally true of the present dispensation? "Inasmuch," He will hereafter say, "as ye have done it unto these my brethren, ye have done it unto me." He, in His Gospel and in His servants, still encounters the contradiction of sinners.

Yet we have perhaps most reason to conclude that He refers simply to the time preceding His advent, before the world was relatively to Him present in it. In the latter part of the previous chapter we found these words: "I came forth from the Father, and am come into the world; again, I leave the world and go to the Father."

"With thine own self." He asks to be raised above all principalities and powers and might and dominion, to be invested with a glory above all finite glory—to be placed, in a word, at the right hand of the Majesty on high, with all power in Heaven and earth, manifestly, as He ever is inherently, equal with God, one with God.

This glory He had in the Scriptures before He came into the world. Daniel saw one like to the Son of man brought before the Ancient of Days, and presented with dominion and glory and a kingdom that all people should serve Him. Isaiah spoke of Him as the Wonderful, the Counselor, the Prince of peace, the mighty God, the everlasting Father. David says: "Thy throne, O God, is for ever and ever."

The views that we obtain of all these words of the Lord Jesus must bear (we may have remarked it before) a certain proportion to our own experience. They mean more or less as we move upon a higher or lower level. We must reach a particular level before we can even vaguely discern the next eminence, and only when we have reached the latter shall we discern a higher. And many, many of these flights are found in a single passage of Scripture. The Lord Jesus has let Himself down to our level, as far as may be, in the words used by Him; but those words participate in His own marvelous nature, and, in the tiniest of them, Alps on Alps arise to the Christian who is pressing forward in the divine life. We need therefore continually to be coming back to the Scriptures which we have once fed upon; our experiences may, in the interval, have so expanded that we shall be prepared to see a higher truth than could formerly be apprehended by us.

"I have manifested thy name unto the men which thou gavest me out of the world." We have here a specification of the work mentioned in the fourth verse: "I have finished the work which thou gavest me to do; I have glorified thee on the earth." He glorified the Father by manifesting His perfections, revealing His true nature. God was manifest in Him. God *was* in Him, and would have been manifest to all had man been what he professes to be.

Man denies that his mind is blinded by the god of this world. But of what value is his denial? It is because he is blinded that he denies it; if he were aware of it, his blindness would be even then passing away. He that made the world was in the world, and the world knew Him not. This settles the whole question. When Christ shall appear in His glory, then the tribes of men will be overwhelmed with confusion; for the simple fact that Christ is glorified shows that their entire life has been a tissue of rebellion and iniquity.

"The men whom thou gavest me out of the world." Here is election, and here we see that had there been no election there would have been no salvation. Sinners are the last persons that should find any fault with this doctrine, for it is this alone that opens the door of hope to them. The doctrine of election never occasioned the perdition of a single soul, unless, indeed, some may have chosen to wrest it to their own destruction. Even then it was not the Bible doctrine that destroyed them, but a figment of their own misguided minds.

Election saves men—destroys none; it does not touch, or approach, or in any way influence, those that are unelected. Election does not make war upon Scripture, but leaves in their integrity all those passages that testify concerning the boundless grace of God and His willingness that all should be saved and come unto the knowledge of the truth. The doctrine of election inspires me with hope because it tells me that God is actually embarked in the great work of saving sinners, without reference to any fitness of theirs. Then, what further encouragement I need I find in the blessed fact that the invitations of the Gospel are addressed unto men generally, and consequently to me in particular. "Whosoever will, let him take the water of life freely"— let him lay hold upon the hand of God stretched forth to save him from this present evil world.

The doctrine of election ought, however, to trouble those who remain in their sins, and who neglect to come to Christ. If the doctrine of election can awaken the careless and worldly-minded—awaken them to anguish and alarm—we may surely bid it Godspeed. Nothing can be more dire, more fatal, than the state of spiritual supineness in which so many are living.

John 17:6. *"I have manifested thy name unto the men which thou gavest me out of the world: thine they were, and thou gavest them me; and they have kept thy word."*

They were given to Christ that He might give unto them eternal life. The expression, "thine they were," does not, then, mean that they were already regenerate before they knew Christ. Some of them probably were the children of God before they became followers of Christ, pious Jews, believing in the coming Savior and waiting for Him. Independently of this, they were all God's property. Sin does not in the least impair the claim of God to all the powers of His creatures. They may abide under the shadow of another master, but it is only during the divine sufferance: sooner or later they must fall into the hand of the living God. Nay, even now there is not a day in which God is not levying tribute upon them and compelling them to declare by acts, if not by words, that He is the Sovereign.

Why this headache? Why this heartache? Why this hunger, this thirst? Why did the fire burn that child—the flood sweep away that pile of timber—the worm destroy that crop—the winds dash in pieces that ship? Whence these manifold humiliations, losses, privations, injuries, that befall the children of this world? There is no unrighteousness with God; He takes not what is not His, smites not those who are beyond His jurisdiction. So far from canceling His title to them, sin makes them His in an additional sense—His to smite, to destroy, if He will. They are also His in this blessed sense, that He may give them to Christ.

"Thou gavest them me." The Jews supposed that the Messiah-ship of the Savior would be announced by some unparalleled gift made by the Father to Him and through Him to them. Earthly supremacy appeared to their carnal minds the greatest of all gifts of God to man, and they expected that the Messiah would be invested with an unequalled authority over the nations, and crown His own peculiar people with honors and dignities and wealth yet unwitnessed. In contrast with all this they saw a few Galileans given to Him. Where is the faith that would not have been staggered by such an issue?

There were teachers in Jerusalem at whose feet were sitting hundreds of the most intelligent and influential persons of the community; Gamaliels who numbered among their disciples the noble, the wealthy, the learned. But the Father gave to Jesus the fishermen, John and James, Peter and Simon, the publican Matthew and a few others of like standing, and the Savior accepted them as a proof of the Father's love and wisdom. For He was to thresh the mountain with a threshing instrument such as no man would have chosen.

There was a youth of great promise perhaps even then in the school of Gamaliel. He would have scorned to identify himself with such a company as that which followed Christ. The Lord afterward condescended to make him one of them, but not without having first taught him to empty himself of all on which he prided himself—to become a fool in the worldly sense, in order that he might become wise in the Christian sense.

"They have kept thy word." It was the Word of God, though received from the lips of Christ. From the hour when first Christ commanded them to follow Him, how many attempts had been made by the adversary to hinder them from keeping Christ's word!

How many "friends" had taken them aside and in "the kindest manner" told them that they would only involve themselves in trouble and disaster if they followed Christ! How many learned Scribes and Pharisees had assured them that they were rushing upon destruction in following One Whose claims to the Christhood could not stand the least investigation! How often had the words of Christ been so obscure and perplexing as to seem to justify the denunciations of His opposers! How many that walked with them for a while had gone back confessing that they had made a great mistake!

How strange the conduct of Christ this very week in Jerusalem! God had disposed all the people to greet Him with hosannas, and had plainly opened a way for Him to the long unoccupied throne of Judah.

273

Yet He entirely omits to avail Himself of this striking providence, and seems ready to throw Himself into the hands of His enemies. But He Who had enabled the disciples to see that Jesus had the words of eternal life, had also enabled them to persevere in that conviction, notwithstanding all the fiery darts of the adversary.

"They have kept thy word." Ah! if it may only be our privilege to hear this testimony from the lips of Christ concerning us! That word is the key that will open to us the pearly gates and all the chambers of happiness in the eternal world. But it often looks mean and worthless, and all manner of agents come to us from the evil one, seeking by all manner of devices to get it from us. One will whisper in our ears, "You are now going into the palace of a distinguished man, and you will meet there a very distinguished circle. There is no one more competent than yourself to move in such a circle, but do throw away that ugly key. You will render yourself ridiculous by it, and in fact it is insulting to them to be flourishing it before their eyes. It is just as though you openly declared your contempt for those blessings of Providence that have been so abundantly bestowed on them."

Another time you are ready to sink in a sea of cares and perplexities. Then a voice comes to you, saying, "Is it possible that you insist on adding to your multitudinous cares the care of keeping that miserable key? You have no proper use of your hands while you persevere in carrying this worthless thing." Another time a very friendly voice says, "I rejoice to see that you have discrimination enough to prefer this homely key to the golden keys that men esteem; but is it not too precious to be carried daily about into the haunts of business? Here is a beautiful casket for it; leave it here in your bedroom, and gaze upon it in your hours of solitude and spiritual refreshment." Another emissary tries to make you swallow an intoxicating or stupefying draught, in the hope that you will then let it fall.

That key everybody despises, and yet no one will suffer you tranquilly to carry it. Wise men will spend the entire day in trying to show you by irrefragable [indisputable] proofs of science that there is no door in the universe that may be opened by that key. They should know far more about the universe than others; they have weighed the worlds in scales and have reconstructed extinct creations that preceded Adam on the earth.

You reply: "I have the testimony of yonder cloud of witnesses looking down upon us from thrones of light. This key admitted them and will me." The man of science says, "Much meditation has made you mad; there is no cloud of witnesses, there are no thrones of light. Here, take this magnifier and sweep the heavens, and convince yourself that there is nothing of the kind." You hold fast to your key and leave the poor man.

Then you meet with a most religious man, who says, "Oh, I am so delighted that you have the key! But you must know that without a little filing in one part and a little soldering in another the key will be of no use. There has been an alteration in the lock to suit our advanced times, and there must be a corresponding alteration in the key. Give me the key, and I will give it the required improvements at once." Still another meets you and says, "You have the right key, only it needs to have the stamp of my church upon it; otherwise the lock will refuse to know it."

Surely, it is wonderful if we are able to keep the very key of Heaven, the Word of God, in the face of all these impediments. But we are kept only as we keep it. To keep it is "to keep ourselves in the love of God."

John 17:7-8. *"Now they have known that all things whatsoever thou hast given me are of thee. For I have given unto them the words which thou gavest me; and they have received them, and have known surely that I came out from thee, and they have believed that thou didst send me."*

There was so much that was human about the Lord Jesus—He was such a veritable man; the play of human emotions was so visible upon His countenance and in the tones of His voice; there was such a spontaneousness about His utterances; there was such an unpretending simplicity in His deportment—that it was difficult for His companions, the apostles, to apprehend the divine nature through all this, except on certain special occasions when the works and words of God were too conspicuous to be unrecognized.

Now, in the last hours of His ministry, they were making rapid progress, and in the days succeeding His resurrection they would make still more rapid progress in the blessed art of discerning athwart [between] the human, the divine. They were now becoming aware that in the chambers of their memories, there was a vast treasury of acts, words, looks and tones bearing no more exalted designation than that which referred them to their Friend, Jesus, which were nevertheless of a value altogether infinite—the human modes, in fact, by which the nature and sentiments of the King of kings, the Lord of Hosts, the God of Abraham, had been expressed. The most precious of all conceivable utterances had fallen abundantly from His lips, and had been flung, slightly appreciated by them, to the lumber-house of memory.

Now it began to dawn upon them that a famished world would come and ask for those sublime gifts of revelation and of salvation entrusted to them by the Most High. This apprehension would have been overwhelming, had it not been for the promise of the Holy Spirit to bring to their remembrance all things whatsoever Christ had said unto them.

"Now they have known that My words were Thy words, *all* My words were Thine; that I have all along been uttering the sentiments, not of a mere Nazarene, but of God Himself." Ah! it was a long and wearisome battle the Savior had to wage against this form of unbelief. It was like a defeat to Him when He saw the idea developing itself in their minds of a Christ human apart from God. "I can of mine own self do nothing. I do always these things that please him. He hath given me a commandment, what I should say. I seek not mine own glory." Had He only been willing to receive glory for Himself as a man, a prophet, a created Messiah, men would have willingly given it. But treason was in the thought; He would not listen to it for a moment. He was in the world that God might be manifest and God be glorified, nor was He content till the idea of Him in the minds of the disciples, like a moon, was brought near to the idea of God, the sun, and He rejoiced greatly as the hour of conjunction drew near.

"They have received"; "have believed"; "have known surely." Faith is simply the heart's reception of the words of Christ. Belief of the truth is knowledge of the truth.

They have received the words. They have consented to receive the words with which Christ came freighted from Heaven. It was not Gabriel, it was Emmanuel Himself, the Lord of lords, Who was the bearer of these heavenly gifts, the words of everlasting life, to man. But after having entered this world, the difficulty was to find anyone that would receive them. This is still the difficulty.

Men are willing that the contents of every other mind should be poured into their intelligences, but who is willing that the contents of the mind of the Son of God, the treasures of wisdom and knowledge that were in Him, should be poured into his mind? No man ever spoke such words as Christ spoke. "Be thou clean," He said to the leper, and immediately he was healed of his leprosy; "Come forth," and Lazarus came forth; "Come out of him," and unclean spirits, legionary in number, fled. What mighty and triumphant words were these! Would you not have supposed that the least word from those lips would be esteemed by men as of incalculable value? Heaven and earth shall pass away, but not one jot or tittle of His words shall pass away.

A day will come when all human hearts shall be examined, and every one in whose heart shall be found words of Christ shall enter into the joy of the Lord, and never more see death, and every one in whose heart Christ's words shall not be found shall have his portion in the lake of fire. And yet men will not receive His words. That is, they will not take them into their hearts; they will not feed upon them; they will not make them a part of their life; they will not allow them to have the authority of truth over them. Have *you* received them, O reader? For instance, this word: "Except a man be born again, he cannot see the kingdom of God." Or this: "As many as are led by the Spirit of God, they are the sons of God." Or this: "He that is born of God hath the witness in himself." Or this: "I would thou wert cold or hot; because thou art lukewarm, I will spue thee out of my mouth." Or this: "Only believe." Or this: "It is more blessed to give than to receive."

Are you Christ's word-bearer in the world? When a question is asked touching your vocation, does the answer spontaneously rise to the lips of men, "Oh, he is one of those that bear the words of Christ"? When a question is asked touching your property, does it occur to men to say, "He has little that we value, but he has something that he esteems above all treasure, and that is the word of Christ"?

If the words of Christ would only dwell quietly in the heart without interfering with the other tenants, many of whom have been there from time immemorial, there would be little opposition made to their entrance. But the various denizens [residents] of the heart all understand perfectly that the word of Christ makes for itself a scourge of small cords and proceeds at once to attack these ancient residents. To receive it is like giving to all these notice to quit. What wonder that these combine to resist unto death this revolutionary and uncompromising element! But these tenants are really the emissaries of Satan and the dire enemies of the heart. They are triumphant mutineers reveling in the palace of which they have taken possession. The word of Christ exposes their true character, and allying itself to the will, expels them and restores the various chambers to peace, love, joy, long-suffering, gentleness, goodness, faith, meekness and temperance.

"The word is nigh thee, even in thy heart and in thy mouth, that if thou shalt confess with thy mouth the Lord Jesus, and shalt believe in thine heart that God hath raised him from the dead, thou shalt be saved."

To take the word concerning Christ crucified into our heart is to take that which will crucify our old and evil nature, and to receive the word concerning a risen Savior is to connect ourselves with Him rising and obtain deliverance from spiritual death.

John 17:9-10. *"I pray for them: I pray not for the world, but for them which thou hast given me; for they are thine. And all mine are thine, and thine are mine; and I am glorified in them."*

Christ prepares richest blessing for the world by praying for His people. His people are the channel through which His grace is diffused in the world. Consequently, the world has no interest that can for a moment be placed in urgency alongside of this—namely, that the people of Christ should be abundantly endued with all heavenly gifts. Christ is most truly interceding for the world when He intercedes for His people. We learn from His own words in this very prayer (verses 21, 23) that when His people are really one in Him, the world will believe on Him as the Sent of God, the Messiah, the Savior. Everywhere Scripture seeks to familiarize us with this idea. "He that believeth on me, out of his belly shall flow rivers of living water"; "he shall be a fountain of life"; "the wilderness and the solitary place shall be glad for him." "Ye are the light of the world."

As Christ prays for His own, so we are to pray for them and labor for them, knowing that, so far from robbing the world by giving our sympathies to the household of faith, we are, on the contrary, consulting its highest interests. And let it not fail to be remarked that the very things which are most to be desired for the disciples of Christ are those which will best fit them to be benefactors of their fellow-men.

"I pray for them whom thou hast given me." They were not made perfect and given to Christ, but given to Him in deepest unworthiness and spiritual ruin that He might make them perfect. They were given to Him to be prayed for by Him.

Can anything be more reassuring to the believer than the thought that he has been given to Christ and is now His property, stamped with His signet? He has been given to Him with all his unworthiness, his depravity, his wretchedness, his helplessness—given to Christ and accepted by Christ. The moment he obtains this assurance, he obtains a solid ground for the conviction that Christ will redeem him from all iniquity and purify him unto Himself. For Christ will not defile Himself by recognizing as His property that which continues vile.

Some generous man may receive into his house a wretched scape-gallows, but it will be with an intention to labor for his recovery. He will not so dishonor himself as to place an unreformable thief and libertine among his children. The moment a thing or a creature becomes identified with us, something of our life goes over into it, so that we are wounded with its wounds, and prospered with its prosperity. If we are given to Christ and recognized by Christ, then may we be sure that He will speedily remove every spot from us that we may be unblemished and holy.

Christ prays for them that have been given Him. Are they, then, to neglect praying for themselves? That would show that they have not been given to Him. Christ prays for them who pray through Him. Our prayers reach the throne of grace through Him, and the blessings of His Gospel reach the world through us.

Christ does everything for us. He dies for us, ascends for us, prays for us. He takes our prayers and makes them His own. The Father hears Him always. These prayers that are put in Christ's hands are very different in form and expression. Some men are very learned in the literature of prayer, but Christ receives with cordiality the prayer from which they would turn away in disgust. Some prayers, as they ascend, are shot at by many an angry arrow of criticism, but they wing their way upward; and are cheerfully presented by Him Whom the Father hears always. Whom Christ prays for, them He prays with; but there are some Christians so advanced that they will by no means be found praying with some for whom Christ prays. But we will hear Christ saying more on this point as we proceed.

"For they are thine; and all mine are thine and thine are mine; and I am glorified in them."

Whatsoever is Mine is Yours, and whatsoever is Yours is Mine.

All true worshippers of God, from the foundation of the world, are Christ's. Without the premeditated sacrifice of Christ, there would have been no communication of the grace of God made to them. "Before Abraham was, I am." Christ was truly, though not at the time so manifestly, the Mediator between God and Abraham as He is between the Father and us. Cornelius was directed to Peter that he might hear words whereby he should be saved—words concerning Christ. Woe unto him that is so bold as to make a distinction, and affirm that what is the Father's is not the Son's, what is the Son's is not the Father's! It is a great error to suppose that you can honor one without honoring the other.

Let me too say, "Whatsoever is mine is Yours, whatsoever is Yours is mine." I have naught but what is Yours. You, O Savior, are free to take and to dispose of all. Let me never see the day when I shall look gloomily at Your hand removing aught or turn a deaf ear to Your voice requiring the surrender of aught. And Yours is mine. Your people are mine. Whom You accept, shall I reject? Shall I not find pleasure in them? Shall I introduce a new doctrine of election, and out of Your elect ones select a minority for recognition and communion? Woe worth the day!

"I am glorified in them." There is an almost oppressive fullness of meaning in these words. Our poor faith staggers under them. Throughout the whole course of our Christian experience these words stand ready to show us great and mighty things which we know not. "Glorify thy Son," He had said before; now He subjoins, "I am glorified in them." It was far from enough that He should put on glory in the presence of the hosts of Heaven. His people are His representatives on earth, and He would be glorified in them.

He is glorified in them whom the Spirit of glory and of God rests upon, when they are His faithful witnesses and testify to all undauntedly and mightily that Jesus is the Christ. He is glorified in them when they get the victory over their own evil tendencies, and with meekness and lowliness of heart take His yoke upon them; when the Spirit of God has a full exhibition in their lives, demonstrating His presence, and thus demonstrating the presence of Christ glorified in Heaven. He is glorified in them when they carry on His own manner of life and go about doing good. He is glorified in them when their faith and consecration are such that they are enabled to do the works that He did, and greater works than these.

282

John 17:11. *"And now I am no more in the world, but these are in the world, and I come to thee. Holy Father, keep through thine own name those whom thou hast given me, that they may be one, as we are."*

He had before said of Himself, "As long as I am in the world I am the light of the world." So great significance belonged to His presence in the world. If the intelligence were suddenly flashed through the world that the sun now shining above our heads would set to rise no more, how dread the consternation that would seize all minds! With what intensity of desire and what bitterness of despair would all gaze upon the western sky, upon the orb of day sinking never more to reappear!

But the Sun of righteousness is, in a sense, immeasurably greater— the Lord of day; the day that disappears with Him embraces infinitely more of our interests; the night that follows His departure is the night of everlasting despair. How should such an announcement thrill through all human hearts! But the announcement does not come by itself. The Savior does not suffer the words to die away upon our ears before He utters healing and compensatory words. You will say, "How can this be? Where in all the realm of infinite truth can He find words rich enough to compensate for such an announcement?" He has found them, nevertheless: "These are in the world" and "I come to thee."

Who, then, are these to whose presence in the world Jesus refers in such a connection? If Jesus be no more in the world, what is it to us whether these disciples of His, these reeds shaken with the wind, be in the world or not? Even the Jews that put Messiah to death did not give themselves any trouble about His disciples that remained behind Him in the world. When the Shepherd is smitten, of what account are the scattered sheep? What virtue or wisdom or valor or power is in them? When the light of day is extinguished, of what account is the glow-worm?

Who are these? Are they not weak and foolish Galileans?—rude, uncultivated fishermen?—frail, erring creatures of dust?—like waves of the sea driven with the wind and tossed? When Greeks and

283

barbarians draw nigh, saying, "We would see Jesus," what manner of reply is this to make to them, "He is no more in the world, but these are in the world"? Jesus was holy, harmless, undefiled and separate from sinners, but these are unable to answer for one in a thousand of their transgressions.

Yes, but join together the two expressions, "These in the world" and "I come to thee." There are the disciples on the earth, and there is Jesus in Heaven—Jesus in Heaven having not merely all power in Heaven, but all power on earth. These who are in the world are indeed most insignificant, but they are united to Christ by faith; they are His instruments, directed by His Spirit. Whatsoever they ask the Father in His Name, it is done for them; they have the Word of Christ; it is theirs to make known the unsearchable riches of Christ.

When He was with them on the earth, He kept them indeed, but had often occasion to deplore the readiness with which they suffered themselves to be swayed by evil impulses. Ascending up on high, He will keep them in another and more glorious sense. They shall be endued with power from above—power to resist temptation, to overcome the evil of their natures, to testify of Him by bold words and mighty deeds, to establish His kingdom among Jews and Gentiles. There was far more of the power and glory and majesty of Christ seen in the streets of Jerusalem on the day of Pentecost than when the Savior in His own blessed Person walked those streets. Christ was then known for the first time by multitudes who had often heard Him speak and seen Him go in and out among them.

How little do we yet understand the great thought expressed in these words which fell from the lips of the departing Savior! How little do we understand that we are to be the representatives of Christ upon the earth, and to make manifest, in our own person, the savor of His Name! "Lo, I am with you always"—with us, not merely in the sense of made known to us, but in the more excellent sense of made known by us. "I am the vine, ye are the branches." How is the Vine made known save by the branches? If we were abiding in Him with anything like perfection of faith, it would be possible for us to say, "He that has seen us has seen Jesus."

But consider that we are representing *a* Jesus. We are either holding forth to the contemplation of men the true Christ or another. There is more in this than a mere figure of speech. We preach the Gospel to mankind, but the Christ of that Gospel is seen by men through the medium of the life we lead. "I am with the Father, and these are in the world to make Me known in My love and power, My wisdom and all-sufficiency."

When the Son of Man cometh, shall He find faith on the earth? Faith in anything like perfection? Faith to grasp the true idea of a Christian life? Faith to fulfill the high vocation bodied forth in this parting prayer? Faith to reproduce in all communities of earth the evidences that Christ is ascended upon high, and is giving good gifts to men? After having experimented upon the belief of His people, in all lands and under all conditions, will it be necessary for Him to say, "Therefore mine own arm brought salvation unto me, and my fury it upheld me. I have trodden the winepress alone, and of the people there was none with me"?

Bring this home to yourself personally. "I am no more in the world, but this one is in the world, and I come to thee." Christ called you and laid His hand on you, and then left you in the world to carry on His life, ascending up on high that you might have power with God. You have a multitude of exceeding great and precious promises, so that you might not be wanting in the means of enjoying perfect and constant communion with Him. He has given unto us all things pertaining unto life and godliness.

You upon the earth and He in Heaven. This is Christ's arrangement, with a view to the fullest revelation of Himself to the sinful souls of men. Do you understand this? Do you rightly conceive your position? Have you risen to the height of this great dignity, this sublime responsibility? Are you praying, aiming, living, so that men may see Jesus in you? Seek, as you value the souls of men, seek to appreciate your position. Make the most of the conditions belonging to this arrangement while you are subject to it. Let the prayer, "Come, Lord Jesus, come quickly," vindicate its own sincerity by a full-hearted, persevering and enlightened endeavor to show the world the utmost possible of Christ.

John 17:11-12. *"Holy Father, keep through thine own name those whom thou hast given me, that they may be one as we are. While I was with them in the world, I kept them in thy name: those that thou gavest me I have kept, and none of them is lost, but the son of perdition; that the Scripture might be fulfilled."*

The holiness of God expresses His opposition to all sin. They only know Him in His holiness who rejoice in the absolute opposition of His nature to all sin. No man knoweth the Father save the Son, in Whom is all His holiness, and save those to whom the Son reveals Him, changing their natures into a conformity with His.

"I have kept those whom thou hast given me in thy name, that they may be one as we are." The good Shepherd, being about to lay down His life, brings His little flock to the Father and consigns them to His care. He knows full well that when the Shepherd is smitten the sheep must be scattered, but not irrecoverably. He invokes the Divine aid in their behalf, so that in the hour of the power of darkness their faith may not utterly expire, and that they may speedily be united and abide safely under the shadow of their Father's wing.

As the disciples had looked with all confidence to Him in every time of peril, and had ascertained by indubitable experiments that there resided in Him all the love, the power and the wisdom that they could possibly need, so let them now look to the Father. For in fact the love, power, wisdom, manifested by Him were the love, the power and the wisdom of the Father. "Have I been so long time with you and yet hast thou not known me, Philip? He that hath seen me hath seen the Father." I have kept them in Your Name; in Your Name let them be kept. Let the knowledge of You be their preservation.

"Keep them, that they may be one as we are." This, then, is the prayer which Jesus offers in our behalf. We need to consider it well, for it is of sovereign importance that we should distinctly understand what we are to aim at. Christ's aim must surely be our aim. Christians are represented as those who are kept by the power of God through faith unto salvation. On this keeping hangs salvation. An error here will send its blighting influence along the entire pathway of our unending existence.

When Christ was in the world, He kept them—from what? He kept them—how?

He kept them from the evil that was in the world. What efforts were made to destroy their confidence in Christ! How subtly, and perhaps unanswerably, did Scribes and Pharisees often cite the Scripture to show them that Jesus could not be the Messiah! How many scriptural difficulties were they called upon to solve! And when they were obliged to confess that they were unable, of themselves, to solve them, with how much derision were they told that it would better become them first to master the revealed will of God, and then set themselves in opposition to the teaching of the masters in Israel!

We may be sure that if many came to Jesus with their objections and their questions, many also came to the disciples when they were absent from Him, and that such faith as they had was exposed to many a fiery dart of the adversary. Jesus was to them a shield, and kept them during this bitter and prolonged conflict. Many others went away. There was a sermon preached by Jesus in the synagogue at Capernaum, and there were muttered objections of the Jews on the same occasion. The result was, that many fell away from Jesus and there was great triumph on the part of His adversaries. It was a very critical moment; the day seemed to go against Jesus altogether, insomuch that many thought the apostles would also fall away. Their faith trembled in the balance, but they resolved to stand by Jesus. "To whom shall we go? thou hast the words of eternal life."

The servant of Christ declaring the Gospel to the heathen may engage in similar discussions and witness similar results. Men that have not the love of the truth in them will fail to feel the force of the arguments used by the defenders of the truth, and they may be cheered by seeing some ill-grounded professors of Christianity apostatize from the faith. But Christ keepeth His own, not by ceasing to declare the truths that give offence, but by giving His people experience of the

287

power of His words in the heart, and deepening their convictions that those words are words of everlasting life.

He kept them by the revelation of Himself to them. Though there was much about Christ that they could not explain, though many of His words were to them mysterious, though His course in many things confounded all their anticipations,—yet they refused to surrender their confidence in Him. If we divide their life of faith into two parts, one preceding His resurrection, the other succeeding, altogether the severest trial of their faith was perhaps during the first part.

Just in the degree in which they were kept united to Christ were they kept united to each other. Just in the degree in which our faith shall be perfected and a more tender and intimate intercourse with Christ established, shall we be inspired with mutual love. We should hardly have expected just here the petition, "That they may be one." But it is most interesting to observe that the two things, the preservation of the disciples and their union, constitute but one desideratum [requirement] in the mind of Christ. These are essentially connected. The scattering of the flock is the destruction of the flock. How much do they therefore sin against Christ who wish to be kept apart from the rest of the flock!

The best evidence that a man is abiding in Christ is found in the tenacity of his attachment to the people of Christ. Where this evidence is not seen, there is reason to fear that the true Christ is not known. And let us not forget that the best evidence of Christian love is by no means afforded when we find ourselves powerfully drawn to those who think just as we do touching the doctrines of religion and modes of worship. A man begins to give irreproachable evidence of Christian love, and shows that the petition of Christ, "That they all may be one," has an echo in his heart only when he begins to find joy and refreshing in the society of those whose sentiments on many minor things run counter to his own, and who are accordant with him only in the matter of loving Christ.

This gives us a wonderful picture of what salvation is. A man cannot be saved by himself. Salvation is a common salvation. The very bond that unites to Christ unites to His people. The new life in the soul wages an unremitting war against selfishness. Every man who truly cries, "Save *me*," learns afterward to cry, "Save *them*." He identifies his interests with those of Christ, consequently with those of all Christians, with those of the truth, with those of humanity, seeing that Christ was a propitiation not for our sins only, but for those of the whole world.

"And none of them is lost but the son of perdition, that the Scripture might be fulfilled." It is not certain that these words, "That the Scripture might be fulfilled," refer to what is said of the son of perdition. They may refer to the words, "I have kept them in thy name." Probably, however, they refer to Judas, as our Lord a little before (13:18) had quoted the Scripture, "He that eateth bread with me hath lifted up his heel against me," applying it to the betrayer.

"The son of perdition." Compare with this similar expressions: "The children of disobedience, the sons of peace." It was the character of Judas that made him a son of perdition. The evil of his nature was germinant within him and manifest to the eye of Christ, long before it was suspected by others. A very slight modification of circumstances would have enabled him to pass unsuspected through life. The manifest Judases in the church are very few, compared with the unsuspected.

The successor of Judas is one who hears daily the words of the Lord Jesus, and is mixed up with the best Christians—not an avowed enemy of Christ, but a greater lover of something else, it may be gold; and when he is obliged to choose between Christ and that rival god, the rival carries the day. But his great study is to avoid coming to such an open election, and, in fact, to retain externally his connection with the one while he continues to enjoy the other.

John 17:13. *"And now come I to thee; and these things I speak in the world, that they might have my joy fulfilled in themselves."*

Out of the depths of this world the voice of the Savior is heard, saying to Him Who sits upon the throne, "I come to thee." He descended into this fallen world, and identified Himself with humanity; and it is with a blissful consciousness that He has grappled to Himself the race, and that in Him humanity will ascend on high to the region where no curse is, that He exclaims, "I come to thee." For we rise with Him. The passage by which He mounts on high is one that remains open behind Him. No hand in Heaven or on earth or in the realm of darkness hath power to close it, until He return in the clouds of Heaven to judge the world.

An expression like that which then follows we have had already: "These things have I spoken unto you that my joy might remain in you, and that your joy might be full," John 15:11. Once more we are called to consider the delightful fact that Jesus, when about to depart out of this world, was chiefly solicitous to endow His disciples with all His own wealth of spiritual blessing. He gave them His peace, His position, His privileges, His joy, His power, His holiness, His Father's words, His Father's care, His Father's love, His union with the Father, His own glory.

This marvelous characteristic of this parting interview should never be lost sight of. And this prayer was uttered chiefly that disciples may understand, if their faith permit, that they are brought unto Him in order that they may step into the position from which He steps, ascending on high that they may there encounter the same glance of love that came to Him from the Father, receive the same words, have the same communion; that they may encounter the same contradiction of sinners, be sustained by the same peace, the same hope.

Christ came not merely that we might have life, but that we might have His life—not merely that we might have forgiveness of sins and unending happiness, but that we might participate in the glorious elements of His own sublime existence. "Abide in me and I in you." "Christ liveth in me." "For me to live is Christ." How little is this understood! The only life that we can obtain from Christ is His life. He is made unto us wisdom, righteousness, sanctification, redemption. We are partakers of His nature as well as of His salvation. The same mind that was in Him is to be in us. In this connection there is a great depth of meaning in the following passage: "Till we all come in the unity of the faith and of the knowledge of the Son of God, unto a perfect man, unto the measure of the stature of the fullness of Christ; that we henceforth be no more children." Is it not time that our hearts gave an echo to this word of Paul, "That we henceforth be no more children"?

"These things I speak in the world." "In the world"—while He was yet in the world, before His crucifixion. He was on the point of becoming a prey to the direst agony. He was about to die a death such as no man had ever known. Yet He tranquilly and lovingly makes arrangements at the throne of grace in behalf of His disciples, that His joy may be fulfilled in them. His prayers were generally addressed in private to the Father. This prayer was uttered audibly, in order that the disciples might be gladdened by hearing Him urge with such serenity of confidence their interests at the throne of God. He knew also that His words would have a place in the everlasting Gospel, and be published among all nations in all languages.

"That they might have joy." "That they might have *my* joy." "That they might have my joy *fulfilled*." We have, then, the unimpeachable testimony of the Son of God to this important fact, that there is in the seventeenth chapter of John provision made for the joy of believers. "Who will show us any good thing?" is the desponding exclamation of many. Even believers often need to learn anew where and how joy is to be found. But mark, it is Christ's joy. If you borrow anything from the world's definition of joy, you will look in vain to the words of Christ for the satisfaction of your soul's need. You must let Christ teach you what joy is and then you shall find His words to be joy-inspiring.

Do you suppose that Christ would select for Himself out of all the joys of the universe those that are inferior? No; His joy is the joy of Heaven; it is from the throne of God; its home is the bosom of God. Surely it is a vain deceit you are practicing upon yourself if, while professing to desire and look forward to the life of Heaven, you neglect to avail yourself of the provision which Christ has made for you in this chapter.

We are told that the word by which we are to be saved is nigh us, even in our heart and in our mouth. The word has various properties. It saves. It also sanctifies. It gives peace. It inspires joy. It renders fruitful. We know that it is to us the word that saves, because it is also the word that sanctifies, the word that imparts joy. But if it be not in our experience a joy-imparting word, why should we cling so confidently to the persuasion that salvation will come by it unto us? It is the word of life, and the life which it communicates is something now possessed, not a thing of the future.

Far be it from me to wish to dampen the confidence of any whose faith is genuine, though small as a grain of mustard-seed. But Christ will save us in His way, not in our way. "This is eternal life," He says, "that they may know thee, the only true God, and Jesus Christ whom thou hast sent." This knowledge we obtain here. Paul counted all things but loss for the excellency of the knowledge of Christ. Not merely at the beginning of his course, but during all the length of it, he had this intense thirst for the knowledge of Christ, maintained in its intensity by the blessed attainments he was continually permitted to make.

See how the joy of Christ was fulfilled in Paul. Paul was raised up to be an example not merely of how much the grace of God would forgive, but also of how much the grace of God would bestow after having forgiven. Paul is just a comment upon the words of Jesus. When Christ says, "They are not of the world," we may turn to Paul, and by the life of the apostle obtain an approximate conception of the meaning of the word. When He says, "Sanctify them through thy truth," Paul will again help us to understand His meaning. When He says, "I am no more in the world, but these are in the world," it will again be profitable to look to the apostle.

Believer, what is your joy? Today's joy? Yesterday's? Look at it, take the measure of it, and ask yourself if it be that joy which Christ here speaks of as His own, for nothing less than that has He made over to you. This joy of yours, is it bright, blessed, sanctifying, strengthening? Does it arm you against temptation, and lift you above care, and fill your devotions with thanksgiving, and facilitate the entrance of your words into the hearts of those to whom you speak concerning Christ? If not, then let me urge you to take your unsatisfactory joys to Christ, lay them at His feet and ask Him for the genuine. Learn to look on everything as an enemy that would tend to keep the joy-chamber of your nature, set apart by Christ for Himself in these words, in the possession of alien joys that have scarce any acquaintance with the crucified One.

John 17:14. *"I have given them thy word; and the world hath hated them, because they are not of the world, even as I am not of the world."*

The Savior gave eyes to the blind, hearing to the deaf, speech to the dumb, health to the multitudes that were suffering from incurable ailments, food to the hungry, deliverance to the tempest-tossed, life to the dead. He showed that He had power over all material wealth by directing His servant to find a piece of money in the mouth of a fish— a miracle that He wrought in order, perhaps, to show the lovers of money His ability to surround Himself with untold wealth and His abnegation of that power. What, then, did He give His disciples? He gave them the Word of God and a heart to receive that Word. He taught them to recognize the words of God in His works. What He valued above all, He taught them so to value. He made them willing to count all things worthless in comparison with the Word of God communicated by Him.

"The Lord hath set apart him that is godly for himself." How? By giving him His Word. By writing His law in his heart. It is thus that the disciples of Christ are made to be "not of the world." The world cannot receive the words of Christ; they are foolishness unto it. Just so far as a man receives the Word of Christ, he receives Christ Himself. When the Word of God dwelleth richly in him, then Christ abideth in his heart, by faith; if Christ abideth in his heart, then is his character assimilated to that of Christ, for Christ dwells in no heart otherwise than as Sovereign, with power to reveal Himself in the words, the works, the ways of man.

Christ speaks of what He has already given me. It is much, it is magnificent in His eyes. What ought it to be in mine? Does it become me to seem to myself a very poor man? Are not the answers to thousands of my prayers to be found in the given Word? Shall I torment the Savior for heavenly things when the heavenly things disguised in earthly words, exhaustless mines of wealth, are around me? How few

Christians have done more than just taste the words of Christ! There is probably not a Christian on the face of the earth who has not despised and neglected far greater blessings than those which he has appropriated. Without faith it is impossible to please God, and the food of faith is His Word.

Some that were prisoners in Lucknow received one day a single leaf of a Bible. With what avidity did they devour the words! How marvelous seemed the promise contained in that scrap of paper! Would it not be an immense gain to many who are now sighing and pining among the countless promises of God's holy volume to be reduced to some similar scrap of Scripture? Were large portions to disappear mysteriously and irrecoverably from their Bibles, day by day, with what alarm and anxiety would they seize upon the diminishing treasure! Should it continue to vanish, entire books of it at a time taking wings and fleeing back to Him that gave it, until scarce a little tract of holy words remained, may we not suppose that these readers would begin to snatch at the words of life with an intensity of desire and of appreciation never before known?

Imagine the ancient prophets, David, Isaiah, Jeremiah, introduced to a company of modern Christians; with what a holy impetuosity would they congratulate them upon their possession of the complete Scriptures, wondering, withal, how they could find time to sleep and to eat! Those ancient prophets felt themselves imprisoned in the incompleteness of the revelation given them, because of the glimpses that they sometimes obtained of the Messianic fullness of time. But how small the number of those who have any very exuberant sense of the blessedness connected with the possession of Christ's Word!

"They are not of the world, even as I am not of the world." This is not a prayer, not the expression of a desire, but the statement of a fact. If we are of the world, we are not Christ's. But many will perhaps say, "It is difficult to determine precisely what is meant by this expression, 'of the world'; different Christians have different conceptions. You must beware, therefore, how you denounce this and that person as being out of Christ because they are in the world."

Is it, then, so difficult to decide this question? Is it at all doubtful what kind of life Christ led? We are not of the world, as He was not of the world.

Christ mingled freely with all classes of men. He did not clothe Himself with a forbidding austerity. He inspired publicans and sinners with confidence and accepted the invitations of Pharisees. But He would not do or say anything, in any society, that might in any way appear to countenance what was wrong in the customs, maxims, aims or religion of men. Nor would He omit to do or say anything whereby He might express His disapprobation of their erroneous sentiments and habits. He pleased not Himself, but studied the pleasure and comfort of all, so far as the interests of truth would permit Him. He was in the world to bear witness of the truth. He would go into any assembly, but never would He neglect the opportunity of teaching men that the great truths concerning God and salvation are topics most suitable for such occasions, and by no means to be excluded. He would not go where the truth of God might not go. He was always Himself—that is, One Who looked upon men as spiritual beings bound to the judgment-seat; sinners, obnoxious to the wrath of God; needing to be born again; needing the pearl of great price; needing to work out their salvation with fear and trembling—these were His views; and to say that He was always true to Himself is to say that He always aimed at the best enunciation of these views.

In like manner His disciples are in the world to bear witness of the truth. They are lights in the world holding forth the Word of Life. Were they of the world, they would not be lights in the world. Light shines in darkness, and the darkness comprehends it not. They will mingle freely with the world, on condition that they shall not be called to yield any recognition to the maxims and sentiments and customs of the world, on condition that they shall not be obliged to suppress any of the great truths that they are set apart to make known.

Is it not a fact that many who are regarded as Christians are freely invited to worldly assemblies? Would they be were it not well understood that they will observe the usages of society, and avoid the introduction of the subject of religion? And if those who profess to be the followers of Christ should realize it to be their duty to bear everywhere witness of the truth, and to discountenance the maxims by which society is constituted, is it not likely that there would be a great revolution in their social taste? We imagine that they would, debarred from that society in which they have ordinarily mingled, look around them for the people of God, and join themselves to them with a heartiness not before exhibited. Then would the ways of Zion no longer languish.

Perhaps the great obstacle to the realization of Christ's desire for the union of His people, expressed in the latter part of this prayer, is in the very prevalent idea that a man may be of the world and yet be a Christian. Our Lord has already sat in judgment upon these worldly Christians; there is no need to wait for the last day; the Word that will then judge is now with us. We are told that Christ's people are not of the world, as He is not of the world, for He has given them His Word, to be borne everywhere by them, and to be uttered by them in their conduct and otherwise; and there is no truce between this Word and the fashion of this world. There is indeed a truce between many who profess to be Christ's word-bearers and the world, but the mistake is in supposing that they are His word-bearers. There are many who are willing enough to confess Christ in nine places if they may be excused from confessing Him in the tenth.

John 17:15-16. *"I pray not that thou shouldst take them out of the world, but that thou shouldst keep them from the evil. They are not of the world, even as I am not of the world."*

Christ's people have been brought out of darkness into God's marvelous light not merely in order to obtain their own salvation, but that they may be lights in the world holding forth the Word of Life; and, just in the degree in which it is desirable that the lights of life should be shed abroad among mankind, is it desirable that those who have been called, and justified, and sanctified, should continue here to prosecute that work for which they have been so carefully fitted, so abundantly qualified.

We sometimes hear the expression that such a one is ripening for glory, and the opinion seems to be entertained by some that rapid progress in sanctification is a sure omen of proximate translation to the better land. There is no place in the universe where holy men are so much needed as they are in this very world of ours, and may we not say that every eminently holy man would, on many accounts, prefer this life and its privileges to the blessedness of Heaven?

"To depart and be with Christ is far better" was the opinion of an eminently holy man, but this was only the half of his opinion, for he hastened to add that beyond this "far better" was another "far better." To be with Christ in glory would be unspeakable gain to himself, but the privilege he now enjoyed of laboring to bring others to the enjoyment of that unspeakable gain would be forfeited by his departure. "To abide in the flesh is more needful for you. And having this confidence, I know that I shall abide and continue with you all, for your furtherance and joy of faith."

As we become like Christ we rejoice in the opportunity of communicating the knowledge of salvation through His blood to perishing sinners. It is indeed the will of Christ that His redeemed ones should be with Him where He is, and behold His glory, in the mansion prepared for them. But we are here called to observe that He declines offering a prayer that they should be removed from the world. It is doubtless His will that they should remain here so long as the interest of His kingdom may be subserved by their presence here.

Some may be ready to remark that persons who give the highest promise of usefulness are often very mysteriously removed. After years of preparation they become, so far as we can see, peculiarly fitted for labor in their particular sphere, and are then cut down on the very threshold of their labors. There are such instances, and doubtless it is necessary that there should be such. In order that this may be a state of probation adapted to promote the largest and best results, it is fitting that every individual, no matter how richly endowed with gifts of the Spirit, should have it impressed upon him, at every step of his life-journey, that he has this treasure in an earthen vessel, and that he may be summoned away from earth at any moment.

It would not be, on the whole, desirable that Christians should have a guarantee of long life in this world, either for themselves or others. The least reflection will show that many evils would be likely to result from any different ordination of Providence than that which compels every servant of Christ, whatever his usefulness or his aspiration, to realize that he has here no abiding city, and may be ushered at any moment into eternity. Were we in a position to ascertain the facts, it would probably appear that the instances to which we have referred are not proportionably so numerous as they appear and that there is, on the whole, a greater measure of life given to Christ's devoted servants than to others.

Christ prays not that His servants should be taken out of the world; what, then, is His prayer? That they may be kept from *the evil*; "the whole world lieth in *wickedness*"; "deliver us from *evil*"; the same word occurs in these three passages. We may add another example: "That he might deliver us from this present *evil* world." And still another: "He that is begotten of God keepeth himself, and that *wicked one* toucheth him not." Possibly, this last translation may be the fittest, in all

299

the instances. The word is similarly rendered in Matt. 13:19: "Then cometh the *wicked one*, and catcheth away that which was sown."

This wicked one is represented in Scripture as the prince of this world; he reigns in the hearts of the children of disobedience. The whole world, with the exception of the people of Christ, lies in willing subjection to him. He is styled the god of this world—has his heavenly places, his angels, his principalities and powers. The passages from Matthew show the nature of his antagonism to the word-bearers of Christ; he seeks to catch away the word out of their heart.

This word is like a signet-ring of their Lord, a pledge of victory. Embraced faithfully, it overcomes the world in the heart of the believer, and embosoms within itself capacities of external conquest that justly alarm the prince of the power of the air. He accordingly rises in his strength to assail that word wherever he discovers it, and the heart in which it has found a lodgment becomes the object of his immediate solicitude. In view of this ever-impending strife, the prayer of Christ ascends to the Father in behalf of those who have received His words: "Keep them from the evil one." If he that is mighty, even the god of this world, has sat down in battle array against the soul in which Christ's word is deposited, let Him that is mightier, even the Lord of hosts, appear for the defense of this soul.

But how does this harmonize with the passage already quoted from John's Epistle: "He that is begotten of God keepeth himself, and that wicked one toucheth him not"? "He keepeth himself"; how is this? Jude has something like this: "Keep yourselves in the love of God." But Jude quickly followed it up with—"Now unto him that is able to keep you from falling."

But let us consider how God keeps His people from the wicked one. He shows them the power of their adversary and inspires them with a hatred of his rule. He shows them His own superior power and the conditions upon which He exerts it. He bids them be strong in the grace that is in Jesus Christ and fight the good fight of faith. They discover that whereas without Christ they can do nothing, through Christ they can do all things. They consider that there are ten thousand promises of the grace of God in the Scriptures, and that if this grace were to be exerted in subduing their adversary without action on their part, there would have been no need of a single promise. They learn accordingly to work out their own salvation with fear and trembling, assured that when they do this God Himself is working in them to will and to do, of His good pleasure. Thus they are kept by the power of God through faith unto salvation.

The Word of God is kept in them by faith; by their own faith they overcome the world, for faith opens the door for the manifestation of the power of God. Be strong in the Lord. Strength, energy, determination, perseverance, wisdom, boldness and many other qualities are manifested by him who, ignoring any strength and wisdom of his own, is nevertheless strong in the Lord and in the power of His might.

John 17:17. *"Sanctify them through thy truth: thy word is truth."*

There is some warrant for reading "the truth" instead of "thy truth." All truth is God's truth. What truth is especially referred to is shown by the statement, "Thy word is truth." If we would know what is God's Word, we are referred to another statement in the context: "I have given them thy word." Have we no other word of God than that which fell from the lips of Jesus? Oh yes: "God, who spake in time past unto the fathers by the prophets, hath in these last days spoken unto us by his Son." "All Scripture is given by inspiration of God." Christ hath borne the same testimony concerning the Scriptures generally as He has concerning His own words. The Word of God bore testimony to Him; He received that testimony; He appealed to the Scriptures of the Old Testament; belief in Moses was a preparation for belief in Him.

What honor He invariably put upon the Word! When He accompanied the two to Emmaus, He did not flash upon them the evidence that Christ was risen but beginning at Moses and descending through all the prophets, He convinced them that nothing had been done to Christ except what had been distinctly predicted. And having compelled them to honor the Scriptures by believing them, He made Himself known to them in the breaking of bread. We are reminded of His own words: "If I have told you earthly things, and ye believe not, how shall ye believe if I tell you of heavenly things?" The earthly things are the things already revealed. God requires us to believe and give expression to the truth already brought before us, ere He will consent to reveal unto us things that properly lie beyond them. There are some who enter the King's highway of prophecy, not by the narrow gate of experimental truth, but by climbing over the wall. Wanting the appointed preparation, they soon wander from the path.

We have said that Christ received testimony from the Word. He both received and gave. And so with His Church; it receives testimony from the Word and gives a response of attestation to the Scriptures. There is a church that says, "It is mine alone to declare what is the

302

word, and no man comes unto the word save by me; faith in me must precede faith in the word." "Ah, but," says the poor sinner, "how know I that you will indeed guide me to the Word? I need testimony concerning *you* before I can blindly follow your testimony. Let me once know that you are the Church of Christ, and that you are infallible, then I can tranquilly surrender myself to your guidance. But who can really testify to me that you are that save God Himself? And where is God's testimony except in His Word? How, then, can I possibly believe in you unless I have a previous faith in God's Word? That Word must guide me to you, not you me to the Word."

Our Savior's prayer in behalf of His people is that they may be made holy. He refers to the means, the Word of God, but He does not mention the agent, the Holy Spirit. There is no mention in the whole of this prayer of the Holy Spirit. But He had previously taught His disciples that none of the things mentioned in these petitions could be accomplished without the Holy Spirit, and He had positively promised that they should receive the Comforter. The disciples had the truth, yet the Savior prays the Father to sanctify them by means of it. In itself it could not sanctify them; they could not sanctify themselves by it; there was to be an altogether additional forth-putting of the divine power, in order that it might be the means of their sanctification.

We must, therefore, ever take the Word of God back to God and ask Him to sanctify us with it. Oh that in all our reading of the Scriptures we might remember to cry mightily to God that our eyes may be opened to behold the wondrous things that are therein! We would think it a great thing if a message should be conveyed to us by some angel from above, to the effect that we might for the mere asking obtain a great addition to the Word of God. Yet we may for the mere asking so obtain the influences of the Spirit of truth that it will be as though a verse of the Scripture became a page and a page became a book. Are there not many among Christians who are reading the Bible with the minimum of the Spirit? Let us ask ourselves as we read whether any power greater than that of our own natural intelligence is employed in writing the words upon our heart.

All you that hunger and thirst after righteousness listen to the blessed words which the great Intercessor addresses to your Father and His Father: "Sanctify them." You know that if you ask anything according to His will, you have the petitions that you desired of Him. The question recurs, "What is His will?" This, then, is the will of God, even your sanctification.

Christ's unchangeable desire in behalf of all His people is that they may be sanctified. This prayer that they may be with Him and see His glory is introduced by a petition for their sanctification. And observe, He places no limit. He does not say, "Sanctify them in part." He draws no line whereto and no farther He would have the work of sanctification proceed. No matter how far the Spirit of God may have carried this work in any one, it is still the privilege of such a one to avail himself of this petition. "He is able (and not unwilling) to do exceeding abundantly above all that we ask or think." Do you fear lest some good brother is carried away by an extravagant conception of what the Lord will do for him? Your fear is vain. Let his thought tower as it may, God engages that His power and grace shall soar beyond it, their limits as distant as ever.

But what is holiness? First let us ask, "What is it that the Spirit of God does with the truth?" All that He does is simply to give it sway over the mind. He does not aim to do anything more than cause the truth to dwell in the mind clothed with the authority that properly belongs to it. The mind is naturally adverse to God's truth, and insists upon perverting it and degrading it and mutilating it. But the Spirit of truth causes the truth to stand up on its feet and to sit down on its throne.

The truth without the Spirit is dead; it is a defenseless carcass in the hands of men. The Spirit makes it to live and to do valiantly. Whatever the truth of God is intended and fitted to accomplish, that is holiness. We are holy just so far as we are living under the power of the truth. A saint is just a true man. He that scorns to be thought a saint declares that he knows not the companionship of truth. He is consecrated to the expression of falsehood. He that is thoroughly under the influence of truth is a thoroughly holy man. But let it be understood that God's Word is truth.

304

John 17:18-20. *"As thou hast sent me into the world, even so have I also sent them into the world. And for their sakes I sanctify myself, that they also might be sanctified through the truth. Neither pray I for these alone, but for them also which shall believe on me through their word."*

"As thou hast sent me into the world, even so have I also sent them into the world." "As I am Your apostle in the world, so these are My apostles in the world." An apostle is simply one sent. They whom we call apostles are distinguished from others, not by their designation, but by their gifts.

Christ, being not of the world, was sent into the world; the apostles were first chosen out of the world, and then sent into it. Christ was anointed for His work by Him that sent Him; the Spirit of God was upon Him; the apostles were endued with power from on high when the Holy Ghost came upon them. As the Father that sent Christ left Him not alone, so Christ promised to be with His disciples even unto the end of the world. As Christ came into the world to seek and to save that which was lost, so the apostles were sent forth to seek the salvation of men.

As the Father acted with infinite wisdom in sending His Son on such a mission, so was the wisdom of God manifested in sending, not angels, but redeemed men—men even in process of redemption—to carry on this mission. As the Father heard the Son always, so it was the privilege of His apostles to know that He Who had sent them, and Who was clothed with all power in Heaven and earth, would hear them always. As the Father manifested Himself to Christ, so Christ would manifest Himself to the apostles. As Christ was sent with His own full accord, saying cheerfully, "Lo, I come to do thy will," so the apostles were heartily content to go forth on the mission assigned them.

As it was in love that the Father committed this work to the Son, so it was in love that the Savior commissioned His disciples to go to the world that hated them and preach the Gospel. As Christ was a

Root out of a dry ground, springing up where no one would have supposed He would, among the rude and despised people of Galilee in prophetless Nazareth, so the disciples were Galileans, and their birth and nurture were much against them in the estimation of educated Jews. Christ spent much of His life as a carpenter, toiling for His daily bread; the disciples were also of the laboring class. Christ testified of the world that it was evil, and a similar testimony is committed to His disciples. Through suffering Christ entered into His glory; through much tribulation the apostles entered into the kingdom of Heaven.

"And for their sakes I sanctify myself that they also might be sanctified through the truth."

Believers are sanctified by the Father, (v. 17). Christ speaks of sanctifying Himself; there must, then, be a difference in the signification of the words. However, the Savior once spoke of Himself as "him whom the Father hath sanctified and sent into the world." The primitive idea in sanctification is separation. "Thou hast set apart him that is godly for thyself"—separation from the world, with a special view to the revelation of the glory of God. Christ was separate from sinners, and the divine recognition of this fact constituted the sanctification referred to in the passage just quoted. "This is my beloved Son in whom I am well pleased"—these words set Him forth as sanctified. His people are separated from sinners by being separated from sin.

Believers are sanctified through the truth, because the truth reveals to them the Lamb of God that taketh away the sin of the world. Beholding as in a glass the glory of the Lord, they are changed into the same image. The light of the glorious Gospel of God shines into their hearts. Christ made the truth what it is by living, speaking, acting and suffering as He did; and it is evident that what He means by His self-sanctification is just this—the revelation of His holy nature in all appropriate ways, so that the record of His life and death should be all that the necessity of the case demanded, with a view to the sanctification of believers.

Let me, then, as I read the Gospels, continually remember that Christ uttered this and that parable, wrought this and that miracle, underwent this and that humiliation, with reference to the sanctification of His people, with reference to my sanctification. Would it not be a profitable employment for us to go carefully and prayerfully through the Gospel with this idea constantly before us? Every individual record is presented to me by the Savior, with an expression of His desire that I may be sanctified by means of it.

"Neither pray I for these alone, but for them also which shall believe on me through their word."

In this, as in other passages, we are unequivocally taught the absolute necessity of the word of the Gospel in order to faith in Christ.

How shall they believe in Him of Whom they have not heard? and how shall they hear without a preacher? Many excuse themselves for the great crime of not making known the Gospel by boldly dismissing the word that assures them that faith is dependent upon hearing. All faith is the reception of some word. God might have revealed the Gospel by dreams or immediate inspiration, to all human beings, but neither this nor anything like it is any part of His plan. He has sometimes made use of visions and of angels to awaken some perishing sinner, but what was the announcement made on such occasions? "Go to such an apostle, send for such an evangelist, and he will tell thee *words whereby thou shalt be saved*." To whom shall we go? You have the words of eternal life; and the words which He gave to them are none other, in fact, than what He here speaks of as "their word"; "I pray for them which shall believe on me through their word."

Every believer believes that Christ intercedes for him. How can he be called a believer if he believes not this? This prayer here recorded is one that we are permitted to hear, but we have faith with regard to those we hear not. In this recorded prayer we have an epitome of the prayers that Jesus offers in behalf of His disciples. "But I wish to know," says some impetuous suppliant, "whether my particular petition is presented by Christ." Not if it be in conflict with the petitions here embodied.

If you pray for something that would tend to impede the work of your sanctification, either Christ must withdraw His prayer for your sanctification or else your prayer must be given to the winds. Happy for you if your prayer be given to the winds! You are perhaps as much indebted to the intercession of Christ for the failure of your petitions as for their success. See to it that your prayers correspond to those which the Saviour here offers for you. After this manner pray you. Christ is not our Mediator save as He is our Teacher. If we insist on urging at the throne of God some prayer that Christ has not taught us to offer—has indeed directed us not to offer—we set aside the mediation of Christ; and however profusely we may mix His Name up with our prayers, He knows us not, knows not these supplications.

What soul-reviving words are these: "I pray for them that believe"! You are one of those, are you not? Do you understand these words? The Son of God in Heaven, on Whom the enraptured eyes of all are fixed, prays for you. You bind Him to the earth, and He feels that He is only half in Heaven while you are on this treacherous earth. He has the keenest sense of all that affects you or threatens you, and He prays for you. This prayer is prayer indeed. You need not take your idea of it from your own prayer. That will give you no clue.

John 17:21. *"That they all may be one; as thou, Father, art in me, and I in thee, that they also may be one in us; that the world may believe that thou hast sent me."*

One is almost overwhelmed with the sublime propositions that crowd upon us in this passage. Look at Christ the man, and consider the intercourse of His soul with God. How wonderful the correspondence that went unceasingly on between the Savior and the Father! There was no part dark in Him—no thought, feeling or imagination that refused to encounter the light that beamed in the look of His Father. "The Father loveth the Son and showeth him all things that himself doeth." "What things soever he doeth, those also doeth the Son likewise." "I know that thou hearest me always." "The Son of man WHO IS in heaven." "Who is in the bosom of the Father."

Christ prays that the believer may occupy on the earth the same blessed position that He occupied relatively to the Father, that there may be between the two the same marvelous intercommunion; the same unfaltering fellowship; the same most intimate union. And in order that there may be this wondrous harmony between God and the believing soul, He prays that that soul may abide in Christ as the Way, the Truth and the Life, may be one in Him as the branch is one in the vine, may make Christ its all in all, and understand how thoroughly Christ has given Himself to it.

He prays thus in behalf not of one believing soul, but of all. And when believers thus, or approximately thus, abide in the Father and in the Son, then will they be found abiding in one another. The union between them will be of such a nature that the world will be arrested by the spectacle and irresistibly compelled to believe on Jesus as the Christ, the only Redeemer of the lost, for they will have before their eyes the spectacle of redemption accomplished.

Here, then, we find the Savior praying for the world, entreating in their behalf the greatest of gifts—faith. We see that in all His intercessions for His people, He has still regard to the salvation of the unawakened multitudes. If for a little He concentrates His attention upon His own, it is that they may be rendered the salt of the earth, and more competent as lights in the world to hold forth the Word of Life to the perishing around. He offers here substantially the prayer which He taught His disciples to offer: "Thy kingdom come, thy will be done on earth as it is in heaven."

If men have in common one supreme aim, this suffices to bind them together. There is union among them when they have an enthusiastic admiration for someone who is leading them through dangers to victory. Though nothing can exceed man's inhumanity to man, yet we see everywhere the evidence that men *can* unite. The name of a man they never saw becomes a rallying word for millions. The Christian, however, knows in Whom he has believed. Christ is precious to the believer, and just in the degree in which He is so are believers drawn to each other. If there be little that is worthy of the name of union among Christians, it is simply because there is a very equivocal union betwixt them and Christ.

The twenty-fifth of Matthew informs us that the great revelation of the judgment day will be that love to Christ is shown by love to His people. They that separate themselves—that build for themselves a little chapel in the grand cathedral of Christ, with separate entrance, and with walls so thick that the praises of the people of God in the great sanctuary cannot be heard by them—simply cut themselves off from beholding the glory of Christ when He shall appear in the midst of the great congregation. They anticipate the judgment, and pronounce beforehand on themselves the sentence, "Depart from me." They shrink from Christ as they shrink from His people. They will say perhaps, "No, we do not shrink from His people; we love them all."

Ah! but let me ask you for information touching the characteristics of Christ's people. Have you not sought the criterion somewhere else than in the pure and simple? There are certain religious modes and forms and formularies that are agreeable to the religious habits of your nature. Have you not boldly settled it that these embody the very doctrine of Christ, so that where they are not, Christ is not? If so, how little you know of the heart of Christ! The heart that was pierced on Calvary was a larger heart than yours. The exigencies of His love are not to be baulked by the trifling differences that appear so formidable to the cabined, cribbed, confined sentiment to which you monstrously apply the name of love.

When the Son of man cometh, shall He find faith on the earth? It is the great question of this hour. A form like unto that of the Son of man is almost discernible athwart the twilight gloom. Shall He find faith on the earth? To give the matter a practical bearing, shall He find faith in you? "Oh, I am a believer!" A believer according to what sense?—yours or Christ's? Christ's definition of a believer is, one that believes in Christ's love to His people and gives proofs of his faith in works that benefit them.

Have you faith to discern the Christ that is now manifest? There is a glorious manifestation of Christ now in the churches, differing from the full manifestation of the last day, since that will leave no room for faith. This, though glorious, is not overwhelming. The true believer discerns this and rejoices greatly in it. He sees Christ in the years of grace that now succeed each other. He hears the voice of Christ saying, with the sound of a trumpet that may be heard to the ends of the earth, "That they all may be one, that the world may believe that thou hast sent me."

John 17:22-23. *"And the glory which thou gavest me I have given them; that they may be one, even as we are one; I in them, and thou in me, that they may be made perfect in one; and that the world may know that thou hast sent me, and hast loved them, as thou hast loved me."*

Christ sought not His own glory, but had ever a single eye to the glory of God; He sought not the honor that comes from man, but that which comes from God only. He could truly say, "I have glorified thee on the earth," His whole life having been devoted to the exhibition of the glory of God.

Conceive for a moment of such a thing as that men, in being drawn to Christ, should be drawn away from God! The Jews affected to have such a fear. "Give God the glory," they said to the man whose eyes Jesus had opened, "as for this Jesus, we know that he is a sinner." Jesus truly testified, "No man can come unto me except the Father which hath sent me, draw him." That which drew men to Christ was an influence from God Himself.

No man need be afraid of yielding to the attraction of Christ, for Christ was God manifest in the flesh. There is nothing more purely divine than is the influence that flows from Him. The Unitarian is afraid lest, forgetting the claims of the Father, we should give excessive honor to Christ. But the very idea of a division of honor between a creature and the Creator is blasphemous. Unless we may give all honor to Christ, and ascribe unto Him all divine perfection and sovereignty, it is a fearful error to give Him the least scintillation of that glory that belongs to God. "I can of mine own self do nothing." "Cursed be he," says the Old Testament, "who putteth his trust in an arm of flesh," that is, in a created arm; who trusts for salvation to anything less than God Himself.

When we look to Jesus, we see a perfect man—perfect in His limitations and necessities, as well as in His endowments and capacities. We see manifested through the medium of this humanity all the Godhead. They that look upon Him as a being midway between man and God reveal only how fatally they are ignorant of God and of Christ.

But what is the glory which Christ here speaks of as given Him by the Father, and by Him to His disciples? There is an incommunicable and there is a communicable glory of Christ. "By him and for him were all things made." "He upholdeth all things by the word of his power." "By himself he purgeth our sins." "He is head over all things to the Church." He was "a lamb without blemish and without spot." "Every knee must bow, and every tongue confess that he is Lord, to the glory of God the Father." But let us look at His communicable glory. "I in them, and thou in me, that they may be made perfect in one." It was Christ's glory to show forth the glory of God, and it is the glory of His people that they may show forth the glory of God in Christ.

Christ does not give to His people any other glory than that which the Father gave to Him, and it does not become His people to seek any other glory. He sought not for Himself the honor which came from man. He seeks it not for His people. All those honors that tend to hinder the perfect union of Christ's people by clothing a portion of them with an exalted worldly position, while other portions are correspondingly depressed, are most pernicious. They take the place of something infinitely more to be desired.

Perfect union should be the great aim of God's people, as it evidently is the great aim of their Leader and Commander. Their salvation, you may say, is His great aim. Yes; but is it not most evident from the words of Christ that the path of salvation and of glory lies through the Beulah land of union? In order that Christ's fervent and reiterated prayer for the union of His followers may be fulfilled, it is necessary that the spirit of glory and of God should so rest upon them that all thought of worldly glory should be flung to the winds.

When once they begin to understand the glory that Christ has given them, the glory of this world shall fade away as a phantom at the rising of the sun. The god of this world has blinded the minds of men, so that the light of the glorious Gospel of God may not shine unto them. The work of God's Spirit is to destroy this blindness and cause them to find all glory in Christ.

Christ gives glory unto His people by giving the Holy Spirit unto them and causing them to embrace the true idea of glory. "His divine power hath given unto us all things that pertain unto life and godliness." If we look into the early chapters of the Apocalypse, it will be made evident to us that the glory which Christ gives to His people is not merely that which invested Him when He was on the earth, but that which He put on when He ascended up on high. They are to participate with Him in all the glory which is to be exhibited by Him in consummating the work of redemption. You will find in Rev. 2:26-27, that the magnificent promises made by Him in the second Psalm are made over by Him to that believer, whoever he be, and wherever, who shall keep His works unto the end.

"That they may be made perfect in 'one.'" Or "unto one." They approach perfection as they approach unity. Perfection is impossible in a state of separation. My life is not wholly given unto me, but a part of it is given to my brother, to be available to me when I abide in him. We have only fragments of blessings in our disunited state, and the complement of these fragments shall be given to us when we come together. This may be an arrangement that we do not approve. We find very good reasons for loving our brother as we do from a distance and from a slight elevation.

Our religion is all interwoven with a multitude of denominational usages that effectually interfere with the manifestation of our love to those brethren who are outside the wickerwork in which we are shrouded; and does it not appear every way better that the Lord should fall in with our arrangements and bless us within our own wickerwork? The Lord has long ago decided what is best, and it is most presumptuous in you to call this matter up again and fly in the face of Christ's decision. Christ will govern His Church according to His own declared principles.

His purpose is that His people shall be perfected in union. While the world stands it will remain impossible for them to obtain anything more, in their state of disintegration, than fragments of blessings.

"I in them." Christ is in His people, and there is a possible manifestation of Christ in His people unto the world of which we have now no conception—something most sublime and glorious, as yet, however, in the region of the possible, for this manifestation can only take place when His people are made perfect in one. When the petition here embodied is fulfilled, then will the New Jerusalem have come down from Heaven, and of that New Jerusalem, Christ will be the glory. Christ in His people is now more mutilated and marred than He is revealed. When it comes to be understood that to believe in Christ is to put on the obligation to love all Christians as Christ hath loved them, then will the heavens and the earth, that are now, prepare to flee away and all things to become new.

John 17:23. *"And that the world may know that thou hast sent me, and hast loved them as thou hast loved me."*

That the world may know that Jesus is the Messiah, the Savior of mankind, the only Mediator between God and man, the Way, the Truth and the Life, the Prince of peace, the King of saints, the Lord of glory, and that it may know that there is nothing in all the universe more precious than the faith by which Christians are united to Christ, inasmuch as they by means of it have access to that same marvelous love which the Father has for His only-begotten—in a word, that the world may feel the force of the saying of Jesus, "One thing is needful," and learn to regard all earthly treasures as utterly insignificant in comparison with the Pearl of great price—the world, the great, busy world, the idolatrous world, the fanatic world, the carnal world, the world of Secularists, Mormons, Spiritualists, Romanists, Greeks and nominal Protestants, the civilized, literary, scientific world, the world in all its countless varieties of culture and of barbarism, with all its social gradations, its honors and dishonors, its pleasures and its miseries, its Pharisees and its Sadducees—that this great world may know how glorious is that salvation which it has so long despised and rejected—how is this magnificent result to be brought about?

What Christian can for a moment be indifferent to this question? Is not the mere announcement that such a result is within the limits of possible realization enough to arouse the dormant energies of all the people of God? How strange it would be if the revelation of this possibility and of the means by which it is to be realized should remain unheeded! How strange if the disciple should assume to be wiser than his Master, and imagine that he may neglect the means here pointed out, and by methods of his own bring to pass the world-wide triumphs of the Gospel! How surprising the art of the great adversary manifested in keeping the followers of Christ unmindful of the indicated means of obtaining so great a victory!

316

"That they may all be one. I in them, and thou in me, that they may be made perfect in one, and that the world may know that thou hast sent me." Generation succeeds generation, century succeeds century, empires rise and fall, new continents are discovered and peopled, but the world remains in subjection to the arch-enemy of God until the disciples of Christ cease to contend among themselves as to who shall be greatest, and learn to love one another as Christ hath loved them. How long must this earth wearily revolve upon its axis until the followers of Christ flow together into one great army, under the sole leadership of the great Captain of their salvation?

Christ's desire is that the world may know that the believer is the object of the same infinite love that rested upon Himself. The question is not yet, "Has the world learned this?" but, "Has the believer himself learned it?" Does his own conception of this love in any degree approach what is here indicated? If he falls immeasurably short in the recognition of it, how is it possible that the unenlightened mass of men will attain to the comprehension of it? Christ seems to take it almost as a matter of course that the believer will know it (perhaps His idea of a believer is one that does this); He is simply arranging for the revelation of the fact to mankind generally.

Surely it is time that you and I made haste to understand what it is to be a Christian. It will not do for us to be living in the outskirts of the region enlightened by the love of God. We belong to the very center of that region. The place that was made for Christ to occupy, full in the beam of God's loving countenance, was made for us to occupy after Him. He stood there that we might know how to stand there. Divine love followed Him thither. Then He drew us to the spot and disappeared, leaving us suffused with the same glorious and irrevocable kindliness of the Godhead that constituted the atmosphere of His own being.

John 17:24. *"Father, I will that they also, whom thou hast given me, be with me where I am; that they may behold my glory, which thou hast given me: for thou lovedst me before the foundation of the world."*

There is a phraseology or mode of address appropriate to be used by a son of tender age, and another that is becoming to him when he is at man's estate and has become the intelligent companion of his father. It is as a son of mature years that the Lord Jesus addresses the Father. There is one mind to the Father and Him; "Father, I will."

"They whom thou hast given me." This is the seventh time our Lord makes use of this expression in this prayer. He loves to look upon His people as the gifts of His Father. The whole universe is to Him an expression of the Father's love, but He prefers to see that love expressed in the gift of repenting souls. It is through their faith that they are given unto Him. O my soul, what a wondrous vocation is this of thine—the exponent of the Father's love to Christ! Jesus, when He looks upon thee, sees in thee just that, and every act of faith on thy part is a new utterance of that love. The manifold affections and exercises of thy new nature constitute a song of love of the Father to the Son. Thou art a harp, as yet imperfect and lacking much, from which the love of the Father to Him that loved thee and gave Himself for thee, shall be sounded forth to all eternity.

Man has intricately mingled his life with the life of this world. He has poured himself into a thousand currents of sin, into a mighty expanse of ungodliness; he has identified himself with countless objects that belong to this apostate world. How much, then, is implied in the giving of him to Christ? He is to be gathered up, as it were, from a thousand places; his affections to be detached from manifold objects; his tendencies to be recalled from a diversity of paths. On the (unnecessary) supposition that the particles of a man's body, diffused through nature at his dissolution, must be reassembled in order that his body may live again, the task would not be greater—infinitely less, in fact—than that of recovering the soul of a man, in all its tastes and tendencies and desires and admirations and faculties, for Christ.

Jesus will not ascend up on high without putting on record this statement of His desire concerning His people—that they may be with Him where He is. And yet we may observe that He says, "Where I am," not "Where I shall be." Doubtless the expression has its echo in Paul's exclamation, "To depart and be with Christ, which is far better." But it does not exclude—it rather includes—this idea that believers may be enabled to move in the same spiritual region in which He moved when upon the earth, to have the same communion with the Father, the same joy, peace, love, patience, that He had.

He that hath in him the hope of that future translation to the presence of the glorified Redeemer will purify himself here below even as He is pure, according to the model of purity left him in the Savior's life. It is when we seek to be meek and lowly as Christ was meek and lowly that we show the genuineness of our aspirations after His celestial glory—when we seek to walk in love as He also did that we give proof of an enlightened desire to be with Him where He is on high.

This will of Jesus relates not merely to the end here specified, but comprehends all that is intermediate between the present position of the believer and that end. The terminus is the throne of Christ; multitudinous steps conduct to that sublime pre-eminence, and the prayer of Jesus accompanies the believer every step of the way.

Your path sometimes plunges abruptly, and to all appearance ruinously, downward, yet perhaps this is one of the very experiences demanded by this word of Jesus: "That they may be with me where I am." The Heaven that Christ has procured for us is not the empty and wretched heaven of this world, nor something made up partly of that and partly of the Christian's hope. To fall from that heaven is no fall, for that heaven and Christ's Heaven are contrary the one to the other. That heaven is merely the region of cloud, and we cannot well see Christ's Heaven from it. To be banished from it is often to be banished to a region where Christ's Heaven for the first time bursts upon us in its appropriate glory.

Let us recall the fifth verse: "And now, O Father, glorify thou me with the glory which I had with thee before the world was." And here: "That they may behold my glory which thou hast given me; for thou lovedst me before the foundation of the world." A comparison of the two passages seems to show that glory and the Father's love are in the Savior's estimation, as nearly as may be, interchangeable terms. We are like-minded with Him when we regard the love of the Father as glory. May we not find a blessing in this thought? God is love; therefore it is impossible that there should be any gift of greater value than His love.

The communication of God's love to the heart is the communication of Heaven. The difference between an angel and a saint yet in the body is that the former is in an atmosphere of love. The prize which is held out to men to animate them in their conflict with the world is divine love. It was for the excellency of the knowledge of this that Paul counted all things but loss. The believer begins, indeed, with the love of God. He finds it, even in infinitude surpassing all knowledge, at the cross of Christ. Nevertheless, God does not throw Himself away upon the penitent sinner, so that He has thenceforward nothing more to bestow.

This prayer of our Lord abundantly teaches us that there are magnificent and undreamt-of prizes of divine love presented to kindle the aspirations and stimulate the efforts of the believer, all along his Heavenward course. And this it is to be a believer, namely, to discern those glorious prizes and catch inspiration and energy from the sight of them.

John 17:25. *"O righteous Father, the world hath not known thee: but I have known thee, and these have known that thou hast sent me."*

Four times in this prayer the Savior addresses the Father as *Father*—once as *holy Father,* once as *righteous Father*, once as the *only true God.* In the great controversy between God and the world, the Savior speaks with the voice of an umpire declaring that God is righteous, and that the world is consequently unrighteous. "That thou mightest be justified when thou speakest and be clear when thou judgest."

It was not merely the testimony of the Savior's lips that God is righteous, but that of His life; for on all occasions, without exception, the will of the Father was enthroned in His heart. "I seek not mine own will, but the will of the Father which hath sent me." Nothing less than that is a satisfactory assertion of the Father's righteousness. Does it not happen to some of us to use language of this kind in prayer, while many a will of the Father, Whom we thus laud, remains unheeded?

Christ is made unto us righteousness, first as our Sponsor, then by reconciling us to every will of God. We are clothed with righteousness in the highest and best sense when we know God to be righteous in all His ways, and show that we know Him thus righteous by walking no more in our own ways, but altogether in His. The cross propitiates God to us and us to God. God was in Christ reconciling the world unto Himself.

"The world hath not known thee: but I have known thee." If Christ knew the Father, it is certain that the world knows Him not, for there is a mighty gulf between Christ's views and those of the world. "As the Father knoweth me, even so know I the Father." His knowledge of the Father was perfect, and it was embodied in all His teachings, in all His acts. "Blessed are the pure in heart, for they shall see God." Look at the conception of Deity expressed in this statement, and then at that which found utterance in the ceremonial observances of the Pharisees. "Blessed are they that hunger and thirst after righteousness; for they shall be filled." Put this conception beside that which reveals itself in the lukewarmness of the great body even of those called Christians. "The Father loveth the Son and hath given all things into his hands."

This is surely very different from the world's conception of God. Men imagine that they can find a far higher throne of God than the throne of grace. The work of redemption appears to them a comparatively little work, down among the pettinesses of divine condescension. Man's nature demands for him an atmosphere infinitely exalted above all mention of sin and salvation. They look for salvation through the contempt of God, rather than through His love. God is too great to stretch down His hand and shut the door of life in the face of any of His creatures that wish to enter.

Utterly different from all this is the only true God made known to us in Christ. His greatness is the greatness of love. The throne on which He receives returning prodigals is the same which the cherubim and seraphim encompass. Had He been capable of condemning His works, He would not have created them. He does not despise sin, He abhors it. "If thy right eye offend thee, pluck it out and cast it from thee," said He Who knew the righteous Father. The world knoweth Him not, for it does not believe that man is called to make any such sacrifices, or that sin is such a deadly enemy.

"I have known thee; and these have known that thou hast sent me." No man knows the Father save the Son and He to whomsoever the Son will reveal Him. That He should give eternal life to as many as Thou hast given Him, and this is life eternal, that they might know Thee, the only true God, and Jesus Christ Whom Thou hast sent. He that recognizes in Jesus the Legate of the Father has already some knowledge of God.

There are many theologians, men even in the ministry, who for a score of years have weekly investigated the sacred record, fathoming its depths and exploring its diversified paths, who know not God so well as the crucified thief who said unto his crucified Lord, "Remember me when thou comest into thy kingdom." The knowledge that enters into faith is that which God calls knowledge; the rest is chaff. All knowledge must be baptized by faith, else it is reprobate. Without faith it is impossible to please God, for without faith it is impossible that the life-giving light of God's countenance should shine into your heart. Oh that ten thousand students of God's Word would this day consider this and check themselves!

"I have known thee." Christ did not know *about* God, He knew God; His thoughts all looked to Him; He dwelt in the pathway of the beams of divine love. Consider, O eager student of the Scriptures, that the mere accumulation of scriptural lore is not the accumulation of treasure in Heaven; whereas all that you receive in faith is treasure both in Heaven and in earth. This is life eternal, to sit at the feet of Jesus by faith and learn of Him. Read with the heart, and in a quarter of an hour your gain will be greater than in many weeks of intellectual study. God is love, and love only can know love; the intellect can make nothing of it. Let love open the door by which alone love can enter. "I rose up to open to my beloved, and my hands dropped with myrrh, and my fingers with sweet-smelling myrrh, upon the handles of the lock." But love can make everything of the intellect, regenerate it, ennoble it, endow it.

"And I have declared unto them thy name." More literally, "I have made known unto them thy name." I have known Thee; these have known that Thou hast sent me, and have received from Me the knowledge of Thee—at least the beginning of that knowledge. In becoming acquainted with Me, they became acquainted with Thee. Thy character has been poured out into the Gospel which records My acts, words and sufferings. This Gospel must be preached in all the world for a witness to all men. The rejection of it is the rejection of the knowledge of God. At last cometh the day when the Lord Jesus shall be revealed from Heaven in flaming fire, taking vengeance on them that *know not God and obey not the Gospel* of our Lord Jesus.

323

John 17:26. *"And I have declared unto them thy name, and will declare it; that the love wherewith thou hast loved me may be in them, and I in them."*

If it becomes us to listen eagerly and reverentially to every word that falls from the Master's lips, we ought surely to give special heed to the last words spoken by Him to His disciples before He entered upon His final sufferings. If we hang breathlessly upon the words of a believer passing into the presence of Jesus, with what rapt attention should we drink in the farewell syllables of Him Who is the great object of faith!

Believers expect that on the dissolution of their bodies their souls shall be translated into the presence of God and the Lamb, and clothed with glory, honor and immortality. They believe that this shall be done for them because Christ hath died and ever lives to make intercession for them. The blood of Jesus Christ cleanseth them from all sin, so that it is not incongruous, but every way admirable, that the Father should make them heirs of everlasting blessedness. The love of the Father to the Son is the guarantee of this magnificent result. As it is a pure impossibility that the Father should make light of the sacrifice offered by His well-beloved Son, so it is impossible that the trust which reposes upon this sacrifice should be dishonored.

Are believers, however, sufficiently impressed with the fact that the sacrifice of the Lamb has had reference not only to the ultimate redemption of their souls, but to the present enjoyment of the things pertaining to life and godliness? What are the silver threads that run most conspicuously through these five chapters? Joy, peace, love, humility, faith, fruitfulness, holiness and union. And now His parting blessing is given in the words, "That the love wherewith thou hast loved me may be in them, and I in them."

He lived, loved, suffered, died, not merely that we might ascend with Him to glory, but that the love of God might descend and rest on us even as it had rested on Him. Why should we, in estimating the value of Christ's mediatorial work, think exclusively or excessively of the glory that shall be revealed in us when we shall have done with earth, losing sight, or almost losing sight, of the mighty revenue of divine love *at present* accruing? We are to honor Christ by seeking for ourselves the things prominently mentioned in His promises and in this prayer. We are to magnify the efficacy of His blood by seeking to have His peace, His joy, His experience of the Father's love.

There is nothing better in Heaven than what Christ here requests for His people. About to depart out of the world, He entreats that the love which had so unceasingly and mightily flowed toward Him during all His pilgrimage here below might not depart with Him and be lost to earth—that the same benignity and complacency and tenderness and sympathy that had looked down to Him from the throne of Heaven might continue to look down upon the earth, even upon those that believed on His Name.

We expect God some day to love us even as He loves His only-begotten. Christ does not ask this for us some day, but now. The atonement of Christ has the value now that it will have in any future day. The blood that was shed on Calvary does not begin by purchasing for us a little love, and then, like the merchandise of this world, rising in value, end by purchasing the whole.

But stay: how can the Father love us as He loves His only-begotten, Who was holy, harmless, undefiled and separate from sinners, the express image of His person and the brightness of His glory? Do you ask me this? I ask you in reply, "How can God love us at all?" There are just as great difficulties to be overcome, just the same in obtaining for us the least love from the Father as in obtaining the utmost. Those difficulties, the believer needs not to be told, are overcome by the crucified One. There are multitudes of semi-believers who have faith to grasp a modicum of love, and think it presumptuous to lift their regards to anything like the love which the Father had for Jesus. It does not dawn upon their minds that such limitation of their faith is neither more nor less than an unwarrantable limitation of the value of Christ's blood. We make approaches to the great love that Christ here entreats for His people just as we make advances in the knowledge of the cross of Christ.

The love of the Father to Christ was not a love that refused to let sorrow make the acquaintance of its object—not one that speedily overwhelmed His enemies with confusion, or that defended Him against the approach of temptation. And the fact that the believer is compassed about with infirmities, sustains losses, encounters reverses, *seems* even to be looked coldly on by the God of providence, is no proof that he is not loved with the love of which Christ was the object.

"I in them." This is the argument of arguments, the yea and amen of all promises. "Behold Me in them, treat Me in them, love Me in them. Do I need to ask You, O righteous Father, to continue loving Me, to entreat You to extend to Me the same loving consideration after the cross as before it? Nothing surely could be more unseemly than to suppose the possibility of the opposite. Well, if Your love to Me can know no end, no diminution, hear Me, then, while I declare that I am in My disciples who dwell upon the earth, and that Your love must seek Me there."

Dost thou take knowledge, O believer, of the wondrous vantage-ground given you by this declaration of Christ? He is in you, and consequently you *must* encounter the full tide of the Father's love to Christ when you draw near to the throne of grace. Only believe. To slight you were to slight Him Who is in you. To stint you with an inadequate measure of good-will were to bring a cloud over the relations of the Father to the Son. Christ is no more in the world, but you are in the world and Christ in you. Draw near, therefore, to the throne of grace with as true a heart and in as full assurance of faith as the holy Son of God Himself did when He tabernacled here.

"I in them." Lord, teach me to recognize You in myself; abide in my heart by faith; let me hasten to repudiate myself, that the place may be fully prepared for You; and teach me to recognize You in my fellow-Christians, to love You in them, to serve You in them.